SHADOWS
OF
DOUBT

D1566259

SHADOWS OF DOUBT

NEGOTIATIONS OF
MASCULINITY
IN AMERICAN
GENRE FILMS

BARRY KEITH GRANT

Wayne State University Press · Detroit

15 14 13 12 11   5 4 3 2 1

LIBRARY OF CONGRESS CATALOGING-IN-PUBLICATION DATA
Grant, Barry Keith, 1947–
Shadows of doubt : negotiations of masculinity in American genre films / Barry Keith Grant.
p. cm. — (Contemporary approaches to film and television series)
Includes bibliographical references and index.
ISBN 978-0-8143-3457-7 (pbk. : alk. paper)
1. Masculinity in motion pictures. 2. Motion pictures—United States—History—20th century.
I. Title.
PN1995.9.M34G73 2010
791.43'6521—dc22
2010015131

∞

Designed and typeset by Charlie Sharp,
Sharp Des!gns, Lansing, Michigan
Composed in Reminga Pro

To Jim, Joan, and Jeannette—
steadfast colleagues through the years

Contents

Acknowledgments

Several friends and colleagues have helped me shape this book. Murray Pomerance nurtured my ideas and provided much help and patience as I worked them out over several years. For providing invaluable feedback on various chapters, I am grateful to Hilary Radner, Christie Milliken, Charles Maland, Alistair Fox, Christine Holmlund, Yvonne Tasker, Christopher Sharrett, and Robert Kolker. The two anonymous readers of the original manuscript provided thoughtful suggestions for revision, and I hope they too will see their wisdom reflected herein. Annie Martin, acquisitions editor at Wayne State University Press, gave her unwavering support for the project from the beginning and throughout the editorial process. Carrie Downes Teefey at the Press and copyeditor Dawn Hall helped immeasurably in the book's production.

My reading of *Red River* in chapter 3 is an elaboration of ideas briefly discussed in my book *Film Genre: From Iconography to Ideology* (London and New York: Wallflower Press, 2007), pp. 66–71.

Chapter 4 is a slightly revised version of the essay "The Classic Hollywood Musical and the 'Problem' of Rock 'n' Roll," which originally appeared in *Journal of Popular Film and Television* 13, no. 4 (1986): 195–205. It is reprinted here with permission of Heldref Publications. The material on *Lonely Boy* was adapted from the essay "From Obscurity in Ottawa to Fame in Freedomland: *Lonely Boy* and the Cultural Meaning of Paul Anka," in *Candid Eyes: Essays on Canadian Documentaries,* ed. Jim Leach and Jeannette Sloniowski (Toronto: University of Toronto Press, 2003), 48–60, and is used with permission of University of Toronto Press.

Chapter 5 was published originally as "Hello, Deli! Shtick Meets Teenpic in *The Delicate Delinquent,*" in *Enfant Terrible! Jerry Lewis and American Film,* ed. Murray Pomerance (New York: New York University Press, 2002), 225–37, and is reprinted with permission of New York University Press.

Chapter 6 is excerpted and revised from "When Worlds Collide," chapter 7 of my book *Voyages of Discovery: The Cinema of Frederick Wiseman* (Urbana: University of Illinois Press, 1992). Copyright © 2008 by the author.

Chapter 7, "Of Men and Monoliths: Science Fiction, Gender, and *2001: A Space Odyssey,*" was first published in *Stanley Kubrick's 2001: A Space Odyssey: New Essays,* ed. Robert Kolker (Oxford University Press, 2006), 69–86, and is reprinted with permission of Oxford University Press.

Chapter 8, "Taking Back the *Night of the Living Dead:* George Romero, Feminism, and the Horror Film," is an updated and slightly revised version of an essay that was first published in *Wide Angle* 14, no. 1 (1992): 64–77. It is reprinted by permission of the Johns Hopkins University Press.

Chapter 9 is a slightly revised version of the essay "Rich and Strange: The Yuppie Horror Film," which first appeared in *Journal of Film and Video* 48, nos. 1–2 (1996), 4–16.

Chapter 10 is an updated version of the essay "Man's Favorite Sport? The Action Films of Kathryn Bigelow," which was first published in *Action and Adventure Cinema,* ed. Yvonne Tasker (London and New York: Routledge, 2004): 371–84. It is reprinted here with the permission of Routledge University Press.

The images from *The Cool World* are used with permission of Frederick Wiseman and Zipporah Films. The stills from *The Fatal Glass of Beer, The Delicate Delinquent,* and *2001: A Space Odyssey* are courtesy of Photofest. All other illustrations are from the personal collection of the author.

Introduction

In the plot of Alfred Hitchcock's *Shadow of a Doubt* (1943), young Charlie Newton (Teresa Wright), a wholesome teenage girl from a small town, discovers that her Uncle Charlie (Joseph Cotten), whom she has always admired and who has come for a rare visit, is in fact a psychopathic serial killer who marries widows and then murders them. Realizing that his niece has discovered his secret, Uncle Charlie attempts to murder her and make it look like an accident, but in the climax she manages to push him in front of an oncoming train and kill him instead. Some critics, following the lead of Robin Wood, have read the film as a work of horror, understanding the murderous Uncle Charlie as the return of the repressed desires and frustrations surging within young Charlie and her family. Certainly Hitchcock provides rich detail in depicting the normative world of the Newton family, the world in which young Charlie feels trapped and yearns for excitement; and as Wood puts it, Uncle Charlie "brings life and excitement into an inert world, but proves to be a devil who must be destroyed."[1] Wood's influential reading focuses on the privileged horror motif of the doppelgänger, the evil twin, by emphasizing the relationship between the two Charlies. For Wood, the paralleling of uncle and niece are "two sides of the same coin," and he explores this idea from a perspective that combines Marxist and Freudian theory to understand Uncle Charlie's sexual pathology as the expression of contradictions inherent in capitalism and the bourgeois family.[2]

The fact that Uncle Charlie shares his pathology with other Hitchcock villains, Norman Bates in *Psycho* (1960) and Bob Rusk (Barry Foster) in *Frenzy* (1972), both of whom also target women as their victims, suggests the trope's importance for the director, particularly as it relates to the complex dynamics of gender in his films. But the repetitive, serial nature of Charlie's violence, and the Newtons' relationship to it, also speaks to the importance of popular culture, including genre movies, in everyday life. Indeed, if Hitchcock's *Rear Window* (1954), as generally acknowledged, is about cinematic spectatorship, then *Shadow of a Doubt* may be understood on one level as being about the consumption of popular culture generally.

In *Shadow of a Doubt,* as Wood observes, each member of the Newton family "inhabits a private, separate dream world, the mother nostalgic for her youth and her adored younger brother, the father living in a fantasy world of detective fiction and real-life crime, the younger daughter perpetually immersed in books."[3] Emma Newton's untroubled memory of the past, an illusion frozen in time, is signified by the nineteenth-century photographs of their parents her brother gives to her as a gift: her images of the past, as Susan Sontag says of photographs, are memento mori testifying "to time's relentless melt" by fixing nostalgically upon a fleeting moment long gone.[4] Analogously, the preoccupation of her husband, Joe (Henry Travers), with pulp crime fiction at the expense of the real world is suggestive of consumers of popular culture who negotiate reality through the lens of genre convention. Despite the dated prelapsarian patina of American small-town wholesomeness and innocence in which the family lives, Mr. Newton is particularly relevant in the context of today's postmodern world in which, as Rick Altman suggests, "the rise of consumerism and the mass media, along with the extraordinary proliferation of narrative entertainment that they have brought, have tilted the typical generic mix of life experience/textual experience radically towards the experience of previous texts."[5] Even Charlie's younger sister, Ann (Edna May Wonacot), a precocious intellectual who looks down her bespectacled nose at her father's pulp fiction, is reading *Ivanhoe*—a popular Romance written by Sir Walter Scott, the author whom Mark Twain blamed for nothing less than inspiring the "jejune romanticism" of Southern chivalry and even the Civil War "with [his] dreams and phantoms . . . with the sillinesses and emptinesses, sham grandeurs, sham gauds, and sham chivalries of a brainless and worthless long-vanished society."[6]

Yet Uncle Charlie himself is a monstrous masculine image of popular culture. Just as he arrives in the Newtons' hometown of Santa Rosa by train, accompanied by the ominous smoke of the engine, so mainstream movies, fueled by the locomotive of capitalist mass culture, come to us as smoke screens, casting their shadows before our eyes. Genre films present an unending series of Uncle Charlies, eternally returning with ritual repetition. Sometimes they cloak their ideology, masquerading as the normative, while others test our worldview by, as young Charlie says, "shaking us all up." At the beginning of Hitchcock's film, young Charlie is reclining lazily in her bed in mid-afternoon, daydreaming of adventure, the model of the most passive spectator; but "growing up" or "maturation" for young Charlie means coming to terms with the real Uncle Charlie behind the dapper façade, with facing the consequences of one's fantasies. In the film's climax, the two wrestle aboard Uncle Charlie's departing train, as he tries to kill his niece because she knows the awful truth about him; she, however, manages to defeat her uncle by pushing him off the train instead. Similarly, the activity of experiencing genre films sometimes forces us to grapple with our culturally entrenched values, beliefs, and assumptions. In this sense, Uncle Charlie is not merely a figure of horror, as Wood describes him; rather, he represents the doubt that lurks everywhere in the shadow play of genre films, not only in horror movies and thrillers but also, as this book shows, in seemingly more upbeat genres such as musicals and comedies.

Today, only the most rigid of ideological critics would regard genre movies and other works of popular culture as necessarily insidious as Scott's fiction was regarded by Twain. While it is true that some genre movies function "to assist in the maintenance of the existing political structure" by encouraging viewers to "cease examining themselves and their surroundings, and to take refuge in fantasy,"[7] not all genre films do so, as such diverse examples as, say, *You Only Live Once* (1937), *All That Heaven Allows* (1955), *Psycho, Little Big Man* (1970), and *Thelma and Louise* (1991) clearly attest. As John Fiske has argued, the very popularity of popular culture texts depends upon people's ability to actively make meanings relevant for them even as those texts "serve the economic interests of the dominant."[8] Classic Hollywood cinema—best represented by genre movies, by far the bulk of its production historically—may be "excessively obvious" in its stylistic norms, as David Bordwell would have it, eschewing ambiguity in style and narrative construction; but as Bordwell himself also observes, this does not mean that as viewers we are passive when we watch Hollywood-style movies since we must actively work to make meaning as we watch. "Classical films call forth activities on the part of the spectator," writes Bordwell. "These activities may be highly standardized and comparatively easy to learn, but we cannot assume that they are simple."[9] And while all genre movies require extratextual knowledge on the part of spectators to decode them, many important ones such as *Scarlet Street* (1945), *Bring Me the Head of Alfredo Garcia* (1974), and *Pennies from Heaven* (1981) demand a particularly sophisticated knowledge of generic norms be mobilized by the spectator in order to understand them fully.[10]

Wood emphasizes the phallic sexuality Uncle Charlie represents in *Shadow of a Doubt,* focusing on such details as the initial shots of him recumbent on the bed of his boardinghouse room fidgeting with a cigar, and how he "becomes erect," abandoning his disguise with a cane and standing upright after getting off the train at the Santa Rosa station.[11] In this book I discuss individual genre films, the genre films of particular directors, and cycles of American genre films in terms of the representational strategies they employ to depict masculine identity and sexuality. In genre movies the ongoing, fundamental issues of gender and sexuality are worked through and along with such other questions as national identity and citizenship, race and class, and contemporary political tensions. All of these issues are addressed to varying degrees in this book, but mostly as they intersect with and inform generic strategies for representing masculine identity and sexuality. Throughout, I have sought to examine the films I discuss *as* genre films—that is, how they express meaning within the representational traditions in which they participate, both within cinema as well as popular culture more broadly.

In her discussion of serial killers and serial killer films, although she does not mention *Shadow of a Doubt* specifically, Annalee Newitz links masculinity to capitalist modes of economic production, arguing that serialized violence "may be a social corollary to working conditions under consumer capitalism."

In making this connection, she follows Wood's Marxist approach. But, interestingly, she also notes former FBI agent Robert Ressler's explanation that he coined the term *serial killer* with the idea of movie serials like *The Phantom* (1943, based on Lee Falk's comic strip) in mind, and then goes on to suggest a further correlation between serial killer narratives, their popularity with American audiences, and the "serialized, unsatisfying fantasy" enacted by real serial killers.[12] Her analysis is persuasive, and, indeed, there is no reason that her analogy might not be extended beyond serial killer narratives specifically to apply to all genre works, even those not concerned explicitly with themes or representations of violence. As Newitz notes, serialized violence "is repetitious, blurs the boundaries between what is natural and artificial, and takes place in a consumer-oriented economy"[13]—a description that also applies to generic works generally and their ideological projects as cultural myths.

In this regard, the serial or repetitive nature of genre films is central to their ideological function and to how they express meaning. Hollywood's historical reliance on sequels, prequels, remakes, series, and cycles, which has characterized its film production throughout its history and continues unabated today, is only the most obvious testament to this ritual function of genre. Genre conventions depend for their existence on their serialized repetition, and in turn this repetition allows individual genre movies to partake of, to modify, to question, and to subvert their generic traditions and the ideology they have tended to endorse. No genre is inherently reactionary or progressive.[14]

After Laura Mulvey's breakthrough article, "Visual Pleasure and Narrative Cinema," in 1975, critics slowly began to consider the representation of masculinity in film as well, beginning with Steve Neale's pioneering essay, "Masculinity as Spectacle," on the male body as site of erotic pleasure.[15] In 1993, exactly a decade after Neale's initial work, Peter Lehman later decried the relative paucity of critical attention to masculinity in movies, and he went on to analyze a number of disparate films focusing on their strategies for representing the male body, especially in relation to the penis.[16] Since then, other critics have employed Judith Butler's notion of gender as performance, thus undermining any stable and monolithic notion of masculine identity. The notion of male masquerade, for example, has been explored by Gaylyn Studlar in her study of male stars during the silent era.[17]

Critics now understand that while representations of masculinity may have been the center from which Others were defined, it was not simply one uncontested construction of masculinity that was at play in movies. Nevertheless, quick to look for cracks in a previously assumed monolithic but mythic representation, many critics identified moments of "crisis" in the representation of masculinity in movies. To take perhaps the most obvious example: film noir, which flourished in the 1940s and '50s, is generally understood by scholars today as being largely about the acute sense of disempowerment men felt returning home from World War II to find that during the war women had left the domestic sphere and entered the workforce in unprecedented numbers. Accordingly, masculinity in film noir is often depicted as a struggle for the male protagonist to maintain his heteronormative identity. As Frank Krutnik argues, film noir offers a series of engagements with "problematic" (that is, nonnormative) aspects of masculine identity, and he concludes that noir's emphasis on male characters who fail to fulfill the ideal oedipal trajectory of the Hollywood master narrative are "perhaps evidence of some kind of crisis of confidence within the contemporary regimentation of male-dominated culture."[18]

But if a "crisis" is, as the Oxford English Dictionary (OED) defines it, "a vitally important or decisive stage" in any given process, a turning point, then the term *crisis* here is perhaps inaccurate, for part of the mythic function of genre movies within mass-mediated society is to address in coded fashion definitions, ideals, and concepts of gender, engaging, like much of popular culture, in a continuous process of ideological testing and negotiation. As Neale so acutely observes, in cinema "there is constant work to channel and regulate identification in relation to sexual division, in relation to the orders of gender, sexuality, and social identity and authority marking patriarchal society."[19] This suggests less that particular genre films and cycles may be seen as reflecting a series of representational crises than that they offer part of an ongoing dialogue with audiences about the ceaseless challenges to and valorization of heteronormative ideals—what I call "negotiations"—in a constantly changing society at specific points in time.

Accordingly, in these pages I implicitly argue that to understand the history of American cinema as a series of masculine crises—perhaps even to think of any particular period in the history of American film, much less individual films such as, say, Martin Scorsese's *Raging Bull* (1980), as expressing a "crisis"[20]—is both inappropriate hyperbole and a serious misunderstanding of Hollywood cinema. Within culture, as R. W. Connell observes in his book

Masculinities, the hegemonic position of a particular model of masculinity is "always contestable." "At any given time," he writes, "one form of masculinity rather than others is culturally exalted," for "when conditions for the defense of patriarchy change, the bases for the dominance of a particular masculinity are eroded."[21] Consequently, we would do well to remember that the key, but apparently too often neglected, word in Neale's point is "constant." One of the primary social functions of genre movies is to engage in a perpetual dialogue around what Connell calls the "currently accepted strategy" for defining and representing masculinity, like femininity, at any and every given historical moment.[22] *Crises* in the representation of masculinity are nothing more than especially insistent "defenses of patriarchy."

It is of course true that genre movies have frequently offered the dominant representation of what Joan Mellen years ago called the "big bad wolf": "a male superior to women, defiant, assertive, and utterly fearless." "Repeatedly through the decades," Mellen writes, "Hollywood has demanded that we admire and imitate males who dominate others, leaders whom the weak are expected to follow. The ideal man of our films is a violent one. To be sexual he has had to be not only tall and strong but frequently brutal, promising to overwhelm a woman by physical force that was at once firm and tender."[23] Whether it is Clark Gable, John Wayne, Humphrey Bogart, or Vin Diesel, the archetype is familiar. Yet, it is also true that at the same time movies have insistently presented this image, they also have consistently questioned it. The ten chapters to follow all explore particular instantiations of this ongoing dialogue in genre movies regarding American masculinity. Arranged chronologically according to the films discussed, these essays cover a wide historical range and several genres, including comedies, musicals, horror, science fiction, westerns, teen movies, and action films. Most focus on specific films and directors, for the intersection of auteur and genre provides an especially rich site for analysis, with a couple discussing specific generic cycles. Some of the films I consider offer important challenges to dominant representations of masculinity, while others reveal an acceptance of or capitulation to them.

The book begins—appropriately, given his significant place in establishing Hollywood's representational codes—with an analysis of D. W. Griffith's films, particularly *Broken Blossoms* (1919), one of his most important features. In chapter 1, I argue that Griffith's tendency toward abstraction in his approach to character encourages an understanding of them as types embodying broad, culturally accepted concepts of class, race, and gender. More specifically, his splitting of masculinity into characters embodying two opposite extremes, represented by the physical Battling Burrows and the spiritual Cheng Huan, is a narrative trope subsequently discernible throughout the history of Holly-wood cinema; but it is particularly revealing in *Broken Blossoms,* which, while focusing on its unfortunate heroine Lucy (Lillian Gish), is as much about the masculinity of its two male protagonists as it is about the oppression of women within patriarchy.

In chapter 2, I consider how two of the most popular film comedians of the 1930s, Groucho Marx and W. C. Fields, deflate the masculine connotations of earlier American comic types, the Yankee and the backwoodsman, and suggest this treatment reflects the erosion of faith in national ideals during the Great Depression. Both comedians animate these two traditional American comic figures to debunk the myths upon which they depend, and as a consequence they undermine the traditional concepts of masculine power and prowess they represent. A close reading of Fields's short *The Fatal Glass of Beer* (1933) shows how the film uses the iconography and conventions of the western in this process of masculine demythification.

The western also informs the discussion in chapter 3 of Howard Hawks, perhaps the most influential Hollywood director in representing traditional masculine ideals on screen. Here I examine Hawks's celebrated notion of professionalism, particularly as it is treated in *Red River* (1948), his first of five westerns. In a close reading of the film I trace its alternative versions of masculine identity, clearly derived from the types established by Griffith decades earlier, and show how the director's interest in the nature of masculine professionalism clashes with the conventions of the form. In the end, I argue, Hawks's masculinist concerns trump the genre's mythic function as the lone western hero is reintegrated into society rather than like, say, Shane, light out for the territory, thus allowing for the perpetuation of the male professional and the restoration of the father in the narrative's oedipal scenario.

In the 1950s, with the rise of youth culture and its predominant form of expression, rock 'n' roll, the prosocial ideology of the film musical, and the mythology of romance upon which it depended, was threatened by a new form of music with connotations of aggressive phallic sexuality. In chapter 4, I explain how the musical, in order to maintain both its commercial viability and mythic functions, had to incorporate rock 'n' roll, and I examine the strategies the genre employed to do so. Discussing several rock musicals, I show how they neutered rock 'n' roll of its phallic implications by stressing its communal aspects in both performance and narratives contexts, and by remolding the sexualized images of male rock stars into safer and more acceptable versions of masculinity.

Teen films and musicals are among the genres that Jerry Lewis mobilized to help create his comic persona in *The Delicate Delinquent* (1957), his first film without former partner Dean Martin. In chapter 5, I consider how the disparate generic elements of *The Delicate Delinquent* work expressively rather than as a failure of conception, in this instance to articulate the conflicts that are inherent within the comic character "Jerry Lewis." In the film, the Lewis persona also struggles with the same masculine alternatives that inform Griffith's film, and his struggle to integrate them in his attempt to mature from teenager to manhood is mirrored in the film's odd, heterogeneous style.

A similar aesthetic tension informs the exploration of black masculine youth in *The Cool World* (1964), the subject of chapter 6. Produced by famed documentary filmmaker Frederick Wiseman and directed by experimental artist Shirley Clarke, *The Cool World* (1964) is about the troubled existence of black youth in Harlem. As with *The Delicate Delinquent,* I argue that the film's disparate influences and consequent generic hybridity are less an aesthetic failure than a telling expression, in this case of the double consciousness that informs the protagonist's conflicted sense of self and, according to black writers and critics, African American identity more broadly. It is precisely the models of masculinity offered to Duke Custis by such icons of white popular culture as his namesake John Wayne in movies like *Red River* that bring into vivid relief the boy's racial marginalization.

Stanley Kubrick's films have consistently offered a harsh critique of masculinity, and in chapter 7, I explore how *2001: A Space Odyssey* (1968) uses the conventions of science fiction in such a way as to encourage us to see the world from a different perspective that the film depicts as stripped of traditional masculinist biases. In his treatment of narrative, production design, and mise-en-scène, Kubrick's film, released the same year as Ursula Le Guin's influential novel, *The Left Hand of Darkness,* was instrumental in the examination of the genre's traditional masculine assumptions that would drive the wave of feminist science fiction literature shortly thereafter.

Just as Kubrick's film critiques phallic masculinity in its use of the science fiction genre, so George A. Romero animates the horror film for a similar purpose. Chapter 8 considers how Romero's auteurist vision, developed in his series of cult zombie movies beginning with *Night of the Living Dead* in 1968, the same year as *2001*, involves the undermining of the masculinist notion of professionalism promoted in Hawks's action films as mindless machismo. Focusing on the 1990 remake of the original film, written by Romero and directed by his longtime special effects collaborator, Tom Savini, I trace the gendered representations in the series of both the living characters and the undead, showing that as women become empowered in the films, the zombies are increasingly cast as metaphors for masculine violence and aggression.

In chapter 9, I examine the cycle of thrillers and erotic thrillers that, beginning in the late 1980s, altered the semantics of the horror film to articulate the anxieties of the era's yuppie generation during a period of economic downturn and male fears of disempowerment both in the workplace and in personal relationships. Conflating economic and gender anxieties within the context of horror, the yuppie horror film emerged out of the perceived challenges to masculinity incited by changing gender relations during the period, as manifest, for example, in the advancement of women in the corporate arena. Reading films like *Fatal Attraction* (1987) as horror films provides another example of how masculine fears are channeled through the convention of genre.

If the book begins by discussing D. W. Griffith, the "father" of classic Hollywood cinema, then it ends, equally as fittingly, with an analysis of the films of Kathryn Bigelow, the only woman director to date who has succeeded in establishing herself as an auteur working within the various action genres traditionally regarded as addressing primarily male spectators. Bigelow's films, from *The Loveless*, a 1983 biker film, to the war film *The Hurt Locker* (2008), her most recent film as of this writing, consistently question the values and assumptions of masculinity, particularly the central importance of violence, that underlie its conventional representation in action films, even as they provide these genres' various pleasures. In their deployment of point of view and the gendered gaze of the camera, as well as through other narrative strategies, Bigelow's films bring these issues to the fore and implicate spectators in their enactment. In a sense, this is what Griffith was doing already in *Broken Blossoms*. The crisis of masculinity has a history at least as long as that of cinema.

Contrasting *Shadow of a Doubt* to Frank Capra's *It's a Wonderful Life* (1946), Robin Wood shows how similar ideological tensions are worked out differently in different genres and by different auteurs. As he notes, while Hitchcock's film is a suspenseful thriller and Capra's a populist comedy, both movies mobilize conventions of yet another genre, film noir, to negotiate the same ideological issue: "the affirmation of family and small-town values that the action called into question." And although the two films may offer strikingly different views of this ideological project, Wood's essential point is to counter the mistaken tendency "to treat the genres as discrete" because "at best, they represent different strategies for dealing with the same ideological tension."[24] My work here is hardly exhaustive, and undoubtedly there are many more chapters that could have been included in this project. But these essays, written over a period of twenty years, show that genre films have continually negotiated concepts of gender, and that questions of masculinity, like notions of femininity, have been central to genre filmmaking throughout the studio era and beyond.

If, then, Hitchcock's *Shadow of a Doubt* is on one level about how genre movies—including, of course, *Shadow of a Doubt* itself—function within popular culture, this book, *Shadows of Doubt,* derives from my tracking Uncle Charlie in American cinema for decades. His appearances here comprise a series of negotiations concerning the definition and nature of masculinity through the popular, shared discourses of genre. And as in all negotiations, the parties involved make gains here and accept concessions there. As these essays show, masculinity in American cinema, indeed, like all cultural categories of identity, has never been monolithic or stable; rather, it is an always-shifting concept, revised and reconstituted by the discourses of popular culture, including movies, as the needs of the historical moment require.

1

Pistols and Stamens

Gender and Genre in D. W. Griffith's *Broken Blossoms*

Where better to begin this book than with the work of David Wark Griffith, often referred to in conventional histories of the cinema as "the father" of mainstream cinema? Griffith is usually cited as a major innovator of the narrative film, having "invented" such now standard techniques as the close-up, parallel editing, and expressive ("rembrandt") lighting. His move from New York to Los Angeles after 1913, along with his stock company, was instrumental in establishing Hollywood as the geographical locus of what has become known as the classic narrative style, a style he was so central in codifying. Although the accuracy of this standard description has been challenged in more recent work on early cinema history, Griffith may be said to be a cinematic "father figure" in a more provocative sense, which is the way his films may be seen to address issues of gender representation that are central to that classic style he is often said to have sired.

Griffith's depiction of gender is rooted in his visual sense, as explained first and best by writer James Agee, for whom Griffith was a visual poet.

For Agee, this accounted for both the director's strengths and weaknesses. Griffith, he observed,

> had no remarkable power of intellect, or delicateness of soul; no subtlety; little restraint; little if any "taste," whether to help his work or harm it; Lord knows (and be thanked) no cleverness; no fundamental capacity, once he had achieved his first astonishing development, for change or growth. . . . His sense of comedy was pathetically crude and numb. He had an exorbitant appetite for violence, for cruelty, and for the Siamese twin of cruelty, a kind of obsessive tenderness which at its worst was all but nauseating.[1]

Nevertheless, and in spite of these "handicaps," Agee goes on to praise Griffith as "a great primitive poet, a man capable, as only great and primitive artists can be, of intuitively perceiving and perfecting the tremendous magical images that underlie the memory and imagination of entire peoples."[2]

Agee cites some of Griffith's images, including the homecoming of the defeated hero in *Birth of a Nation* (1915) and the climactic chase on the ice floe in *Way Down East* (1920), which he sees as being shaped by the director's instinctive ability to translate into visual terms feelings that reside in the audience's collective unconscious. What Agee is getting at becomes clear when looking, for example, at the scene in *Birth of a Nation* to which he refers. When the Little Colonel returns to his devastated Southern home after the Civil War, the front door is at the right edge of the frame rather than, as one might expect, in the center; after a momentary, emotionally poignant delay, the door opens and the arms of his sister and mother reach out to embrace him as the shot fades to black. By composing the shot so that the specific detail of their faces are excluded, hidden behind the door at the side of the frame, Griffith manages to articulate a more general feeling of returning home—of being welcomed by "the bosom" of one's family, as Mr. Peacock describes it in John Ford's *Stagecoach* (1939). Although Agee doesn't comment on the gendered nature of the image, his essential point is that Griffith has managed in his visualization of the event to elevate it above and beyond a specific representation of the arrival home of this particular soldier.

Griffith's films on occasion overtly invite the audience to view his images in precisely this abstract, more generalized manner. *Way Down East,* for instance, begins with the introduction of Lillian Gish's character with intertitles explaining that "we call her 'Anna'—we might have called her 'Woman'" and that all the characters are "nowhere yet everywhere." The most famous example is, of course, the repeated image in *Intolerance* (1916) of Gish rocking a cradle; the shot functions as a thematic linking device that connects the film's four distinct narratives, each set in a different time and place. A reference to the transcendental vision of Walt Whitman's poem "Out of the Cradle Endlessly Rocking," Gish's image in *Intolerance* never represents an actual, embodied character within the diegesis, like the other actors, but rather, the abstract, universal desire for nurturance and security.

Agee's notion of Griffith as a cinematic poet whose images capture the concrete objects before the camera yet at the same time resonate with larger, cultural values and experiences coincides with Andrew Sarris's view of director John Ford. According to Sarris, Ford's work captures both "the twitches of life and the silhouette of legend"; thus, he says, Ford's films are poetic largely because they possess a "double vision" that at once depicts specific events and "the abstraction of history."[3] A similar claim can be made for many of Griffith's films, even if they lack the overt metaphorical status given to Gish in *Intolerance.* Griffith had a penchant for broad theatricalism, which was ingrained by a decade of experience on the stage, largely in melodramatic potboilers. This influence, which Agee correctly observes Griffith could never shed despite his other advances in cinematic technique,[4] perhaps, ironically, worked to the director's advantage, pushing his characters, as Sarris might say, toward the legendary as opposed to the literal.

Indeed, we might say that Griffith's films are on one level poetic medita- tions about the very business of gender construction that Steve Neale notes is central to the ideological work of movies generally.[5] Significantly, the primary genre within which Griffith worked was that of the "woman's film." Scott Simmon claims that through approximately one-quarter of the 450 one- and two-reelers that Griffith made for Biograph from 1908 to 1913, he virtually defined the genre. Griffith was producing three films a week at a time when the role of women was dramatically changing, as they began to move out of the domestic sphere into public space.[6] For Simmon, Griffith's influence in this regard is so pronounced that he redubs him, with intentional irony, "Father of the Woman's Film." It certainly is true that one of Griffith's major contributions to the history of the cinema was the image of Victorian femininity that became etched into the collective imagination of his era. This image was the product of a combination of Victorian melodrama and the code of southern gentility that informed his upbringing in Kentucky. As film historian Lewis Jacobs observed, Griffith consistently cast "mere slips of girls, fifteen or sixteen years old, blond and wide-eyed. . . . All his heroines—Mary Pickford, Mae Marsh, Lillian Gish, Blanche Sweet—were, at least in Griffith's eye, the pale, helpless, slim-bodied heroines of the nineteenth-century English poets."[7] Critics have remarked that this unchanging image of women was largely responsible for Griffith's precipitous decline as a director in the 1920s, when it came to seem jarringly out of tune with the Jazz Age, the era of the newly liberated flapper.

Jacobs's description is true of none of Griffith's actresses more than Lillian Gish. She embodied the period's idealized image of female beauty as fully as, say, the illustrations of Charles Dana Gibson did before her. In her autobiography, Gish reports Griffith's instructions to her that one of her characters be understood to represent "the essence of all girlhood, not just one girl," and that she attempt to embody "the essence of virginity."[8] Clearly, Griffith succeeded. For many scholars of film acting, Gish was such a great star because of her ability to represent qualities, beyond her particular character in any given film, of womanhood itself. Richard Dyer, for example, writes that "before [Gish] is a real person, she is an essence," while for James Naremore, she is "the perfect incarnation of WASP beauty."[9]

Because of the looming importance of Gish's image, many would agree with Simmon's claim that "it is evident from Griffith's woman's films—both from their numbers and their narratives—that women not men were central to his career-long project."[10] Yet I would argue that Griffith's films are equally concerned with the representation of men. In fact, Griffith's representations of male characters were rather similar to his treatment of women; inevitably, while they do focus emphatically on women, his films also address questions of masculinity. In standard melodramatic fashion, Griffith's characters, both men and women, are clearly divided between good and evil, and the narratives of his films are built on assumptions about moral absolutes. This includes the era's values of gender and sexuality that he internalized as completely as he did the racist perspective evident in the climax of *Birth of a Nation* when the Ku Klux Klan comes to the rescue of virtuous Southern womanhood like John Ford's cavalry in the climax of *Stagecoach.* Tellingly, *Way Down East* begins by expressing the hope that its story of a naive young woman's seduction will make men realize the pain and suffering *"our* selfishness" may cause (my emphasis).

Griffith's films, like the genre system itself, tend to present what Naremore describes as "a trenchantly binary world."[11] In terms of representing gender, if women in Griffith's films are either virtuous or fallen, madonnas or whores, his male characters also are depicted in two analogous, broadly opposite ways: as lusting brutes—Joan Mellen's big bad wolves—or as sensitive, if not effeminized, gentle souls. This pattern is obvious in the appositely titled prehistoric film *Man's Genesis* (1912), wherein the more sensitive and gentle male, named Weakhands, sets us on the path to civilization by conquering the sexual threat of the villain, named Brute Force, who carries a club and wants to take women by physical coercion. For biographer Robert M. Henderson, Griffith was strongly attracted to the story of primitive man and his struggles.[12] He remade *Man's Genesis* as a follow-up to his more well known western, *The Battle of Elderbush Gulch* (both 1913), originally calling it, with its obvious Freudian overtones, *Wars of the Primal Tribes. Way Down East* offers the opposing characters of the womanizing Lennox Sanderson (Lowell Sherman) and the timid Professor (Creighton Hale), with the hero David Bartlett (Richard Barthelmess) as the ideal synthesis, a model for, as another introductory intertitle tells us, the "man-animal" who has yet to reach the "high standard" of heterosexual monogamy (itself posited as the enlightening gift of Christianity) to aspire to. A similar masculine binary informs Griffith's prototypical gangster film, *The Musketeers of Pig Alley* (1912), in which The Little Lady (Gish) finds herself caught between duty to her unassertive husband, identified only as "the musician" (Walter Miller), who is easy prey to the ways of the street, and returning a favor by protecting the cocky criminal Snapper Kid (Elmer Booth) from the police. The same masculine duality informs Griffith's racist representations of the Other, as in the conflict between the swarthy Indians who threaten to rape the white women in *The Battle of Elderbush Gulch* and the libidinous blacks in *Birth of a Nation,* most notably the stereotypical buck Gus (a white actor in blackface), who pursues the virginal white maiden Flora Cameron (Mae Marsh) through the woods until she chooses to plunge to her death from a cliff in order to avoid the proverbial fate worse than death.

This design is especially interesting in *Broken Blossoms, or The Yellow Man and the Girl* (1919), one of Griffith's most "poetic" films in Agee's sense. In first-run screenings, audiences were cued to regard the film as poetic abstraction even before the projector started, as it was preceded by a live prologue and a one-act ballet, written by Griffith, titled "The Dance of Life and Death," featuring Fate, "a spider of destiny," and a young girl bound "with the chains of everyday existence." Griffith wrote the adaptation himself, including the florid insert titles that offer ample evidence of the faults in the director's sensibility enumerated by Agee. An intimate drama with only three central characters in a variation of the typical Griffith romantic triangle, *Broken Blossoms* was a deliberate move away from the epic sweep of the earlier *Birth of a Nation* and *Intolerance*. Significantly, it was Griffith's first film to be released through United Artists, the company he formed with Charlie Chaplin, Douglas Fairbanks, and Mary Pickford in 1919, although he initially made the film for Adolph Zukor's Artcraft Pictures Corporation and then had to buy back the rights. The film was important for Griffith; at the very beginning an insert title tells us that he did not merely direct the film, but that it was made under his "personal direction."

Adopted from Thomas Burke's story, "The Chink and the Child," from his 1917 collection *Limehouse Nights, Broken Blossoms* tells the story of a gentle, idealistic Chinese youth, Cheng Huan (Barthelmess), who decides to journey to England for the purpose of offering spiritual enlightenment to decadent, violent westerners. Reduced to being a shopkeeper in the Limehouse slum of London, he becomes enamored of a young local girl, Lucy (Lillian Gish), who is physically abused by her stepfather, a swaggering boxer named Battling Burrows (Donald Crisp). After one of her beatings at the strong hands of Burrows, Lucy staggers into Cheng's shop and collapses. He proceeds to nurse and care for her, but Burrows discovers her whereabouts and, assuming "the worst," drags Lucy back home, where in a rage he beats her to death. Inconsolable, the previously peaceful Cheng Huan kills Burrows and then commits suicide.

Griffith chose to make *Broken Blossoms* in part because of the reception of *Birth of a Nation* as racist by some audiences. Many black viewers as well as former abolitionists mounted protests when *Birth* was shown in several northern cities, and riots occurred in more than one instance. A concerned Griffith responded by publishing a pamphlet titled "Free Speech in America" as well as by making his next film, *Intolerance,* the title of which expresses its unambiguous moral lesson. Certainly *Broken Blossoms*, as Julia Lesage has noted, was a deliberate attempt to counter the prevailing "yellow peril" representations of Asians then prevalent in cinema and other popular media, most notably in Sax Rohmer's series of Fu Manchu novels that had achieved wide popularity by the time Griffith made his film. Images of American Chinatowns as places of lurking evil were already conventional in the silent era and have been understood as a response to the competition in the labor force represented by large numbers of Chinese immigrants, particularly in the west, and to the threat of Japan to American imperialist expansion in the Pacific. But while in *Broken Blossoms* this racist view may be that of the bigoted Burrows and the other inhabitants of Limehouse who view Cheng Huan as just "another chink storekeeper," it is not that of the film. Indeed, Griffith's major alteration of Burke's narrative, as Lesage notes, was to change the Yellow Man from a "'worthless drifter of an Oriental' to a poetic, peaceful Buddhist lover of beauty," thus making him a decidedly more sympathetic figure.[13] (Of course, the casting of a white actor, Richard Barthelmess, as the Yellow Man is a choice determined by the casting practices of an inherently racist film industry. If the film works to minimize racial difference, it does so strictly from a white perspective.)

Karl Brown, a frequent cameraman for Griffith who worked on *Broken Blossoms,* has written that this film "*was* a fantasy, a dream, a vision of archetypical beings out of the long inherited memory of the human race. No such people as we saw on the screen were ever alive in the workaday world of today or of any other day. They were as Griffith had explained to me in that dark projection room, misty, misty. . . . They were the creatures of a poetic imagination that had at very long last found its outlet in its own terms. It was a parable in poetry, timeless and eternally true."[14] These "creatures" are clearly conceived and performed, in E. M. Forster's terms, as "flat," that is, as representative types or caricatures rather than as psychologically "round" individuals.

The narrative announces itself as a moral exemplum at the outset, as another early title asks the viewer, "But do we not ourselves use the whip of unkind words and deeds? So, perhaps, Battling may even carry a message of warning." In other words, we are intended to understand the character of Battling Burrows as an exaggerated, more obvious version of an aspect of real men. This idea is powerfully expressed when in the film's climax Burrows's friends come into the police station to report the murder, and the bobbies are gathered around a newspaper proclaiming the latest war news in a banner headline that reads "Better Than Last Week, Only 40,000 Casualties"—a clear comment on the carnage of World War I. As if in a reverse zoom from a big close-up to an extreme long shot, suddenly, startlingly, Burrows's aggression is here put into a more global perspective.

As already mentioned, the fear of racial miscegenation, of that unspeakable "fate worse than death," looms large in Griffith's melodramatic world. This fate does in fact occur in *Birth of a Nation,* and almost comes to past in *The Battle of Elderbush Gulch,* the mise-en-scène of which influenced the famous scene in *Stagecoach* where the gambler Hatfield is about to kill Lucy Mallory when it looks as if the stage is going to be overrun by Indians. This fear is also at the dramatic center of *Broken Blossoms*—especially since it threatens an innocent waif whom Griffith describes in an intertitle as "alabaster," whom Cheng renames White Blossom, and who is portrayed by the actress Dyer accurately calls a *white* star, "the supreme instance" of Hollywood's "equation of light, virtue and femininity."[15]

If, for Laura Mulvey, women are constituted as objects of the male gaze by narrative cinema—the style of which Griffith was a major progenitor—then *Broken Blossoms* is a clear demonstration of women as what she calls "to-be-looked-at-ness."[16] Most obviously, the two important secondary characters, Evil Eye and Spying One (their names signaling the importance of vision), both ensnare Lucy by looking at her: the former examines her lasciviously; the latter sees her supine, seemingly contented, in Cheng's quarters above his shop and informs Burrows, setting in motion the tragedy to come. Even Cheng perceives Lucy as "a vision"; returning home from the opium den, "with perhaps a whiff of the lillied pipe still in his brain," as one of Griffith's insert titles tells us, he rubs his eyes when he first sees her to make sure she isn't merely a hallucination, a vision of beauty in the literal sense.

Lucy comes to understand her own identity as an object of the male gaze. Somehow, in an inchoate way, she perceives her limited, powerless position within patriarchy—a dawning realization, I would argue, also gained by the attentive viewer. Early in the film Griffith privileges Lucy's consciousness, visualizing her thoughts about the two options offered to her as a poor woman. We see her first recalling a conversation with a harried housewife and mother who, picking lice from the heads of unkempt children and scrubbing laundry under the watchful eye of a stern husband, tells her not to get married; and then we see her memory of a pair of prostitutes, faces thickly painted with makeup, who warn her not to follow in the footsteps of streetwalkers like them. Lucy contemplates these two unappealing alternatives while sitting on the dock, a place full of jutting pylons, ship masts, a man sawing a log, and even a tall, erect sailor smoking a pipe—a space, that is, surrounded and constrained by powerful phallic imagery. The neighborhood, the bounded world in which she lives, is a thoroughly patriarchal one. It is no wonder that Lucy frequently is lit from below, a visual expression of her ghastly entrapment, a restriction also suggested by the heavy rope upon which she sits so dejectedly on the dock ("a young girl trapped by the chains of everyday existence," according to the intertitle). Later, in Cheng's room, as her own sexual identity begins to dawn on her, Lucy contemplates herself in a mirror—a gesture that, according to art historian John Berger, is the patriarchal projection of the male emphasis on female beauty onto the female and disavowed as *her* narcissism and vanity.[17] And when Lucy is physically threatened by the macho Burrows, she seeks to mollify him by putting on a happy face, her fingers forcing the corners of her mouth upward, an image more "suitable" to her femininity. One could not ask for a more explicit—that is, "poetic"—image of the oppression of women within patriarchy as this one of Lucy forcing a pitiful excuse of a smile upon her countenance, even as it becomes a ghastly grin that simultaneously makes it strange.

Significantly, though, in *Broken Blossoms* spectacle and performance are shown to be equally a defining aspect of masculinity as well. Most important in this regard is the film's use of boxing, both as Battling's profession and as social metaphor. Writing about masculinity in film noir, Frank Krutnik notes that boxing "represents a primitive form of masculine testing . . . an enclosed arena of masculine performance."[18] In his analysis of Martin Scorsese's *Raging Bull* (1980), Robin Wood sees boxing as important for masculine self-definition, describing the sport as "ritualized violence in which one man attempts to smash the near-naked body of another for the satisfaction (surely fundamentally erotic) of a predominantly male mass audience."[19] Whereas wrestling, for Roland Barthes, is a theatrical event, a kind of passion play enacting the metaphysical conflict of good and evil,[20] boxing addresses the more material issues of the body and its importance to a gendered masculine identity.

In *Broken Blossoms,* although, as Lesage notes, nakedly aggressive masculine sexuality is displaced onto working-class white males, the film's representation of boxing is more focused on the sport's opportunity for the enactment of masculine identity than on class difference.[21] The images of boxing make explicit the ways in which masculinity is schematized in terms of performance

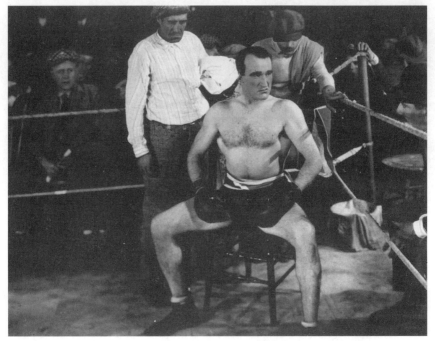

Donald Crisp as the swaggering Battling Burrows in *Broken Blossoms* (1919).

throughout the film. Battling, the embodiment of pure physicality, fights for a living. His body language is always forceful, his carriage erect. His very name (Burrows) suggests the earthiness signified visually by his cauliflower ear and awful table manners, including sticking his finger in his mouth to clean his teeth after eating. Burrows is base, animalistic; it is no coincidence that his boxing opponent in the urban jungle is, appropriately, the Limehouse Tiger. Fittingly, Donald Crisp—who later would famously portray the family patriarch in Ford's *How Green Was My Valley* (1941)—plays Burrows in a manner more broad than any of the other actors, constantly thrusting his limbs outward, swaggering across the frame during the boxing match, and puffing his chest out ridiculously as he is attended to between rounds.[22] It matters little whether Crisp's performance is the result of Griffith's instructions to him, his own conception of the role, the influence of contemporary codes of melodramatic style, or a combination of all of these, for it is entirely consistent with the film's deconstructive project.

Cheng is Burrows's opposite in every way. Where Burrows is hyper-masculine, Cheng is effeminate. If Burrows protests to his manager when caught drinking with some female companions, "Wot yer want me to do, pick violets?" then Cheng, we are told, sees in Lucy the flower to which the rest of Limehouse is blind. Stopping to smell the flowers, so to speak, Cheng Huan represents the loftier spiritual and aesthetic side of man's nature. His movements are more fluid, his posture and physical gestures, unlike the outwardly thrusting Burrows, are contained, his body curled inward (not unlike Lucy when she sits despondently by the dock, contemplating her own oppression). Throughout, Cheng is associated with fragile, ornate finery and the ethereality of dreams. He is often photographed with the Sartov lens, named for the photographer Hendrick Sartov who, in his portraits of none other than Lillian Gish, pioneered the soft-focus style usually reserved for female stars in the classic Hollywood era. Cheng is also shot, as Dudley Andrew has noted, "with curved masking [irising], diffused lighting, or a black background," which has the effect of isolating him from the mise-en-scène.[23] This compositional isolation further effeminizes Cheng by distancing him from the masculine trajectory of mastery over the physical environment, of getting the job done, that is characteristic of classic Hollywood film.

As the dramatic action rises, Griffith crosscuts between Burrows in the ring with the Tiger and Cheng above his shop at the moment he is almost overtaken by his desire for Lucy. This montage makes explicit the thematic contrast between the two men, articulating the tension between the physical and the spiritual, the "body and soul"—a tension that Leger Grindon sees as constituting the dramatic center of the boxing film as a genre.[24] In *Broken Blossoms,* of course, Burrows is the body, Cheng the soul—but this relationship is more complex than at first it may seem. In Griffith's crosscutting, if one of the actions—the boxing match—is a publicly performed spectacle, then the other, a seemingly private, intimate moment, is revealed to be just as involved with the performative in relation to masculinity. The crosscutting here, in other words, serves both as a contrast *and* a comparison, articulating a relation between the crosscut images far richer than many of Griffith's earlier experiments with thematic montage, including even *Intolerance*. Griffith cuts back and forth between the two actions three times, drawing a precise parallel in each instance: in the first, Burrows's blood is rising, as is Cheng's; in the second, Burrows and the Tiger spar, while Cheng begins to advance toward

Richard Barthelmess as the kinder, gentler Cheng Huan (*Broken Blossoms*).

Lucy and the camera, at war with himself; and then, after Cheng masters his sexual desire for Lucy and withdraws, Burrows knocks out his opponent. The film here insightfully shows that Cheng's struggle with his desire is a physical battle as tough as prizefighting, the pressure of social propriety and racial boundaries as palpable as the wildly cheering crowd at the boxing match.

Thus both Burrows and Cheng are conscious of their social identities, their everyday performance of self, no less than Lucy. When his manager suggests that Burrows retire early from the pub to rest before his rematch with the Limehouse Tiger, Burrows responds by distancing himself from any perceived "feminine" weakness with his sarcastic comment about picking violets. And just as Burrows fights for the pleasure of his audience, clearly playing to them as he struts around the ring, so Cheng is self-conscious of himself as a visible minority. Griffith's intertitle at the dramatic moment when Cheng conquers his passion ("His love remains a pure and holy thing—even his worst foe says this") is better understood as coming from Cheng's interior point of view, as if Cheng were thinking, "I'd better not put myself into a position wherein the white racists of Limehouse can accuse me of miscegenation," than merely as emanating from Griffith's own unconsciously internalized racism. No matter how feminized Cheng may be, he cannot escape being viewed by dominant culture as another masculine Other who poses a sexual threat to pure white womanhood. In one of the saddest moments of the film, Lucy, unaware of her ideological collusion, affectionately refers to Cheng Huan as "Chinky." Through the crosscutting during the boxing match, then, *Broken Blossoms* shows that the constraints of ideology are as powerful as a prizefighter's body blows.

Concerning the dangers of male sexuality, *Broken Blossoms* is representative of Griffith's work generally. At every level, his films are riven with the tension between desire and restraint. Griffith at once idealized his women as pure, frail Victorian heroines who are to be protected by upright men, but at the same time he subjected them to a kind of sadistic violation by putting them in dangerous situations from which they had to be rescued in the rousing climax. As Simmon rightly notes, while Griffith's woman's films moralize about women moving into public space, through the very apparatus of the cinematic medium, and its ability to manufacture star images, Griffith subjected them to the harsh control of a male gaze. As a result, observes Simmon, "the story line takes its stand against what the filmgoing situation promotes—the public display of women."[25] Further, in so many of the "last-minute rescues" for which Griffith was known, an aggressive male seeks to penetrate the locked doors of a cowering female, clearly a metaphoric indulgence in the prospect of rape, while the inevitable rescue is a denial of the wish. This repressed meaning bursts forth with startling clarity, perhaps most obviously, in *An Unseen Enemy* (1912), wherein two orphaned adolescent sisters (Lillian and Dorothy Gish) cower in fear in a locked room as a gun threatens them by poking through a hole in the wall.[26]

Clearly Griffith's films functioned as a screen for his personal obsessions and anxieties, most of which centered on his ambivalent attitude toward women. According to Russell Merritt, Griffith's work was "blatant" in its autobiographical aspect and functioned as "a form of therapy" for the director to work through "an adolescence marked by feelings of unexpressed anger, acute humiliation, and fear of women."[27] A psychoanalytic reading of *Broken Blossoms* surely would lead to understanding the film as reflecting the sexual tensions within its maker, for it fits into this pattern of sexual threat more provocatively than most of Griffith's films. Nevertheless, the film's true importance is to be found in the ways in which in it Griffith translates—or "poeticizes"—his personal concerns into culturally relevant imagery. Perhaps the result of its dreamlike nature, the latent sexual and gender content comes to the surface in *Broken Blossoms* with particular clarity.

In her perceptive analysis of the film, Lesage shows how the climax represents a male rape fantasy. For her, "this is one of the most emotionally powerful sequences of sexual assault on film."[28] Certainly Burrows's beating of Lucy is strongly marked as phallic aggression; he brandishes the bullwhip at crotch level and penetrates the locked door with an ax, anticipating by decades Jack Torrence, another problematic patriarchal figure, in Stanley Kubrick's *The Shining* (1980). After the beating, Burrows holds his whip limply at his waist, in a kind of postcoital detumescence. Cheng's death, the result of a rare instance of an unsuccessful last-minute rescue, is the price he must pay for his desire. Before rushing out to confront Burrows, Cheng suddenly, and surprisingly, pulls a gun from within an ornate chest of his Oriental finery and clutches it to his own chest, a wonderfully "poetic" image of masculine aggression now unrepressed. (Significantly, Burke's story, by contrast, concludes with Burrows being fatally bitten by a poisonous snake, earlier left in his bed by Cheng Huan, *after* the Chinaman commits suicide.) In the film, when Cheng shoots Burrows, there are photos of boxers on the wall behind him, a comment on his altered nature. He has become what he beheld, made over into an aggressive, violent male no different from the roughhousing American sailors from whom he shrinks in horror at the beginning of the film. The binary conflict is resolved, as in the narrative of most genre films, but here the ending is tragic because of the character's failure to attain a normative masculine identity.

Crucially, Cheng's romantic idealization of Lucy is shown to be equally as debilitating to women as Burrows's beatings. If one debases her, bringing her to her knees through physical abuse, the other possesses and entraps her by literally raising her on a pedestal as an object of romantic worship—precisely

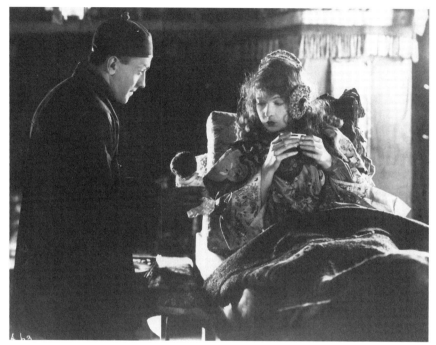

Lucy (Lillian Gish) is worshipped on Cheng Huan's pedestal (*Broken Blossoms*).

the two strategies of sadism and fetishistic scopophilia available to patriarchal representation, as identified by Mulvey.[29] The clothes and finery with which Cheng adorns her are, in Mary Ann Doane's terms, a masquerade of feminine beauty.[30] Either way, she is an object deprived of subjectivity within a masculine discourse, not unlike the little doll she pathetically clutches and which serves as a poignant objective correlative of her own position within a male network of gazes. No matter which way Lucy may turn, she cannot escape being the embodiment of "to-be-looked-at-ness." She is in each case what a man wants her to be: servant, little girl, woman, movie star.

In his book on star acting, Charles Affron describes *Broken Blossoms* as a "poetic" film in large part because of the actors' ability to represent allegorical concepts rather than realistic individual beings, to leave "the realm of representational acting" for "that realm . . . in which the actor becomes metaphor itself."[31] To be more specific, in *Broken Blossoms* the actors become metaphors of culturally defined gender positions. And because they enact roles that are defined *as* roles, as performed, the film ultimately questions ideological assumptions about what masculinity, as well as femininity, "naturally" is. Masculinity, in *Broken Blossoms,* is consequently decentered as the stable term from which the feminine Other is defined. Just as patriarchy defines and limits women and femininity through the gaze and performance, so *Broken Blossoms* says that men are subject to the same processes in order to attain a masculine identity. The boxing ring becomes the stage on which masculine identity is performed. The boxers are cheered on by an applauding crowd, mostly of men; those in the front rows are discernibly better dressed, implying the privilege of class difference but also the shared acceptance of masculine ideology. It is not coincidental that Spying One tells Burrows where he saw Lucy, and that he plants the idea in Burrows's mind that she has been "dishonored" by an Oriental man, in the boxing ring after Burrows's sparring practice. And, given the outcome of the plot, the film suggests further that our culture's valorization of a particular type of aggressive masculinity, the big bad wolf, comes at a great price.

Thus, where Lesage sees in *Broken Blossoms* an instance of patriarchal discourse that must be deconstructed, I see a text that is an act of deconstruction, for it reveals masculine as well as feminine roles as socially determined. *Broken Blossoms,* I would argue, is a radical film, particularly noteworthy for calling into question the notions of gender difference that inform so much of popular cinema, including Griffith's. It holds up to examination alternative versions of masculinity, which Griffith himself offered in so many of his earlier films. The binary view of masculinity that *Broken Blossoms* interrogates became a convention that cut across numerous genres and periods. Variations of it are to be found, for example, in the classic gangster film's opposition of two friends from the hood, one criminal and the other law-abiding, as with James Cagney's Tom Powers and childhood friend Matt Doyle in *The Public Enemy* (1931); in the screwball comedy's opposition between the charming rogue and the milquetoast, as represented by Cary Grant and Ralph Bellamy, respectively, in *His Girl Friday* (1940); in film noir's contrast between the tough guy and the fall guy, as in the relationship between Dan Duryea's sleazy pimp and Edward G. Robinson's meek clerk in Fritz Lang's *Scarlet Street* (1945); in the contrast between two kinds of professional leaders, as embodied by John Wayne and Montgomery Clift, in Howard Hawks's western, *Red River* (1948) (discussed more fully in chapter 3); and so on. *Broken Blossoms,* structured by binary oppositions between the Occident and the Orient, between Christ and Buddha, between the big bad wolf and little meek sheep, is as "trenchantly binary" as any Hollywood genre movie; yet while it may be true that Griffith's vision, as David Cook observes, reduced human history to a melodramatic struggle between Good and Evil, and "structured the cinema . . . [in] the way most of us still perceive it,"[32] *Broken Blossoms* offers alternative versions of masculinity for our consideration, and, astonishingly, finds them both wanting.

While Hollywood films, as Neale says, generally work to construct and reinforce patriarchal definitions of gender by naturalizing them, *Broken Blossoms* is one of those rare films that makes these constructions visible, by foregrounding their very enactment—not unlike the later melodramas of Max Ophuls, Douglas Sirk, and Rainer Werner Fassbinder. In mainstream cinema generally, as Neale writes, "masculinity, as an ideal, at least, is implicitly known,"[33] but this is not the case with *Broken Blossoms.* To what extent this may have been conscious on the part of its maker, of course we cannot say; but certainly, in the end, *Broken Blossoms* is profoundly more "poetic" than James Agee, or even D. W. Griffith himself, ever intended.

Walking Small

W. C. Fields, Groucho Marx, and the Emasculation
of the American Comic Tradition

Fields of Dreams

It has been observed that the rise of the gangster film in the early 1930s, after the onset of the Great Depression, revealed a general disillusionment with the American Dream, that nexus of cultural values equating happiness, material wealth, career success, and bourgeois comfort, and the claim that anyone could achieve it in America. This individualism and expansive optimism was fuelled by the open spaces of the American frontier, but by the 1920s, when the gangster film as a distinct genre began to take shape with such silent films as Josef von Sternberg's *Underworld* (1927) and *Thunderbolt* (1929), the frontier was already consigned to history, officially declared closed following the census of 1890. Gangster films constituted, on one level, a cultural response to the closing of the frontier, for its protagonists embraced a pioneer individualism placed in a contemporary setting. Movie gangsters, then, remained remarkably American in spirit, for they were, at the same time, unethical businessmen, a newer breed of Robber Barons seeking the American Dream amid the dangers and opportunities of the new urban wilderness. In John Huston's *Key Largo* (1948), when gangster Johnny Rocco (Edward G. Robinson) asks why he needs the drug shipment for which he is holding the inhabitants of a Florida hotel hostage when he is already rich, he promptly replies, like any contemporary corporate CEO, that the simple reason is because he wants more.[1]

If, as President Calvin Coolidge had declared, "The chief business of the American people is business," then even during the Depression business continued. In both the movies and the real world, the closing of the frontier, the space that historian Frederick Jackson Turner argued was so important as a social and economic "safety-valve" for the American psyche, was followed by the opening of the bootlegger's spigots.[2] As the criminal lawyer Alonzo Emmerich (Louis Calhern) observes in another Huston crime film, *The Asphalt Jungle* (1950), "Crime is merely a left-handed form of human endeavor." With pragmatic American know-how, the gangster reconciled the myth of the American Dream with historical reality and in so doing retained his status as family breadwinner and mythic wielder of phallic power.

Yet the American Dream had been shown as fading before Black Tuesday in October 1929, already receding beyond reach like the unobtainable green light at the end of Daisy's dock in F. Scott Fitzgerald's *The Great Gatsby* (1925). In Fitzgerald's novel, the eponymous Gatsby, a rich, mysterious businessman who may have earned his fortune as a bootlegger by fixing the 1919 World Series or through a number of other questionable ventures, attempts the Horatio Alger transformation of working-class nobody to host of the rich and famous at his posh Long Island mansion in order to create his own American dream home with his lost love, Daisy. As a sign of his success, he proudly displays his collection of shirts to her as if his wealth and impressive sartorial taste is an index of his worth as a human being, recalling the gaggle of movie gangsters from Little Caesar (Robinson) onward who are fitted for new suits once they take over the gang and their careers are on the rise. But as in the gangster film, so for Gatsby, clothes do not make the man, and his dream ultimately fails, as we are told by Nick Carraway, the novel's narrator, because of "the colossal vitality of his illusion"[3]—that is, because of the insistence with which Gatsby maintains his take on the American Dream despite the reality of Daisy's marriage to another man and the inevitable passage of time.

If gangster movies stubbornly clung to the vitality of the illusion regarding the American Dream, comedies at the time often were more critical of it. Certainly Frank Capra, perhaps the most prominent director of the era, eloquently defended American tradition, espousing democracy, individualism, and capitalism in a series of populist comedies that includes *Mr. Deeds Goes to Town* (1936), *Mr. Smith Goes to Washington* (1939), and *Meet John Doe* (1941), in which the little guy emerges as hero and is able to bring about change within "the system." And, too, John Ford celebrated with nostalgic charm a vision of Americana in *Doctor Bull* (1933), *Judge Priest* (1934), and *Steamboat Round the Bend* (1935), all starring Will Rogers, that bore little relation to contemporary reality. The harmony of Ford's mythical America is summed up visually at the end of *Drums along the Mohawk* (1939), when the new American flag is hoisted for the first time as the gathered crowd looks on in awed respect, including a burly smith (workingman), black woman, and even Native American, who salutes it.

In contrast, though, screwball comedies, which had their greatest popularity in the 1930s, took aim at a variety of social institutions, depicting them as restrictive and staid. A few comedies were bold enough to address social and economic issues of the day, such as *My Man Godfrey* (1936), about a group of wealthy socialites who bring home a "forgotten man" as part of a scavenger hunt, and *The Devil and Miss Jones* (1941), in which the rich boss of a department store goes "underground" as a worker to discover who has been unionizing his employees and ends up becoming sympathetic to them. Both movies, it might be argued, dealt with class difference in America more directly than many contemporaneous dramatic films did. But screwball comedies are occasionally even more radical in their implications. The collapse of the brontosaurus skeleton being assembled by paleontologist David Huxley (Cary Grant) at the end of Howard Hawks's *Bringing Up Baby* (1938), brought about by the wacky Susan (Katharine Hepburn), is, in Robin Wood's famous reading, a vivid summary image of the carnivalesque implications of screwball comedy: "The dry bones represent his life-work and are an image of his way of life, destroyed finally by the eruption of the Id."[4]

The trajectory of the silent era's greatest comic figure, Charlie Chaplin's Tramp, in the same decade reveals the extent to which film comedy had changed, had become more socially conscious. Charlie cherished traditional values with a cloying sentimentality not unlike D. W. Griffith's, but in the

1930s he capitulated to contemporary economic realities. Charlie, like Chaplin himself, was the embodiment of the American Dream, someone who did pick himself up by his own bootstraps—even if in his movies he used his cane on occasion to help him do so. In his earlier films social problems are resolved with a swift kick in the pants, but by the 1930s such solutions are impossible. In *Modern Times* (1936), Charlie simultaneously desires and parodies a comfortable, middle-class life and a happy marriage. Early in the film Charlie could still dream of living with the gamin (Paulette Goddard) in a neat middle-class cottage, represented in a bucolic vision complete with grapes growing in abundant profusion outside the kitchen window and a cow obligingly coming to the back door to deliver fresh milk. Chaplin's dream imagery focuses on a house not only because the Tramp and the gamin are homeless, but also because it is the locus of American visions of success. Indeed, for some historians, "the house has been . . . the dominant symbol for American culture," representing nothing less than the American Dream itself.[5]

By contrast, Groucho Marx, never one to succumb even momentarily to romantic illusion, is considerably more cynical about home and hearth. Playing a shady real estate salesman in *The Cocoanuts* (1929), he promises in his pitch that "you can have any kind of a home you want to"; "you can even have stucco," he adds, but quickly admits, "oh, how you can get stucco" buying a house from the likes of him. For Groucho, the foundation of the dream home is already rotten. His questionable approach to selling real estate undercuts Charlie's more naive faith and sentimentalism, and underscores the fact that the moral values of Chaplin's Tramp are rooted in pre-Depression optimism. The appropriately titled *Modern Times,* made in the middle of the decade, was Chaplin's first attempt at explicit social commentary—the image of Charlie caught in the huge gears of a machine became iconographic of twentieth-century feelings of alienation and disempowerment—and so, at film's end, Chaplin makes his final appearance as the Tramp when, after being victimized by machinery both mechanical and social throughout the film, he is pushed aside by an auto as he heads on down the road. Already in the modern times of the 1930s plans were in process for a national system of interstate highways that would facilitate Walt Whitman's open road, an example of "progress" that, Chaplin knew, would leave the Tramp in its dust.

If the sentimental Chaplin was out of place, an anachronism, during the Depression, the comedies of the streetwise Marx brothers found their

métier in the period's collective social anxiety and doubt. The Italian im-
migrant persona of Chico Marx spoke to European-Americans' aspiration
for assimilation in the American melting pot. At the same time, the brothers'
nose-thumbing humor employs a carnivalesque chaos wherein sacred cows
are roasted mercilessly. *Duck Soup* (1933), unquestionably the most trenchant
in the series of the Marxist critiques, has been called an "anarchic comedy,"
with good reason. As Rufus T. Firefly, president of the mythical country of
Fredonia, Groucho proclaims in the film, "Whatever it is—I'm against it."
The country's war with the neighboring nation of Sylvania begins because
of a trifling personal incident, when President Firefly insults that country's
ambassador (Louis Calhern) during one of Groucho's verbal cascades. Death
and destruction, albeit in a comic mode, follow as a result. In the big battle,
the four Marx brothers wear a series of different military uniforms from
different times and nations, a jumbled pastiche of military iconography suggesting a universal criticism of militarism and patriotism. The first time we
see Groucho in the climactic battle scene, he is wearing a Revolutionary War
uniform with a Confederate Army cap, which later on becomes a coonskin
cap (with the tail snipped off by Harpo)—a frontier icon that becomes more
cogent given the treatment it receives at the beginning of *Go West* (1940),
their western parody discussed below. Indeed, *Duck Soup* depicts the very
concepts of nationalism and patriotism as little more than absurd: "While
you're out there risking life and limb amid shot and shell, we'll be in here,
thinking what a sucker you are," says President Firefly to Pinky (Harpo), who
has been "volunteered" to infiltrate enemy lines in a losing battle—a joke that
underscores the self-interest of state power.

The comedies of W. C. Fields also undermined the values of the American
Dream, particularly in its family aspect. Andrew Bergman, Gerald Mast, and
Raymond Durgnat, among the few critics to have written on Fields at any
length, all agree that the comedian's humor often has as its target a debunking
of the basic values of the American way of life, especially the home and the
family. *The Bank Dick* (1940), according to Mast, is "the culmination of Fields's
studies of small-town, proper, moralistic Americana"; "if the beginning of the
film burlesques the propriety of the Protestant ethic, its ending burlesques
the American Dream of happiness through wealth."[6] The Marx brothers avoid
family ties and domesticity, and Groucho's wooing of Margaret Dumont
always has an ulterior motive, usually money, and is patently insincere—"Mrs.

Rittenhouse," he confesses to her in *Animal Crackers* (1930), "ever since I met you, I've swept you off my feet"—but Fields is typically shackled with family. Being head of the household is an ordeal for Fields, and complications arise for him as the harried family patriarch in, for example, *You're Telling Me!* and *It's a Gift* (both 1934). In the former, he plays inventor Sam Bisbee, who with misdirected American ingenuity seeks to support his family with inventions like collapsible spoons and keyhole finders for drunks while dealing with his daughter's problematic love life; and in the latter, he is Harold Bissonette, proprietor of a small-town general store who is besieged beyond endurance by his shrewish wife, cloying children, and annoying customers.

While critics such as Mast and Durgnat have offered some of the most useful theoretical frameworks we have for considering film comedy in general, in writing about Fields they often fail to get beyond mere recapitulation, cheerfully recounting some of the comedian's routines involving his endearing misanthropy. Even Simon Louvish's monograph on *It's a Gift* largely fails to go beyond such celebration.[7] I suggest that if the Marx brothers critique the American Dream by deflating the pretensions of high culture, whether the rarefied atmosphere of opera in *A Night at the Opera* (1935) or the hallowed halls of the university in *Horse Feathers* (1932) ("I think you know what the trustees can do with their suggestions," says Groucho as Professor Quincy Adams Wagstaff, when he moves from the ranks of faculty to assume the headship of Huxley College), the comic films of W. C. Fields also undermine its cherished values, largely through their inflection of popular culture's idealized images of American masculinity. Fields's comedy plays off established American comic traditions involving triumphant and heroic comic archetypes of American masculinity that bespeak the self-image of the body politic.

Founding Fathers

In his essay "Laughter," Henri Bergson writes that "the comic comes into being just when society and the individual, freed from the worry of self-preservation, begin to regard themselves as works of art."[8] Indeed, as the United States began to develop national self-confidence after the Revolutionary War, truly indigenous art began to flourish. In 1787, the same year as the Constitutional Convention in Philadelphia, there appeared the first American theatrical comedy, *The Contrast,* by Royall Tyler—"A Citizen of the United States," as he is proudly described on the title page of the first published edition of the play. Also the first American play to be performed by professional actors, it created the wholly original character of Brother Jonathan, a homespun sage who mocks Americans' emulation of British fashion. The character of Jonathan established the soon-to-become familiar pattern, which survived for over a century on the American stage (and that appears, somewhat altered, in later fiction, most notably in the work of James Fenimore Cooper and Henry James), in which a plain New Englander outwits the foppish Englishman or American Anglophile, here embodied in the character of Mr. Dimple. Tyler's aim is clearly expressed in his prologue:

> *Exult each patriot heart!—this night is shewn*
> *A piece, which we may fairly call our own; . . .*
> *Why should our thoughts to distant countries roam,*
> *When each refinement may be found at home?*[9]

In the play, Jessamy, manservant to Mr. Dimple, who has been educated in Europe, tells his counterpart Jonathan, servant to Revolutionary War hero Colonel Manly, that he doesn't have "the graces"—to which Jonathan replies with cracker-barrel simplicity and pride that he has no intention of converting. With such repartee, Jonathan and subsequent comic New Englanders solidified the character of the sharp-witted Yankee who invariably represented honesty, plain dealing, common sense, industriousness, and egalitarianism. In short, American culture had begun, with characteristic exuberance, to depict itself with the character of Manly's man, Jonathan.

The Yankee's costume, according to Constance Rourke, consisted almost invariably of "a white bell-crowned hat, a coat with long tails that was usually blue, eccentric red and white trousers, and long boot-strap," eventually evolving into the patriotic icon of Uncle Sam. The Yankee actors and writers spoke in elaborate yet pithy colloquial monologues that, influenced in part by Benjamin Franklin, came to contain so much homespun wisdom that the comic Yankee was looked upon as a virtual oracle. As Rourke puts it, "His slanting dialect, homely metaphor, the penetrating rhythms of his speech . . . [created laughter that] also created a fresh sense of unity. . . . He was a symbol of triumph, of adaptability, of irrepressible life—of many qualities needed to induce confidence and self-possession among a new and unamalgamated people."[10]

However, as the nineteenth century progressed and the nation continued its westward expansion, sectionalism inevitably became more pronounced in American culture and politics. Consequently, westerners grew to dislike the Yankee for claiming to be *the* representative American figure. Western newspapers were full of stories disparaging him, and partly in response to Brother Jonathan and the East, the West developed the figure of the backwoodsman. He was a mighty being conjured by the American imagination to help tame the frontier and achieve Manifest Destiny. Stories about the backwoodsman were tall tales, wild hyperbolic statements concerning his size and strength, exaggerations befitting the scale of the American frontier. The scope of his exploits was literally cosmic, his mastery of the wilderness extending to the very heavens; he could unfreeze the Earth in its celestial path on a cold morning as easily as wrestle a bear. His speech was lusty, proud, expansive; and as Walt Whitman proclaims in "Song of Myself," he shouted his "barbaric yawp over the roofs of the world."[11]

The most popular backwoodsman figure was, of course, Davy Crockett. The historical Crockett, a celebrated frontiersman, soldier, and congressman, was quickly replaced by the mythical Crockett after his death at the Alamo in 1835, becoming a figure of such imaginative proportion that "the greatest writer of the age [Herman Melville] could compare him to a hero of Greek mythology and mean it not only as a joke, but as a serious statement about democratic heroism."[12] Crockett almanacs, which appeared from his death and into the mid-1850s, told in boisterous colloquial language of his grand adventures, but bore little resemblance to the facts of his life. So, for example, one day when "It war then so antediluvian and premature cold that my upper and lower teeth an' tongue war all collapsed together as tight as a friz oyster," the mythical Crockett took the warm blood of a bear he'd recently killed, poured it over the sun's face, and "give the airth's cog-wheel one kick backward, till I got the sun loose." Crockett then lights his pipe with the sun and cooks some bear steaks with a piece of sunrise in his pocket.[13] The Crockett myth reached its zenith in the 1870s with Frank H. Murdoch's extremely successful stage drama *Davy Crockett,* the popularity of which is alluded to in the second film version of *The Alamo* (2004) when one volunteer confuses the impossible exploits of a stage Crockett with the actual person.

Almost a century later, when such national self-confidence eroded against the hard realities of the Depression, film comedy reflected the change of attitude in part by demythifying these two traditional, heroic national comic types. In the hands of comedians like Groucho Marx and W. C. Fields, Manley's man Jonathan is emasculated and the backwoodsman is cut down to size, both shown as impotent against the day's dire economic straits. Groucho and Fields worked within these two established comic traditions to create personae that themselves were statements of a loss of faith in the American system. Much of the idiosyncratic presence of the two comedians can be related to these two comic traditions, to which they would have been exposed given their background on the stage. The Marx Brothers were signed by Paramount for their first film, *The Cocoanuts,* largely because of the success of its staged original, and Fields also came to Hollywood after years dwelling, as Durgnat puts it, in "the regions where theatre interbreeds with vaudeville."[14]

Sons of the Pioneers

Because W. C. Fields's comic persona exists within clearly defined American comic traditions, it follows that the meaning of his films derives to a large extent from the relation of his individual comic talent to these traditions, the particular inflections that he brings to them. Approaching the film work of a comedian like Fields in terms of his comic persona shows he often worked within and against the robust sense of masculinity constructed by traditional American humor in order to offer social commentary within comedy.

As Lawrence Alloway has observed, in the cinema, "The star . . . is, when photographed, continually present in a more powerful form than the individual roles he or she may be playing."[15] This may be particularly true in the case of comedian comedy, which involves spectator recognition simultaneously of the comedian as person and celebrity, the comic persona of the comedian, and the particular character the comedian is enacting in a given film. Certainly Fields, like the Marx brothers (Zeppo, alas, is excluded because his persona was that he didn't have one), presented a consistent comic persona from film to film. Just as Groucho is always Groucho, whether he is Capt. Jeffrey T. Spaulding, Otis B. Driftwood, or Dr. Hugo Z. Quackenbush, so Fields is always the irascible and misanthropic "W. C. Fields" whether he is called Professor

Eustace McGargle, Larsen E. Whipsnade, or, indeed, W. C. Fields. His personality remained constant regardless of the specific character he happened to be playing. For comic theorist Maurice Charney, "Repetition may be the single most important mechanism in comedy,"[16] and in movie comedy repetition extends beyond gesture in a particular performance to include the developing persona of the comedian who performs it in numerous films.

Gerald Mast notes that because physical action in comedy is "far more important than Aristotle accorded 'melody' and 'spectacle' in the drama," therefore "the essential comic object was the human body."[17] This is perhaps especially true in the case of comedian comedy, as the very term for this form of comedy suggests. Another way of saying this is that Fields is the auteur of most of the films in which he appears, rather than their directors or writers. Fields in fact did write the screenplays for several of his films (including *My Little Chickadee* [1940], co-written with Mae West, and *The Bank Dick,* the latter under the pseudonym of Mahatma Kane Jeeves), but, in auteurist terms, it is primarily his body that was his "stylo"—just as Groucho literally wrote upon his body with his greasepaint moustache. Like Groucho's, Fields's image remained remarkably consistent despite working with a number of directors, including Edward Cline, Clyde Bruckman, and Norman Taurog, all Hollywood reliables who churned out competent if uninspired studio product. Fields's auteurist status relies upon the mise-en-scène of his own image rather than on, say, the plastic manipulation of the film medium.

Hence the importance of costume, which was so crucial to Fields's image. According to Charney, "Comedy is so fastidious about costume because, in such a highly conventional form, it is one of the chief means of characterization."[18] For both Groucho and Fields, costume was integral to their thematic preoccupation with the American Dream. Groucho's clothes, typically a tuxedo jacket with tails, recalls the Yankee's standard outfit, as does Fields's typical costume—top hat, loud (often checkered) trousers, coat with tails—as can be seen in such films as *Poppy* (1936) and even as early as his first short, *Pool Sharks* (1915). Looked at in this way, Groucho in *The Cocoanuts* and Fields in *My Little Chickadee* are comic versions of Melville's satanic Confidence-Man—the Yankee peddler as Groucho's conniving real estate salesman or Fields's less-than-honed cardsharp Cuthbert J. Twillie in *My Little Chickadee*. This reliance on costume suggests that the films of the Marx brothers and W. C. Fields are not, as Andrew Sarris claims, "more verbal than visual";[19] for while the mise-en-scène of their films may not be as sophisticated as, say, Buster Keaton's or Jacques Tati's, they do rely on the physical presence of their bodies as well as their voices for comic meaning.

Certainly, the two comedians' verbal delivery was crucial to their humor, and it is what Roland Barthes would call the very grain of their voices that also connects to these earlier comic traditions.[20] Once movies discovered sound, the stage was set, as it were, for comedians to exploit the important verbal component of traditional American humor, which Groucho and Fields did to the fullest, not only by utilizing comic speech (puns, non sequiturs, and so on) but also by speaking in ways that invoked specific traditional types of American humor. Groucho's staccato, aggressive delivery, along with his sur-realist string of puns and word associations, as well as his occasional confiding directly to the audience, are reminiscent of the Yankee's oracular manner of speech. His inevitable deflating of the pretentious sophistication of the bourgeoisie, iconographically represented by perfect foil Margaret Dumont (an inspired instance of Hollywood casting that rivals any capitalist fat cat created by Eisensteinian typage) updates the traditional contrast between the Yankee and the Englishman to suit the economic anxiety of working-class audiences during the Depression. Fields's comic delivery works similarly. Durgnat vividly describes his voice as "an alcohol-grated larynx rasping like a rusty lavatory chain,"[21] and with Fields's misanthropic mutterings the Yankee monologue becomes a snarl under the breath, the wisdom more private than public, shared only begrudgingly.

Toward the end of *The Great Gatsby,* Nick Carroway realizes "that this has been a story of the West, after all."[22] And even as the comic personae of Groucho and Fields invoked the tradition of the comic Yankee, both comedi-ans also worked with the figure of the backwoodsman, primarily by parodying the western genre and its cowboy hero, also infused with the backwoodsman's mythic frontier abilities. Both comedians made films satirizing the American Dream as it became located in the myth of the American West.

In *Go West* the Marx brothers expose the corruption and avarice underlying the promise of western opportunity. The film's opening title informs us that "in 1851, Horace Greeley uttered a phrase that did much to change the history of these United States. He said: 'Go west, young man, go west.' This is the story of three men who made Horace Greeley sorry he said it." The opening scene takes place in a railroad station, with the brothers looking to buy tickets for the train (the "New York and Western Railroad") going to "the west." The generality of their destination as "the west" instead of any specific place suggests that the film is about the mythic West rather than the geographic one, a reading encouraged by the music that at this point consists of nondiegetic strings playing a few notes of Stephen Foster's "Oh, Susannah."

At the station, Joe (Chico) and his brother Rusty (Harpo) meet S. Quentin Quale (Groucho), to whom they explain that Rusty is carrying a shovel because, as gold is lying in the streets out west, he is going to pick some up and send it back home. Reinforced by his mock-Italian accent, Joe's vision of the West evokes the naive myths held by many poor European immigrants to America in the nineteenth century and even into the next. Groucho is the city slicker—the Yankee—who tries to scam the other passengers by telling them the lineup at the ticket counter is at the other end of the station. But Groucho quickly becomes the tenderfoot who is himself fleeced—literally, as in the climax of the scene Harpo cuts open Groucho's trousers with a pair of scissors in order to access the money in his pocket. As Groucho reflects, "All I wanted to do was to go west, not go broke." Later, we see Harpo and Chico toiling away with their shovels—hardly the fantasy they earlier had envisioned—in the dusty earth of Dead Man's Gulch, which, with its obvious set and patently painted backdrop, looks like a stylized combination of Death Valley and Monument Valley. Unbeknownst to them, their claim is actually valuable because the railroad wants to lay tracks through it, but crooked interests in the town vie for possession of the deed. Like the false western backdrop, it is only through narrative convenience that they are able to portray the fulfillment of the Dream.

As a parody of westerns and their traditional ideology, Fields's *My Little Chickadee* is more disappointing. The film opens promisingly, with Fields as Cuthbert J. Twillie engaging in some comic business with the bustle of a female passenger in the close quarters of a stagecoach, vaguely referencing the coach scenes in John Ford's *Stagecoach* (1939), released the year before to both critical acclaim and commercial success. The subsequent scenes involving the desiring and desirous Flower Belle Lee (Mae West), who is sent out of town by the self-righteous locals, also recalls *Stagecoach*'s depiction of the stern women of the Law and Order League who force the prostitute-with-a-heart-of-gold, Dallas (Claire Trevor), and the drunken Doc Boone (Thomas Mitchell) out of Tonto. In *My Little Chickadee* the group is headed by the perfectly cast Margaret

The Marx Brothers debunk the western in *Go West* (1940).

Hamilton, already etched in the popular imagination as the mean-spirited Elmira Gulch and the Wicked Witch in the previous year's *The Wizard of Oz*. Unfortunately, however, *My Little Chickadee* then settles all too quickly into a series of individual comic schticks by the two stars, some of them (Fields in bed with a goat, for example) less successful than others (West as the schoolmarm teaching a class), but most having little to do with the western itself. Ultimately the film is a clash of two auteurs, which is presumably why Andrew Sarris finds the pairing of Fields and West "more funny/peculiar than funny/ha ha."[23]

By comparison, *It's a Gift* is more scathing toward American mythology. In the film Fields is Harold Bissonette, an eastern grocer who packs up his burdensome family and heads for California, only to discover that the promised land is not so promising. He buys a California orange ranch by mail, but arrives there to find that it is merely a shack on a stretch of sun-baked desert. The film ends "happily," meeting the requirements of its comic structure, but the newfound wealth that provides this resolution is achieved, as in *Go West*, through mere happenstance (as the film's title implies), so that the absence of any hard work and commitment on Fields's part undercuts the Horatio Alger ideal of success through the perfect combination of luck and pluck.

Strange Brew

Perhaps the Fields film that most brilliantly works the backwoodsman tradition is *The Fatal Glass of Beer* (1933). Chaplin's *The Gold Rush* (1925) already brought comedy to the frontier, but *The Gold Rush* is a comedy set in the west whereas *The Fatal Glass of Beer* is a comedy about the West—or more accurately, the mythic west of popular culture. One of four Fields shorts produced by Mack Sennett at Paramount between 1932 and 1933 (the others being *The Dentist* [1932], *The Pharmacist,* and *The Barber Shop* [both 1933]) and directed by Clyde Bruckman, the script was written by Fields himself. Ostensibly a parody of a stage melodrama titled "Stolen Bonds," the film had its gestation as early as 1928 with a skit by the same name in Earl Carroll's *Vanities* featuring Fields as "a prospector in a snow-bound cabin."[24]

The comic intelligence at work in *The Fatal Glass of Beer,* largely missed by audiences of the day, is the result of the manner in which Fields articulates Depression America's self-doubts by incorporating aspects of both the Yankee and the backwoodsman traditions. The minimal plot has Fields as a "northwoods trapper"[25] named Snavely, whose reformed son Chester (George Chandler) is returning home to their frontier cabin from the corrupting influence of the city where he stole bonds from his employer and succumbed to drinking one beer. At the time of its release, and for some time afterward, *The Fatal Glass of Beer* was considered one of Fields's lesser films. Contemporary reviews tended to agree that it was "two reels of film and twenty minutes wasted"; that it had "no story, no acting, and as a whole . . . nothing."[26] Decades later, however, the film came to be regarded as one of Fields's best, rating italics in Sarris's indispensable *The American Cinema.* Andrew Bergman discerned its thematic core, observing that in its short twenty-one minutes, "Fields obliterates the legend of the pioneer and the qualities that composed the legend," although he does not discuss how the film's humor works within its generic contexts.[27]

The film's depiction of the snow and the Mountie parody the Hollywood

W. C. Fields mocks pioneer mythology in *The Fatal Glass of Beer* (1933).

convention of representing Canada as "that vast, mythical region, never geographically defined, which it invented and called the Northwoods."[28] Inspired by writers such as James Oliver Curwood, the Northwoods, according to Canadian cultural historian Pierre Berton, was an identifiable genre in the silent era, wherein "Canada seemed to be covered by a kind of perpetual blanket of white—an unbelievably vast drift that began almost at the border and through which the Big Snow People plodded about like denizens of Lower Slobbovia."[29] This description certainly fits the corpulent Fields, burdened in the film by his heavy coat, fur cap, and mittens; but the Canadian icons are mere red herrings, for the movie is, of course, actually about Depression America, the time and place in which it was made.

Before the release of *The Fatal Glass of Beer* Fields had appeared in his typical Yankee-like costume in such films as Griffith's *Sally of the Sawdust* (1925), *Million Dollar Legs,* and *If I Had a Million* (both 1932). Therefore, the movie audiences of 1933, even as now, would tend to envision Fields in this way, as a cynical Yankee/vaudevillian. But here, in *The Fatal Glass,* Fields wears the clothing and equipment of the backwoodsman—an image strengthened for those who know that earlier in his career, in the Ziegfeld Follies, Fields had been partners with Will Rogers.[30] In *The Fatal Glass,* then, the effect is as if Fields were wearing the outfits of both the Yankee and the backwoodsman simultaneously, as if the one were superimposed over the other. Traditionally, though, the mythic figure of the backwoodsman was wiry and energetic, and the Yankee was strapping and strong; Fields, as the physical embodiment of these comic types, is strikingly inappropriate. With his bulbous nose, bloated body, and quirky movements, Fields visually betrays ill health in the body politic—as the narrative of *The Fatal Glass* indeed confirms.

Within the film is a visualization of the son Chester's fate in the city, accompanied by Fields's singing the tune "The Fatal Glass of Beer." The song is essentially a shaggy-dog story, telling of the evils of drink and concluding with the moral, "Don't break people's tambourines." Durgnat remarks that Fields "can almost claim to have developed the shaggy-dog joke to its highest pitch of inanity"; and in the present context, the use of the shaggy-dog joke by Fields becomes the very reverse of the backwoodsman's traditional comic method, the tall tale.[31] Where the latter builds its narrative through exaggeration, the former is anticlimactic, dying in its tracks with a punch line that is also a non sequitur. Thus, the very form of Fields's joke here is itself a deflation of the myth behind the character telling it. Indeed, Fields's discourse, parodying the westerner's colloquial speech, consistently undercuts the pioneer figure he seems to represent. At the beginning of the movie, for example, there is the business about the "golden nugate." Fields also underscores the fact that he is performing or parodying backwoods colloquial discourse by stepping out of it: when he enters the Trading Post he says, "Hello thar" several times, as might any pioneer—at least as represented by Hollywood—yet when he picks up the telephone, he utters a typically nasty, urban "Hullo" as if the misanthropic "Fields" has momentarily broken through the character.

The first time Fields asks, "Is it snowing out?" when a blizzard is clearly in progress, we understand that the pioneer is no longer in control of his environment, much less the universe, as Crockett had been. Rather, his repeated statement that "it ain't a fit night out for man nor beast" always results in a flurry of studio snow flying directly into his face. Even when, after several instances, he flinches to fend off the inevitable faceful of snow, the snow

For pioneer Fields, "it ain't a fit not out for man nor beast" (*The Fatal Glass of Beer*).

outsmarts him and pelts him only after he lets his guard down. The visual gag about the dachshund on the dogsled team further suggests the diminution of the pioneer's power and significance.

These gags must be considered in the context of the narrative on which they hang, thus connecting Snavely's ineptitude in the face of nature with his dishonesty and cupidity. Bergman argues, mistakenly I think, that in *The Fatal Glass of Beer*, "The tough, silent pioneer is transformed into a sucker, a dunce,"[32] for Fields's Snavely is plainly too culpable to be considered either a victim or a fool. After all, at the end Fields and his pioneer wife, Chester's mother (Rosemary Theby), pummel their poor son and toss him out into the storm when they find out that in a gesture of remorse he had returned the bonds he stole in the city. Even the basic emotions of Chester's parents are patently dishonest. In its deadpan delivery, the hilarious good-night dialogue between Ma, Pa, and Chester Snavely implies the subtextual opposite, insincerity; and indeed, as we discover, they have taken Chester in only because they thought there was something in it for them. Before tossing Chester unceremoniously into the snow when they find he has returned empty-handed, both Ma and Pa Snavely try to trick Chester into revealing where the bonds are hidden, each claiming as motive the desire to protect the other from emotional pain. And so the traditional family here is both organized around self-interest and disintegrates because of it. As Berton points out, the mythical Northwoods as depicted by Hollywood was supposedly "untainted by the crass influences of civilization, although rape, murder, theft, lust, greed, passion, violence, and torture seem to have been exploited to the full in almost every reel of every film made about the northland,"[33] and *The Fatal Glass of Beer* cleverly parodies this corruption in the wilderness.

Conclusion

Material success in *The Fatal Glass of Beer* is no longer based on the Horatio Alger model; it seems possible, rather, only through downright dishonesty. Fields thus manages in this short movie to satirize both the family and the American Dream—that is to say, values associated with the East and the West, respectively—by neatly combining and mocking in his character aspects of the two male figures that had traditionally represented these regions in American humor. Demythologization was taking place in American cinema well before the end of the classic studio era and the disillusioned 1970s that John Cawelti famously discusses,[34] and by employing this mode in *The Fatal Glass of Beer* Fields is able to offer a sweeping condemnation of America's frontier ideology.

Andrew Bergman writes that Fields's comic intelligence was based on "his intuition that the 'enemy' was not so easy to find: it appeared to be the whole vague universe."[35] But, as I have argued, Fields's business here is not nearly so metaphysical. He shows that the American man is no longer the master of his fate because he has not been able to weather the storm of the Depression and keep his values intact. The very title of Fields's *Never Give a Sucker an Even Break* (1941) expresses his philosophy that "a thing worth having is worth cheating for," and has ineluctable associations with showman P. T. Barnum's cynical version of capitalism and the American Dream. In *Letters from an American Farmer* (1782), one of the first books about America by a European, J. Hector St. John de Crèvecoeur imagines an Englishman coming to the New World for the first time and being impressed by the industriousness of the typical American, which is "unfettered and unrestrained, because each person works for himself." For Crèvecoeur, the American's work ethic results from the fact that "his labour is founded on the basis of nature, *self-interest*" (emphasis in the original). This, he concludes, is the special quality that characterizes the American, "this new man." This description is certainly true of Fields's backwoodsman who, dwelling in what Crèvecoeur calls "the freedom of the woods," has reduced the American Adam to an emasculated crook.[36]

The challenges to the American Dream created by the Great Depression strained the expansive optimism of America's comic characters. Chaplin needs a millionaire to help him attain his love for the blind girl in *City Lights* (1931), and his films after *Modern Times*—*The Great Dictator* (1940) and *Monsieur Verdoux* (1947)—grow discernibly darker in their moral vision before settling into the bittersweet self-reflection of *Limelight* (1952). By the end of the war, Capra's optimism had so eroded that in *It's a Wonderful Life* (1946) his populist poetry could be maintained only with the agency of a literal deus ex machina, the angel Clarence (the avuncular Henry Travers), who has to earn his wings through divine intervention in the life of typical American family man George Bailey (James Stewart). George, like Fields's Pa Snavely in *The Fatal Glass of Beer,* is a modern backwoodsman, a small-town fellow unable to follow his dream and "lasso the moon," as he at first boasts to Mary (Donna Reed). The later work of these comic filmmakers reflects the same cynicism toward the American Dream as expressed, in different ways, in the films of the W. C. Fields and the Marx Brothers. If Bergson is correct in saying that a society's comic sense coalesces as self-reflexive art when it achieves a sense of security, it seems to follow that in times of acute stress, as during the Depression, this very art would be undercut and questioned.

Cock and Bull Story

Howard Hawks's *Red River,* Professionalism, and the Western

When one talks about the heroes of *Red River,* or *Rio Bravo,* or *Hatari,* one is talking about Hawks himself. The professionalism of his heroes is shared by the director. They get on with the job without any unnecessary nonsense. So does Hawks. He can say what he wants to through actions, because his is a cinema of action. . . . Finally everything that can be said in presenting Hawks boils down to one simple statement: here is a man.

—*Movie* 5

Epic in scope, Howard Hawks's *Red River* (1948) tells the story of the first drive along the Chisholm Trail, a route used to drive cattle from Texas to Abilene, Kansas, in the 1860s through 1870s. Starring John Wayne as Tom Dunson, a westerner who establishes his own ranch on the Texas frontier in 1851, the film's sweeping narrative spans the initial settling of the West to the taming of the frontier and the development of a more complex post–Civil War market economy. For many, including apparently John Ford, who had already directed the actor in several pictures, *Red River* was the film that showed that Wayne could act. Peter Bogdanovich honored it by making it the movie referred to in his film *The Last Picture Show* (1971), about the passing of the classic western. And in Wayne's last film, *The Shootist* (1976), the actor, already dying of cancer, played an aging gunfighter dying of cancer whose early life as a shootist, or professional gunfighter, is illustrated with clips from earlier Wayne films, including the scene in *Red River,* discussed below, where Wayne as Dunson faces off against two of Diego's men.

Red River has been interpreted in the context of the Fordist culture of the postwar era, specifically David Riesman's distinction between the inner- and outer-directed man in his book *The Lonely Crowd,* published in 1950. Both Peter Biskind and Michael Coyne approach *Red River* from this angle, though surprisingly neither critic mentions the cattle herd as metaphor for the creeping conformism of the postwar era.[1] In the film John Wayne walks tall and takes land from others for his herd just as herds of middle-class families were moving into Levittowns and the many other suburban developments that began filling up the land across America after World War II. Surely, as Robert Sklar has argued, the film's story of a dramatic cattle drive may be seen as a microcosm for the American economy and empire.[2] Coyne adds that the domestic economy experienced a beef shortage two years before the film's release, giving the plot extra pertinence.[3] Wayne's impassioned speech about beef for the nation ("good beef for hungry people. Beef to make 'em strong . . . make 'em grow") all but makes this interpretation explicit, although the beef for the nation in *Red River* also represents the new world order of rapidly expanding international markets for American goods at a time when the nation was flexing its muscle in the process of emerging as one of the world's two postwar superpowers. In his famous speech upon leaving politics in 1961, President Dwight Eisenhower warned the nation of what he called "the military-industrial complex," and these intertwined interests, which had mushroomed in the postwar era, are prefigured by Wayne's Tom Dunson, a man of both fearsome gun-fighting skill and bold entrepreneurial vision.

Stagecoach (1939), made toward the end of the Great Depression, is, as Chuck Maland has shown, a liberal, New Deal western, criticizing big business in the figure of the embezzling banker Gatewood, who says government should leave big business alone.[4] But *Red River,* made only a decade later, is an unrepentant apology for Robber Baron tactics. The cattle buyer Melville

(Harry Carey Sr.), representative for the Greenwood Trading Co., is honest and straightforward, willing to pay top dollar for Matt's cattle because he has "earned it," paralleling Dunson's reasoning for adding Matt's name to the brand at the end. In the film the locomotive, the paradigmatic icon of the machine in the garden, the marker of civilization and industrialism on the frontier, is presented as unambiguously positive. Towns spring up along the railroad, including Wichita, where Matt can successfully deliver his product to market. The locomotive's billowing black smoke and deafening whistle do not despoil the landscape in *Red River* so much as boldly announce the triumphant advance of industry. The victory of the iron horse over the frontier in fact would culminate a mere three years after the time *Red River* is set, when the final golden spike of the transcontinental railroad was driven at Promontory Point, Utah, on May 10, 1869; but the film's masculinized vision of progress is an address to postwar expansionism as vigorous as King Vidor's delirious adaptation of Ayn Rand's *The Fountainhead* (1949), made into a film the year after *Red River*.

Sklar suggests that the plot of *Red River* may be read in the context of the career of its director, Howard Hawks, who aspired after World War II to work independently of the Hollywood studio system, which necessarily meant finding a way to get his product to market, just as in the plot Dunson must get his cattle to the railroad.[5] Hawks was cofounder of Monterey Productions, the company that produced *Red River*. The film turned out to be the only one ever released by Monterey, as it ultimately cost triple the projected budget by almost $1 million, and then generated a couple of lawsuits from groups waiting to be paid for services provided for location shooting. As well, millionaire Howard Hughes, owner of RKO, filed an injunction against Hawks, claiming that Hawks stole the ending of the film from *The Outlaw* (1943), which was written by Hawks and partially directed by Hughes. In the climactic scene of *The Outlaw,* Doc Halliday (Walter Huston) tries to force longtime friend Billy the Kid (Jack Beutel), as a result of their rivalry for Mexican spitfire Jane Russell, into drawing his gun by winging Billy's hand and blowing off a section of each earlobe (whereas in *Red River* Dunson only grazes Matt's cheek with a shot). Although Hawks eventually convinced Hughes to drop his lawsuit, the legal wrangle caused further delay and expense as the ending of the film, discussed in detail below, was recut. Ultimately, Hawks got his product to market through the independent distribution company United Artists, and *Red*

River would go on to gross approximately $10 million.[6] But whether or not the film is an allegory of Hawks's trailblazing struggle for creative independence, *Red River* is clearly a personal film for the director, and it is at this intersecting site between auteur and genre, between Hawks and the western, that the film is particularly interesting for the tensions it displays, as Hawks brings his interest in the nature of masculine professionalism to the well-established conventions of the western.

As the film begins, Dunson leaves the wagon train with which he is heading west, as well as his fiancée, to build his own cattle ranch. After his departure, the wagon train is attacked by Indians and everyone is killed, except for a boy, Matthew Garth (Mickey Kuhn), whom Dunson and his friend "Groot" Nadine (Walter Brennan) find wandering in shock the next day. Dunson takes the boy on ("he'll do") just as he takes the land he wants from the Mexican aristocrat who currently owns it, and begins his herd. Fifteen years later, with the help of his now-grown adopted son Matt (Montgomery Clift), Dunson begins an unprecedented cattle drive north to Wichita. Dunson grows more tyrannical on the drive, threatening its success, eventually forcing Matt to intercede and take charge. Against the wishes of Dunson, who is wounded in a gun battle with some deserting hands, Matt decides to change their destination and drive the cattle to Abilene, hearing that the railroad has now reached that far west. Dunson vows to kill Matt for "betraying" him, although Matt completes the drive successfully, falling in love with Tess Millay (Joanne Dru), a woman he meets in another wagon train along the way. Dunson rides into town seemingly determined to kill Matt, but in their climactic showdown, at the last minute he relents, the two men are reconciled, and Matt receives Dunson's blessing to marry Tess as well as the addition of his initials on the ranch brand.

Hawks is the only major auteur whose style—apart from the anomalous expressionist flourishes in *Scarface* (1932)—is essentially functional and utilitarian, entirely subsumed by the demands of narrative. He was fond of boasting that in all of his films there is not a single flashback, and he famously defined a good director as "someone who doesn't annoy you." In answer to what advice he would give young directors, he said, "get the scene the hell over with as soon as possible."[7] Yet despite the absence of a distinct visual style, Hawks is the model auteur, one of only two "great" directors for the auteurist critics of *Movie* (the other was Hitchcock).[8] Peter Wollen and other auteurists have long noted that Hawks worked in virtually every genre, and part of the reason for

The patriarchal Tom Dunson (John Wayne) looms over young Matt (Mickey Kuhn) in *Red River* (1948).

the auteurist cult around the director is his ability to work within so many different genres and still express his distinctive concerns, including, most centrally, questions of gender roles and the concept of professionalism. This is precisely why, for Wollen, "The test case for the auteur theory is provided by the work of Howard Hawks."[9]

Hawks was comfortable working within the given constraints of genre, and he forayed into most of the major ones in Hollywood cinema, including detective noirs (*The Big Sleep,* 1946), gangster films (*Scarface*), adventure movies (*The Crowd Roars,* 1932; *Hatari!* 1962), war films (*Sergeant York,* 1941; *Air Force,* 1943), historical epics (*Land of the Pharaohs,* 1955), musicals (*Gentlemen Prefer Blondes,* 1953), and, of course, westerns. Along with Frank Capra, he was the most important director of screwball comedies, a genre he helped invent with *Twentieth Century* in 1934 and to which he contributed many of the best films. By the time Hawks made *Red River* he had honed his craft working within the genre system for more than two decades. In Robin Wood's influential reading of the relation between Hawks's comedies and his adventure films, the screwball comedies are the flip side or inverse of professionalism. In the action movies, women typically represent an emotional or sexual aspect that is distinctly nonprofessional, a "lure of irresponsibility" that threatens to distract men from getting their job done; while in the comedies, however, desire, emotionalism, and irrationality are again coded as feminine, but these qualities are celebrated as a refreshing release or liberation from the demands of professionalism.[10] But if professionalism suggests repression in the screwball comedies, in the adventure films, getting the job done is paramount, whether it is defeating the alien in *The Thing from Another World* (1951, produced by Hawks with directorial credit given to Christian Nyby, editor of several of Hawks's films including *Red River*), defending the jail in *Rio Bravo* (1959), navigating a keelboat up the uncharted Missouri River in *The Big Sky* (1952), or driving the cattle to market, as in the case of *Red River*.

Hawks's male groups have their own inner dynamics, and value and morality follow from accomplishing the task at hand by working as a team. This means that Hawks's groups live on what Molly Haskell calls an "existential precipice,"[11] always defining meaning in terms of action, not unlike what Ernest Hemingway, who was one of Hawks's buddies, would call "grace under pressure" in the bullring. Perhaps the essential Hawksian moment occurs in *The Thing,* when the men spread apart and with outstretched arms trace the shape of the spaceship in the ice and find they have formed a perfect circle. This fellowship of the ring is an essential Hawksian image in that it expresses at once the solidarity of the masculine group and male bonding, and its simultaneous exclusion of the Other, whether woman or alien "super-carrot."

Despite working in so many genres, remarkably, if we discount Howard Hughes's *The Outlaw, Red River* was Hawks's first western after having directed thirty films over two decades, beginning with *The Road to Glory* in 1926. Nevertheless, the western was a genre that became increasingly attractive to Hawks, for he returned to it four years after *Red River* with *The Big Sky* and then toward the end of his career directed a trilogy of them, *Rio Bravo* in 1959, *El Dorado* in 1967, and *Rio Lobo* in 1970. Clearly Hawks felt an affinity for the western, explaining that "westerns just happen to be something that I like."[12] But just what was it that Hawks found so attractive in the western?

Certainly Hawks's code of masculine professionalism fits nicely with Frederick Jackson Turner's influential thesis regarding the importance of the

The Fellowship of *The Thing* (1951) as the perfect expression of the Hawksian male group.

frontier in American history. For Turner, the frontier acted as a crucible that both tested and forged a distinctively American national character. While Turner emphasizes the qualities of self-reliance and rugged individualism forged by frontier life, Hawks focuses on the group qualities that allow for what Turner would call the frontier's "nucleus of settlement" on "the outer edge of the wave—the meeting point between savagery and civilization."[13] Lewis Mumford's description of American pioneers as "stripped Europeans" who had to shed Old World assumptions and values to survive in the wilderness suggests that existential precipice on which Hawks's action heroes find themselves.[14] And, of course, the major themes of the western, including the proper use of violence and the task of "taming the wilderness," enacted by the traditional "code" of the western hero, dovetails perfectly with Hawks's concern with the nature of professionalism and getting the job done.

Although Wollen, oddly, never refers to *Red River* in his discussion of the Hawksian universe, the cattle drive offers an archetypal Hawksian professional situation, as the men must take the cattle on an epic journey through a dangerous land of outlaws, Indians, and natural threats. Just as, in Ford's *Stagecoach,* the journey brings together a group of disparate individuals who forge a new democratic union, so in *Red River* a group of different men are brought together for the common purpose of the cattle drive. Richard Thompson's description of the typical Hawksian world clearly applies to *Red River:*

> In the prototypical Hawksian drama, there is a mature authority figure. He is a professional who draws his heroic stature from his job, a job which is his entire role in life and by which he chooses to be identified and judged. He is surrounded by demi-heroes, trying to acquire full heroic status, or redeem it after a fall, or merely to act out their roles as hangers-on of heroes. As the drama unrolls in the job-world, the airport or racetrack or safari station, a woman appears, a professional, aggressive, competent woman, and she and the hero fall in love through a series of sharp-tongued sparring matches, feeling each other out while maintaining their hardboiled exteriors. The woman must adapt herself to the man's job, since it is the projection of the man into the world; and the man must understand the woman's human needs.[15]

In *Red River,* as in *Stagecoach,* the group must face the Turneresque crucibles of Indians, internal dissention, and natural elements to accomplish their task and arrive at their destination safely. Hawks suggests the cattle outfit as a social microcosm, a cross-section of American men, by showing some ethnic diversity in its makeup, including a cowboy named Laredo; Fernandez, a Latino; an Irishman (who, after punching another cowboy who mocks his hat, a derby rather than the traditional Stetson, offers to help the man to his feet); and a Native American, albeit in the unfortunately stereotypical role of comic relief. At the outset of the drive, Hawks emphasizes the group *as* a group in a bravura pan shot that, significantly, *encircles* all the men before the drive begins. Hawks does allow each participant his own close-up, privileging their individual surge of exultation as the drive commences, but he first establishes their interconnectedness. Unlike the group in *Stagecoach,* the group in *Red River* is all male, an indication of the significant differences in the vision of the two films' respective directors. Ford and his male heroes appreciate the "feminine" values of home and family—"let's not forget the ladies, bless them," as the whiskey drummer Peacock reminds everyone in *Stagecoach*—but women have no place on Hawks's frontier, which is just another space for testing masculine prowess, much like the race track, the Andes, or the Antarctic.

In *The Thing,* the outstretched arms of all the men on the ice also reveal the emphasis on gesture in Hawks's films, the crucial element of what Manny Farber referred to as the director's "poetic sense of action," particularly as it relates to homosocial bonding.[16] Lacking an overt camera style, Hawks's films emphasize the importance of gesture, which is especially significant in the various action genres since in them actions tends to speak louder than words, revealing their moral and spiritual values through physical engagement. Marius Bewley's observation that the action in James Fenimore Cooper's Leatherstocking Tales represents "the intensified motion of life in which the spiritual and moral faculties of men are no less engaged than their physical selves"[17] is equally true of action movies, especially those of Hawks—and, too, of the movies by the directors most influenced by Hawks, including Walter Hill, John Woo, and John Carpenter, who not coincidentally directed the remake of *The Thing* (1982). Jacques Rivette has said that when we watch Hawks's action films, "we are not concerned with John Wayne's thoughts as he walks toward Montgomery Clift at the end of *Red River,* or of Bogart's thoughts as he beats somebody up: our attention is directed solely to the precision of each step—the exact rhythm of the walk—of each blow—and to the gradual collapse of the battered body."[18] His observation hints at the extent to which in *Red River* hands and gestures specifically bespeak male prowess and power.

As in *The Thing,* the bonding of men in *Red River* is often expressed through hands, by how they move and what they do: the way Dunson rubs his holster when he asks for the shovel and Bible after killing one of Don Diego's men, for example, or how Matt rubs his nose like Dunson and rolls cigarettes for him (a gesture reiterated in *Rio Bravo,* when Dude [Dean Martin], no longer the town drunk and a reborn professional, is able to roll his own cigarette at the film's end). During the Indian attack, Groot tosses his knife to Dunson, who catches it without even looking while fighting an Indian in the river and then stabs him in one smooth motion, the "red river" now taking on more ominous connotations of blood. Dunson's unhesitating yet completely implausible catch of Groot's knife-toss (this shot was possibly reversed in printing to create the effect) is a clear sacrifice of realism in favor of authorial expression—an early indication of the tensions embodied in the climax, as discussed below—and is echoed later when Groot tosses Dunson a rifle to shoot it out with the trio of mutineers on the drive (again, a gesture repeated years later in *Rio Bravo* when Ricky Nelson tosses a rifle to Wayne). In *Red River,* as in the later film, the perfectly synchronized toss and catch indicates the bond between Dunson and Groot, who explains their relationship to the wagon master in the opening scene by saying "Me and Dunson—well, it's me and Dunson."

Given Hawks's emphasis on gesture in action, the power of men's hands is often indicative of masculine sexual potency in his films. This is literally the case in *The Thing*, where the alien propagates through seeds from the palms of its hands, paralleled in the romantic subplot when Capt. Hendy (Kenneth Tobey) is accused of making "like an octopus" with the scientist's attractive assistant, Nikki (Margaret Sheridan). In *Red River*, referring to the accomplishment of erecting his cattle ranch on the frontier, Dunson says, "I built something with my own hands." Just before Buster (Noah Beery Jr.) comes riding in with word of a wagon train with "women and coffee" ahead, Matt bends down and in a close-up we see that he has picked up a horned toad—a visual pun clearly connecting hands with sexuality. On the drive, although Matt resists the temptation to shoot the deserting Teeler, he points out his hand was shaking; however, his maturation gives him the steadiness to resist Dunson's taunts in their climactic confrontation. At the end of the film Dunson adds Matt's name to the Red River "D" brand with his hand in the earth, the very stuff from which he had built his enterprise fifteen years earlier, now that Dunson believes Matt has become a man.

Bunk Keneally (Ivan Parry), Groot's assistant cook, provides the group's encounter with the lure of irresponsibility. Here, rather than representing it as the feminine, irresponsibility is depicted as immaturity, a metaphor Hawks later literalized in *Monkey Business* (1952) in the form of a youth serum that causes people to physically regress to childhood. Again emphasizing the importance of hands and of gesture, Bunk steals sugar by licking his finger and sticking it in the sugar barrel. Catching him, Groot observes that "having a sweet tooth is almost as bad as a whiskey tongue or liking a woman"—a line that has considerable resonance in the Hawksian universe, especially, again, in *Rio Bravo* where Dude suffers from both. In *Red River*, Bunk's childish habit causes a disastrous stampede when he tries to get one more fingerful of sugar and accidentally knocks over some pots and pans with a clatter, setting off the already anxious cattle. The stampede causes the death of Dan Lattimer (Harry Carey Jr.), an endearingly innocent young man who was going to use his wages upon completion of the drive to buy a pair of red shoes for his wife. Hawks here borrows a convention from the war film, a genre with which he was familiar earlier in the decade, to emphasize the mawkish sentimentality of the stampede's disastrous aftermath. When the men return to camp after rounding up the cattle and file silently past Bunk, the campfire casts their shadows onto him, and a wagon canopy behind him, like a film screen, the projection of his guilt for betraying the group. The next morning, Dunson angrily accuses Bunk of "stealing sugar like a kid" and wants to tie him to a wagon wheel for a spanking, saying, "Well, they whip kids to teach 'em better."

Tess Malloy is the ideal Hawksian woman, tough *like* a man but aware that she is not as tough *as* a man. Tess knows her place within the group and acts appropriately in the crucible of action. We first see her shooting during the Indian attack on the wagon train, but when Matt rides in she quickly realizes she is not as good a shot and promptly switches to loading rifles for him. In some silly banter in the heat of the attack, she chides Matt for his inexplicable rudeness, and when her shoulder is pierced by an arrow, she hardly misses a beat, glancing at it disdainfully before finishing her complaint and, before passing out, slapping Matt across the face like Dunson had done fifteen years earlier. She does not lure Matt into irresponsibility (although Dunson initially mistakes her as doing so: when they first meet, as he says, "nothing you can say or do . . .") and, of course, it is she who interrupts the climactic showdown between Dunson and Matt by telling them to accept their mutual love.

Red River is all about the masculine values of professionalism and leadership, and the dialogue is filled with typically Hawksian remarks about being good enough, exploring what Wollen calls Hawks's major theme, "the problem of heroism."[19] The film does so through the contrasting versions of masculinity represented by the film's two main characters, Dunson and Matt. Early in the film, Dunson assesses the young Matt when he gives him back his gun, saying with laconic certainty, "He'll do." We know, then, that Matt is good enough, but in what context will "he do"? And, concomitantly, when will the clearly capable Dunson *not* do? The film's examination of these questions is explored in the tension between Matt and Dunson as two different kinds of heroes, leaders, and men, coded respectively as feminine and masculine—one who embraces a policy of walking softly, the other of carrying a big stick (Dunson does point out to Tess that his gun is bigger than the little pistol she has hidden in her arm sling in their first meeting).

At the beginning of the film, Dunson is the heroic pioneer, necessary for carving out the frontier, for helping in the establishment of civilization.

Dunson and Matt (Montgomery Clift) are opposite kinds of leaders in *Red River*.

Dunson leaves the wagon train, striking out on his own to begin his own herd. Someone must blaze the trails the wagon trains will follow, and if it is to be anyone it is Dunson, whose Daniel Boone–like status is suggested by his fringed buckskins. When Dunson separates from the wagon train, the wagon master thinks of insisting he stay, but Groot says, "When his mind is made up, there's nothing you can do about it—watch out he don't stomp on you on his way out." The undeterrable Dunson himself insists that "nothing you can say or do" will change his mind, reminiscent of Davy Crockett's motto, "First be sure you're right, then go ahead." (Of course, Wayne later would play Crockett in his own film, *The Alamo,* in 1960.) The indomitable Dunson—too good a gun to argue with, as Groot reminds the wagon master—is the one man professional enough to get this job of wilderness taming done.

The film suggests that the rugged individualism needed to hew out the wilderness requires a man like Dunson, for the wilderness in *Red River* is a harsh and lawless place. As we learn, the frontier along the Missouri border contains the dual threats of thieves and Indians. There are, admittedly, two brief scenes of exquisite visual lyricism in the film: first, the opening scene with Dunson and Fen (Colleen Gray), his fiancée, the wagon train behind them winding its way through the valley; and second, when Dunson reads from the Bible over a grave as the shadows of the passing clouds sweep across the hills behind him. These two moments are among the most beautiful uses of landscape in the history of the western, but otherwise the wilderness in *Red River* wholly lacks the sublimity of the Fordian frontier, with the iconic mittens and buttes of Monument Valley majestically thrusting skyward.[20] Rather, Hawks's frontier in *Red River* is a harsh and contested space, one characterized by a Darwinian struggle where only the fittest, or the fastest, survive. The Red River itself seems less important for being a cherished font, a source of water in a harsh, dry land, than a place to use strategically in a fight against enemies, as we see when Dunson and Groot, preparing for a nighttime attack by the Indians who had raided the wagon train, employ it as a convenient defensive barrier to have at their backs.

Early in Ford's *The Man Who Shot Liberty Valance* (1962), the young and idealistic lawyer Ranse Stoddard (James Stewart) first arrives in the West traveling by Overland stage, a vehicle with the potential for forging democratic unity, as *Stagecoach* had shown years earlier. But the coach is held up by a gang of robbers, led by the notorious outlaw Valance (Lee Marvin), who emerge from behind the rocks as if a threat arising from the landscape. When Stoddard chivalrously tries to defend the honor of a widow being robbed of a keepsake, he is viciously whipped by Valance, who says, "I'll teach you law—Western law." In a violent rage, Valance rips apart Stoddard's law books, forcing Stoddard to eat his own words, the letter of the Law, by stuffing the pages in Ranse's mouth. Stoddard is helpless in the face of such brutality, and it is the westerner Tom Doniphon (John Wayne) who subsequently but secretly shoots Liberty Valance. Later, with the territory now peaceful and seeking statehood, Doniphon realizes that changing times call for a lawman, not a gunman, and he willingly fades into obscurity while Stoddard becomes the state's celebrated senator. But before this can happen, Doniphon is needed to vanquish that which threatens to destroy western democracy and the Law—the valence of liberty—as surely as Tom Dunson is needed to establish it in *Red River*.

In *Red River,* in order to grow the beef that's good for the nation, as we hear in voice-over from Dunson, the western hero must be, in Hawks's terms, "good enough" to take and keep the land. So, no sooner does Dunson stake his claim than he is challenged by two of Don Diego's men, who ride in from the horizon, like Liberty Valance seemingly emerging from the wilderness as if in response to Dunson's claim upon it. Dunson asks them what Diego's right to the land is. "Many years ago by grant and patent from the King of Spain . . ." explains one of the men, to which Dunson interrupts, "You mean he took it from whoever had it before. Now I'm taking it from him." The line may be read as an indication of the existential precipice upon which the Hawksian hero is tested—and perhaps, more radically, as a surprisingly precise yet no doubt unintentional deconstruction of the colonialist ideology of American expansionism and Manifest Destiny. As the opponents square off, there is no place to hide on the flat expanse of Texas plain; only the most professional is good enough to take this land, to keep it, and to raise the beef that will nurture the nation. In the gunfight Dunson kills one of the men, and the next morning the first thing we see are buzzards circling overhead. Later, when the scene fades in after the passage of fifteen years, the elapsed time is marked not only by Dunson rising from a crouched position with the stiffness of age and discernibly graying temples, but also by the landscape, which is now marked by seven graves—the graves of men, Groot tells us, who over the years had tried to take the land away from Dunson.

For most critics, Dunson is wrong when he leaves his fiancée, Fen, behind with the wagon train to carve out civilization. William R. Meyer's comment that "since Dunson made a horrible mistake and lost the girl he loved, he felt an obsessive need to fulfill every one of his other goals,"[21] is typical in seeing Dunson's later stubborn ruthlessness as the result of a broken heart ("like knives sticking in you," as both Dunson and Tess say in the film). It is true that Dunson's guilt at Fen's death seals him off from emotional understanding and contact later, partly making him the hard, intransigent character he becomes; however, I want to argue that the film presents Dunson's decision as correct, although difficult, and consistent with the Hawksian view of masculine professionalism.

At the beginning of the film, in the first of the two magnificent images I referred to above, when Dunson is about to leave the wagon train and strike out on his own, Fen asks to go along. She appeals to Dunson solely in terms of sexual desire. "The sun only shines half the time," and "the other half is night," she murmurs enticingly when he takes her in his arms to say goodbye.

But Dunson resists temptation, aware of the evident dangers of the frontier, dangers that the film subsequently shows to be the case. The wagon train slowly moving behind the couple evokes the epic journey westward of the course of empire, and reminds us that nothing less than the establishment of American civilization is at stake here. As if in support of Dunson's decision, the film thereafter alternates scenes of day and night, demonstrating that the dangers of the frontier may present themselves at any time. The attack on the wagon train occurs in broad daylight, but then in the next scene it is under cover of night when the Indians attack Dunson and Groot by the river. Later, during the stampede, which also occurs at night, as the men awake and scramble for their horses, one cowboy runs past the camera in his long johns and gun belt, an image that reminds us that danger is ever-present. During the attack by the Indians on Dunson and Groot, Dunson pauses to mourn Fen when he finds the bracelet he had given to her upon leaving now on the wrist of an Indian he has just killed; but the sharp report of a gunshot quickly recalls him to action, the dangers of the frontier too immediate to afford the luxury of emotional reverie.

Dunson's indomitability, the film insists, is necessary for establishing that initial, tenuous foothold of civilization. As Matthew reminds Mr. Melville after the successful conclusion of the drive, Dunson "told men what to do and made them do it. Otherwise we wouldn't have gotten as far as we did." Dunson, celebrated by Hawks as indispensable to the project of westward expansion, is the essential American male D. H. Lawrence described as "hard, isolate, stoic, and a killer."[22] Matt hypothesizes that Dunson is set against him, his own adopted son, because "he doesn't know who to fight," suggesting that Dunson always has to be fighting someone.

It is only fifteen years later, on the cattle drive, that the film says, along with Groot, "you is wrong, Mr. Dunson." After all, it is only because Dunson managed in the first place to take and keep the land that civilization has sprung up around the Red River D Ranch. Dunson's "good beef for the nation" speech suggests a complex national economy, one with the industrial means with which to distribute the beef across the country now that the Civil War is over. On the drive, Teeler tells Dunson that he's crazy because "this herd don't belong to you. It belongs to every poor hopin', prayin' cattleman in the whole wide State." Even some of Diego's cattle have been rounded up—the one-time foreign cattle baron now just one competitor among many others in an open market. It is only in this more complex, "civilized" context that Dunson seems to grow increasingly tyrannical. Like Valance when he whips Stoddard in *Liberty Valance,* Dunson declares to the would-be deserters he wants to hang, "I am the law." Dunson is briefly depicted as "villainous" during this latter part of the film, wearing a black shirt and black hat and with a gang of anonymous gunmen riding behind him. Wounded in the leg during the drive, Dunson's monomania now takes on the epic proportions of Herman Melville's Ahab, the obsessive one-legged captain who also would scuttle his command in his singular pursuit of personal vengeance.

In obvious contrast to Dunson, Matthew Garth practices a more demo-cratic form of leadership. When the cowhand Buster comes galloping back to the herd with the good news about women and coffee being just a day's ride up the trail, all the men impulsively want to rush ahead. Hawks suggests that there is some sense of urgency in their desire, because earlier there are complaints about the coffee tasting like "muck" and immediately before, Matt picks up the toad. But Matt stops the men from rushing off, deciding instead that that they will all go together, as an ideal Hawksian professional group. A more benevolent capitalist, Matt is willing to risk the entire herd by having all the men help when they find the wagon train under attack by Indians. Like Cooper's Hawkeye, Matt knows that "Life is an obligation which friends often owe to each other in the wilderness."[23] Now he becomes the trailblazer—literally, along the Chisholm Trail, and metaphorically, embracing a new cooperative group ethic that is unthinkable for a man like Dunson.

Biskind, Coyne, and Gerald Mast all discuss the conflict between Dunson and Matthew as the transition from a tyrannical and autocratic method of leadership to one of liberal consensus. As Biskind puts it, "Matt is the captain of a team, whereas Dunson is the general of an army," the former "more the son of Spock than of Wayne."[24] Sklar describes this aspect of the two men as a contrast between the rigidity of contracts and the fluidity of compacts: Dunson holds men to their words while Matt is open to compromise and revaluation. Dunson judges his right to leave the wagon train at the beginning of the film because he hadn't signed an agreement, just as he later expects anyone who signs onto his drive to finish it. The Red River brand itself becomes a kind of contract that Matt must fulfill.

By contrast, Matt, in Sklar's words, seeks "to pursue a common purpose, a tacit community of shared goals enforceable more by moral or social suasion than by law."[25] Thus, when Matt takes over the drive, Dunson says Matt will not be able to finish it because he is "soft," a quality the film codes as feminine. Matt has the cow to Dunson's bull, as well as the bracelet that Dunson had initially given to Fen and recovered later from the Indian he kills in the river. When Dunson and Groot find young Matt the morning after the Indian attack, wandering aimlessly and rambling incoherently, he seems to have succumbed to hysteria, a condition associated in Freudian psychoanalysis with women. To bring him back to reality, Dunson slaps him in the face, a gesture repeated later by Tess. Visually, Matt's curved posture is frequently opposed to Dunson's arthritic rigidity, recalling the contrasting body language of Cheng Huan and Battling Burrows in Griffith's *Broken Blossoms* (1919), discussed in chapter 1. There are several close-ups of Clift's face in soft focus, yet in classic Hollywood cinema such Sartov shots are usually reserved for enhancing the glamour of female stars. Most striking is the scene where Tess comes to visit Matt at night while he is keeping watch, looking for signs of the pursuing Dunson. Matt is shown in a reclining position, opening up emotionally as Tess sits above him, *his* face in soft focus with the dew forming on his skin, the one receiving the kiss, not giving it.

André Bazin dubbed a cycle of postwar westerns "the superwestern," which he defined as "a western that would be ashamed to be just itself, and looks for some additional interest to justify its existence—an aesthetic, sociological, moral, psychological, political, or erotic interest, in short some quality extrinsic to the genre and which is supposed to enrich it." Regarding the erotic, he cites both *The Outlaw* and *Duel in the Sun* (1946) as examples, but although *Red River* does have a romantic subplot, Bazin describes it as a "western masterpiece" with nothing baroque or decadent about it.[26] Yet Bazin is here characteristically insightful, because the heterosexual romance means little in *Red River;* Hawks is really interested in the love story between the two men, which is the way he has described other of his films. In the "love scene" between Matt and Tess, when she joins him while he takes his shift guarding the herd, the dialogue refers more to Matt's love for Dunson than for her. According to Wollen, "the undercurrent of homosexuality in Hawks's films is never crystallized,"[27] but it certainly comes close to the surface in the scene in which Cherry Valance (John Ireland) and Matt exchange and examine each other's guns ("Nice, very nice," avers Cherry). And the film ends with images not of the newly formed heterosexual couple, Matt and Tess, but of the two reconciled men and the revised Red River D brand as a symbolic expression of their homosocial union.

The conflict between Dunson and Matt promises to reach its climax in a showdown, perhaps the western genre's most familiar convention. *Red River* obligingly foreshadows such a climax and indeed heartily encourages viewers' expectations for it. Yet in the end Hawks gives us reconciliation rather than confrontation in a denouement that Peter John Dyer tellingly describes as "the effeminate clowning of a sham showdown."[28] In fact, there are two anticipated showdowns in the film, both of which fail to materialize. The first, between Matt and the hired gun, Cherry, is foreshadowed by Dunson, who says they will "paw at each other for a while" and then inevitably clash. Yet as the film unfolds Matt and Cherry seem to have mutual respect for each other's skill with a gun and they get along rather well. Once Matt takes over the drive, Cherry supports him completely. In the climax, as Dunson marches into town to confront Matt in the other showdown that doesn't happen, the generally sympathetic Cherry is either shot in the gut by Wayne or superficially wounded—we cannot tell for sure—but in either case he disappears from the movie, entirely forgotten by Hawks as the director turns his attention to the reconciliatory horseplay between Matt and Dunson that replaces the customary shootout on Main Street.

Although a few critics, most notably Mast, have defended the ending, most regard it as a particular disappointment and the film's biggest flaw.[29] What is in fact going on at the end of *Red River*? It would seem that if generic logic requires the resolution of a shootout, the auteur's traditional notions of masculinity supersede it. At the end of *Red River,* the thrust of the script, if not the entire genre, goes overboard to accommodate the happy ending that Hawks had said he wanted. In the original story upon which Borden Chase's script is based, Dunson is fatally wounded by Cherry and then taken home to his ranch to die. What Hawks does to the ending of *Red River* is a striking instance of the auteur struggling with the genre, with Hawks's masculinist concerns taking precedence over the genre's mythic function. *Red River* permits the lone western hero to be reintegrated into society rather than like, say, Shane, lighting out for the territory, although it is an ending that leaves many aficionados of the western hanging, like Grant and Hepburn on the scaffolding at the end of *Bringing Up Baby* (1938). From a Hawksian perspective, though, this narrative closure allows for the perpetuation of the male professional and the restoration of the father in the narrative's oedipal scenario.

In his analysis of William Wyler's *The Westerner* (1940), Raymond Bellour says that "the bad father . . . must die, in the final confrontation, so that the couple can be formed; he even has his double, his reverse image: the good father . . . who makes possible the entry into the genealogy, the continuity between generations."[30] Whether Bellour's further assertion that the film's oedipal trajectory is characteristic of Hollywood cinema generally is true or not, it certainly applies to *Red River,* where the good and bad fathers are collapsed into the paternal figure of Dunson, who towers over a young Matt in a rare Hawks low-angle shot, and instantly becomes a father figure providing life lessons to the boy ("Don't ever trust anybody 'til you know 'em") as he gives the boy's gun, which he had taken from him by subterfuge, back to him.

Guns are represented as the embodiment of the phallic order in the film, and Dunson has the reputation of being the best. He gives Matt, the young squirt, the gun of the Mexican he kills to replace the little one Matt had but which Dunson had taken away. Matt strokes the new gun suggestively while Dunson does the same with his holstered weapon. Because Dunson is the embodiment of patriarchal masculinity, no one in the film, including Matt, disputes his right to ownership of the herd, or the necessity of Matt to "earn" his initial on the Red River D brand, even though the herd could not have come to exist in the first place without Matt's cow. At the end of the film, the good father part of Dunson triumphs, and he passes on his wisdom and estate to his adopted son, while teaching him how to be a man in a capitalist economy.

The "love scene" between Matt and Tess concludes with a discreet fadeout, suggesting that Matt has become a man sexually, that he is indeed heterosexual, but the promised heterosexual union of Matt and Tess seems more an obligatory gesture required by dominant ideology than a matter of conviction. Indeed, as already mentioned, Matt speaks to Tess of his feelings for Dunson as much as for her. In the final showdown, when the passive Matt, knocked off his feet by Dunson's punches, gets up, literally stands up "like a man" and finally fights back, the sage Groot cheers that "everything's gonna be alright." Hawks himself said of the ending, "I didn't know any other way to end it. I certainly would have hated to kill one of them."[31] In the end, disavowing generic convention, with Matt now fully a man, Tess functions for Hawks essentially to facilitate the reconciliation between the two men. Thus, this "story of a man with a bull and a boy with a cow," as the fictional tome *Early Tales of Texas* informs us, is really another cock-and-bull story about men assuming their place within the patriarchal order in the Hawksian universe.

All Shook Up

The Classic Hollywood Musical, Male Desire,
and the "Problem" of Rock 'n' Roll

Although many discussions of the musical in the 1930s consider its communal celebration as an attempted antidote to Depression worries, rather few have gone beyond the analysis of later individual films to address the relation of the genre to subsequent cultural events. This is perhaps explained by the general consensus that by the mid-1950s the "golden age" of the musical had ended, and that the musicals made after this period are by and large greatly inferior to their predecessors. But it is surprising that so much criticism of the musical has virtually ignored the genre's relation to the rise of rock 'n' roll, a phenomenon of popular music that at least equaled, if not surpassed in its impact, the cultural acceptance of Swing twenty years earlier, and that happened simultaneously with the decline of the musical film.

Since Thomas Doherty's 1998 book *Teenagers and Teenpics,* a few others have addressed some aspects of the complex relationship between popular film and popular music.[1] However, the work that has given us useful paradigms for understanding the musical as a genre have failed to take rock 'n' roll adequately into account. Jane Feuer's otherwise excellent book, *The Hollywood Musical,* for example, provides a good deal of useful information about musical theater and popular dance, and how these forms influenced the film musical, but, except for one passing reference, it is as if rock 'n' roll never existed.[2] Conversely, the few critical discussions of rock movies that have appeared, although generally entertaining and informative, fail to address the relation of these films to the musical as a genre.[3] Rick Altman's hypothetical remark, "When is a musical not a musical? When it has Elvis Presley in it,"[4] seems to express a more entrenched critical opinion than one might expect—perhaps because of the apparently still widely held view that rock music is a more "lowbrow" cultural form. In this chapter, then, I want to look closely at how rock 'n' roll impacted the musical film. My argument is that rock 'n' roll, initially antithetical to both the musical's themes and conventions, nevertheless was rather quickly fitted to the genre's established elements, thus safely modulating the aggressive masculine sexuality it connoted.

Thematically, musicals have been concerned with articulating a sense of community and defining the parameters of sexual desire, the two themes of course being intimately related. As much of the important work on the musical has demonstrated, the genre's notion of community is addressed and worked out in both the plot and musical sequences in a number of specific opposi- tions, the most crucial being social (elitist/democratic) and sexual (desire/ restraint).[5] Both conflicts are typically embodied in the two romantic leads, their difference in outlook resulting in their inability to commit themselves to a relationship. The social opposition is often defined as the conflict between elite and popular art, and is resolved by formulating an ideal of middlebrow entertainment. Examples range from the tap versus ballet conflict in *Shall We Dance* (1937) to the political dimension added to *Silk Stockings* (1957). Narrative closure is attained when the couple's differences are somehow resolved, usually through the mediating power of musical performance; often, then, a marital union or its promise brings with it an integration of the plot's conflicting values.

This social conflict and its resolution are parallel to the genre's other ideological function whereby the socially acceptable limits of masculine desire are defined and delimited. Unrestrained sexual desire obviously poses a threat to the dominant ideology of heterosexuality and monogamy insistently repre- sented in classic Hollywood cinema generally and musicals most emphatically.

Musicals acknowledge such desire but only for the purpose of containing it.[6] In musicals, desire is pushed into the background, much like the shadow doubles of Gene Raymond and Dolores del Rio in *Flying Down to Rio* (1933), who express the secret longings of the "real" characters. "The apotheosis of romance," as Pauline Kael has described it,[7] the genre consistently depicts people offering expansive yet controlled expression of their feelings. One of the essential satisfactions provided by the musical, then, is that it seems to celebrate the exuberant expression of sexuality (metaphorically in the production numbers) while at the same time maintaining social stability (in the narrative). Dancing in the classic musical is thus an ideologically loaded metaphor; not only does it solve the problem of censorship for the genre more satisfactorily than the clumsy fade-out, but also, to imagine that making love is always as smooth as, say, an Astaire and Rogers's pas de deux, even when diegetically improvised (what Feuer calls the engineering of bricolage), makes both courting and mating seem considerably less problematic than they often are in reality.[8]

The 1950s presented the musical with a difficult problem in the emergence of a new form of popular music—rock 'n' roll. To the youth of the period, as well as their parents, rock music seemed to express the biological imperatives of sex in a distinctive rhythmic, verbal, and visual language. It was a new musical form that naturally appealed to a sexually awakening population of adolescents growing up in a generally repressive decade. The very term "rock 'n' roll" (despite Alan Freed's claim to have coined it), like the earlier "jass" (then "jazz"), "in the groove," and other phrases, was slang for sexual intercourse. Like Hollywood cinema, rock music developed a range of conventions for dealing with sexuality. But the codes of Hollywood were much more genteel and euphemistic; many rock lyrics, by contrast, were shockingly explicit, and while others may have made little denotative sense—as in Little Richard's "Awop Bopa Loo Bop A Lop Bam Boom"—the meaning of what Walt Whitman would have called that "barbaric yawp" was clear enough. Above all, rock's driving rhythm, with that backbeat you couldn't lose, was felt to be a disturbingly straightforward expression of raw male sexuality.

Rock's four most important early stars signified undeniably assertive sexual meanings. Pounding his piano in a frenzy—cabinet as well as keys—Jerry Lee Lewis sang that a woman left him breathless and began "High School Confidential" with the unambiguous invitation to "Open up, honey, it's your lover boy me that's knockin'." The gyrations of Elvis's pelvis were so notorious that his performance of "Hound Dog" on *The Milton Berle Show* was regarded by many as obscene, and, subsequently, Ed Sullivan refused to allow Presley to be photographed on his show from below the waist. With outrageous exhibitionism and a raucous shouting vocal style, Little Richard clearly celebrated the fact that "Good Golly, Miss Molly / She sure likes to ball" and that Long Tall Sally is "built for speed / She got everything that Uncle John need." And Chuck Berry, smoothly spreading his legs so that he could pluck his obviously phallic guitar between them, praised his own appeal in "Brown Eyed Handsome Man" and admitted about his car/woman "Maybelline" that "The rainwater blowin' all under my hood / . . . was doin' my motor good." Clearly, rock 'n' roll treated sexuality more openly, less euphemistically, than the June/moon/spoon, let's-knock-knees strategies of earlier popular music.

However, this is not to suggest that rock was different from other forms of popular culture in that it constituted a "direct" expression of "natural"—that is, ideologically free—sexuality. The notion that rock 'n' roll contained "the magic that will free your soul" was not a fact but an interpretation, a cluster of values read into the music by 1960s hippie bands like The Lovin' Spoonful. George Berger's exuberant dance on the dinner table of the middle-class suburbanites while singing the praises of the body electric in "I Got Life" in Milos Forman's *Hair* (1979) is the summary image of this view. Actually, from its inception, rock, although perhaps comparatively liberated in relation to other forms of popular music, has, like genre films, been determined by dominant ideology; it is generally patriarchal, heterosexual, and romantic, thus reinforcing (at least until some New Wave music in the 1980s) traditionally sexist distinctions between masculine sexuality as aggressive and dominant and feminine sexuality as passive and submissive.[9] But the important point here is that rock 'n' roll was perceived as a direct expression of sexuality by frightened cultural reactionaries in the 1950s. Unlike previous forms of popular music, rock seemed to provide and allow for a sexual release rather than sublimation. Religious leaders such as the Rev. Jimmy Snow delivered strong sermons against the "evil" feelings released by rock music; southern white racists claimed that it was a plot inspired by the NAACP; and cities such as Cleveland resurrected old ordinances preventing teenagers from dancing in public.

Two film images of the period perfectly sum up this fearful response to the masculine sexuality of rock. Although not actually a musical, *The Blackboard*

Jerri Jordan (Jayne Mansfield) heats up the iceman in *The Girl Can't Help It* (1956).

Jungle (1955) was the first Hollywood movie to make use of rock by featuring Bill Haley and His Comets' "Rock Around the Clock" on its soundtrack. In the film, a group of young toughs, with whom Haley's music is continually associated, destroys the music teacher's priceless jazz records in a shocking explosion of violence. "Haven't you heard that music soothes the savage beast?" gang leader Artie West (Vic Morrow) wryly asks "The Teach" (Glenn Ford). Quite different in tone, Frank Tashlin's *The Girl Can't Help It* was released the following year and features performances by a number of rock stars including Little Richard, who sings the title song as Jayne Mansfield jiggle-walks down the street. Staring at her, the enthralled iceman cometh as his blocks of ice melt, the warm water flowing out of his truck, and a milk bottle in the milkman's hand pops open and overflows. The irony here is that Mansfield plays a nice girl who just wants to get married; nevertheless, rock music is strongly associated with the sexual desire aroused in men by the very sight of her. Together, these images show that if rock 'n' roll were sexually charged, then it was inevitably linked to the destructive and violent impulses it also unleashed. Tom Ewell's voice, as he attempts to explain to the film viewer the refined pleasures of classical music at the beginning of *The Girl Can't Help It,* is overwhelmed by the increasing volume of the up-tempo music emanating from the juke box behind him—a comic but incisive comment on the commonly expressed concern of the day that the primitive qualities of rock 'n' roll threatened to subvert more civilized values by releasing what D. W. Griffith in *Way Down East,* as discussed in chapter 1, had called "the man-animal."

Some of the best musicals appeared in the early 1950s: *An American in Paris* (1951), *Singin' in the Rain* (1952), *Gentlemen Prefer Blondes* and *The Band Wagon* (both 1953), and *It's Always Fair Weather* and *Oklahoma!* (both 1955). But then, quite suddenly it seemed, beginning in the second half of the decade the genre suffered a surprising decline in production, quality, and popularity. A number of not entirely satisfactory explanations for this development have been offered. Andrew Dowdy, for example, suggests that in the 1950s musicals became too remote from contemporary life.[10] Their settings, he says, tended to be more removed from the audience's experience than even the Astaire-Rogers fantasies had been. They were set in an impossibly romanticized Paris (*So This Is Paris* [1954], *An American in Paris, Gigi* [1958]) or distanced by nostalgia (*By the Light of the Silvery Moon* [1953]). But surely this had been equally true of earlier musicals: *Roman Scandals* (1933), *Meet Me in St. Louis* (1944), and *Take Me Out to the Ball Game* (1949), to name a few, are set in the past of Hollywood's imagination or informed by a similar nostalgia. Indeed, a romanticized or exotic setting, influenced partly by the operetta, had been a convention of the genre since Ernst Lubitsch and the Jeanette McDonald–Nelson Eddy vehicles.

Another hypothesis has been offered by Michael Wood, who observes that by the mid-1950s "it was beginning to seem impossible to break into a general song and dance in America, even metaphorically."[11] Clearly, the dominance in that decade of the science fiction film attests to the multiple anxieties seething beneath the surface of Eisenhower America. But it had been difficult times that had given rise to the musical film in the first place. Just as Nero fiddled while Rome burned, so American popular culture had always managed to whistle in the dark, to sing its own praises during times of crisis.

More significant, I think, are the statistics offered by Dowdy. He reports that in 1943 Hollywood released sixty-five musicals; a decade later the number was down to thirty-eight; by 1963 there were only four, "with two of these dismal flops and one a singing cartoon."[12] This is a long way from the early years of sound production, when "the studios turned out musicals like sausages."[13] The musical production was declining even as the use of color and widescreen, technical advances that should have worked to the genre's advantage, were becoming increasingly common. It is true that by the late 1930s rising costs were making the production of lavish musicals prohibitive, yet it was not this economic constraint that threatened the musical's existence; Busby Berkeley's later musicals at MGM, beginning in 1939 with *Babes in Arms,* showed that even with greatly reduced budgets musicals could still be both innovative and commercially successful. In the late 1960s studios were still spending huge sums on musicals they hoped would be blockbusters: *Star!* (1968), for instance, cost 20th Century Fox $15 million and *Hello, Dolly!* (1969) cost the same studio $23 million in 1968.

The rapid decline of musicals in the late 1950s seems to me more likely explained by the existence of an ever-widening gap between the music in the musicals the studios were making and the music an increasing percentage of the nation was actually listening to—rock 'n' roll. Since the 1950s, the youth audience, loosely defined as ten- to thirty-five-year-olds—the same group that constitutes rock's primary audience—has accounted for approximately 80 percent of total movie tickets bought. Obviously Hollywood needed to incorporate rock music into its films to attract the majority of its potential audience, just as, by the same logic, American filmmakers in more recent years have emphasized the production of new teen movies. As well, rock music in films in the 1950s could provide an alternative to the growing competition of television, which had been perceived as a rival since its commercial introduction in the previous decade. Television for the most part presented the tamer popular music on its variety shows, while Dick Clark's nationally syndicated *American Bandstand* (ABC-TV, 1957–89) was one of television's longest-running shows and the most successful daytime program of its time. In short, rock music offered Hollywood a way to compete with television for the youth audience it needed without spending the exorbitant sums of money required for biblical epics or other "movies are better than ever" counter-TV strategies. Finally, as the studios were later bought up by entertainment conglomerates that also sold records—Warner Bros. by Warner Communications, for example, or Columbia Pictures by MCA—it became even more in the studios' self-interest to promote rock music in movies.

In the late 1960s, after the British Invasion had made rock even more popular, such musicals as *Dr. Doolittle* (1967), *Hello, Dolly!, Paint Your Wagon* (1969), and *Goodbye, Mr. Chips* (1969) were all commercially unsuccessful, while the two Beatles films with Richard Lester, *A Hard Day's Night* (1964) and *Help!* (1965), were extremely popular. In 1970 *Woodstock* grossed an impressive $23 million. Likewise, in the early 1970s, with the exception of *Fiddler on the Roof* (1971), most other musicals, such as *The Boy Friend* (1971), *1776* (1972), and *The Little Prince* (1974), proved commercially disappointing, while George Lucas's *American Graffiti* (1973), featuring a continuous soundtrack of rock oldies, grossed a whopping $75 million. Also in 1973, *Superfly* became the first rock soundtrack LP to outgross its movie. It would seem that the musicals that flopped did so primarily because they ignored the music that the majority of consumers who supported both the record and film industries were listening to. Many of these unsuccessful musicals were either adaptations of Broadway plays or similar in style to them; and Broadway, with the exception of *Bye, Bye, Birdie* and *Hair,* had virtually ignored new developments in popular music. (Unlike Hollywood, Broadway was able to get away with this oversight longer, only because it could accommodate a much smaller—and generally older—audience, which it drew from selected New Yorkers and the endless flow of tourists.)

As Elvis Presley's new contract with RCA proved as early as 1955, rock 'n' roll possessed enormous commercial potential. But as a musical style, it worked against the conventions developed by the musical genre for dealing with issues of masculine sexuality. Hollywood studios, then, were faced with the problem of wanting to incorporate into established generic formulas a musical form that appeared to be in opposition to the conservative ideology of the genre. But although the problem may have seemed difficult, two solutions were quickly found: the stressing of rock's potential for community, and the taming of rock's energy through a deliberate molding of its stars. Both approaches defused the masculine sexuality of rock, allowing it to be contained more easily within the musical's system of conventions; and consequently, rock 'n' roll changed more than did the musical film.

Despite the economic imperatives that motivated their production, the caution and disdain with which rock 'n' roll was generally viewed is revealed by the speed and lack of quality that characterized the making of early rock movies. Films such as *Rock Around the Clock* (1956), *Don't Knock the Rock* (1956), and *Rock, Rock, Rock* (1957) were all poorly directed, low budget affairs analogous to the initial treatment of the music by the major record labels (Columbia, Mercury, RCA, Capitol). The filmmakers' lack of creativity further encouraged these early rock musicals to fall back upon established generic convention. (The remakes of *A Star Is Born* [1976] with Kris Kristofferson and Barbra Streisand, *The Wiz* [1978] with Diana Ross and Michael Jackson, and *The Jazz Singer* [1980] with Neil Diamond are later examples of a similar strategy but employ higher production values.) Thus it is relatively easy to read the ideological tensions at work in these films.

In *Don't Knock the Rock,* for example, rock 'n' roll has been banned locally because the adults distrust it. "Rock and roll is for morons," an old man asserts, while an irate mother declares that "children should be seen and not heard." Alan Freed, the ubiquitous hero of many of these films, arrives to host "A Pageant of Art and Culture" by the town's teenagers at the local high school. The youths begin the pageant with a display of classic paintings and then perform a series of traditional dances, concluding with a demonstration of the Charleston. The old squares soon get the point: one man immediately jumps up and admits to the kids, "You're right, we're really a bunch of narrow-minded fools." The movie employs elements from both the backstage musical and the Astaire-Rogers films to resolve its conflict. From the former (as reworked in the Judy Garland/Mickey Rooney vehicles) it takes the putting-on-the-show narrative and the climactic big-chance concert; from the latter, an updated thematic opposition that motivates the plot, the teenagers simply replacing Jolson or Astaire, adults generally replacing Edward Everett Horton and elite values. Typically, the resolution of the plot has the adults realizing that rock music is not so destructive after all and accepting it.

Similarly, in *Rock, Rock, Rock,* Freed consents to do his Rock and Roll Party TV show from the local high school gym. In this movie the generation gap with its conflicting values is minimized from the beginning. Tuesday Weld's dad already digs rock 'n' roll (including, significantly, Frankie Lymon's "I'm Not a Juvenile Delinquent"), while the second tune in the film, "Baby Wants to Rock," is sung by Weld's five-year-old sister ("I don't want a lollipop in my hand / I just wanna dance to a rockin' band"), thus demonstrating a cultural unity spanning three generations. In the climax Freed, in emphatic close-up, speaks of rock 'n' roll as a cultural melting pot, almost a microcosm of America—in his words, "a river of music which has absorbed many streams," recalling Paul Whiteman's whitewashing of jazz as a "melting pot" in *The King of Jazz* (1930).[14]

Rock 'n' roll helps bring people together in *Don't Knock the Rock* (1956).

Consistently in early rock musicals old and young people, or traditional and new values, come together with a redefinition of rock as harmless after all, something closer to middlebrow (as well as middle-of-the-road) pop.

Many later rock musicals, consciously or unconsciously, hark back to these conventions of both classic musicals and earlier rock movies. Randall Kleiser's *Grease* (1978) is a particularly good example. As in the Astaire-Rogers films, the plot in *Grease* serves to delay the romantic union of the couple, Danny Zucko (John Travolta) and Sandy Olsson (Olivia Newton-John), through a series of misunderstandings. A number of 1950s icons of popular culture (Eve Arden, Sid Caesar) are cleverly cast, including Edd "Kookie" Byrnes as an aging TV personality who brings his rock 'n' roll TV show (National Bandstand) to the local high school gym. Such casting establishes a clear continuity with the rock films of the 1950s. In his black leather jacket, jeans, T-shirt, and laconic posture, Travolta represents the values associated with rock music, while the prim Newton-John (and here again the casting, despite her subsequent pop hit "Physical," serves the movie well) embodies the values of mainstream pop. At the drive-in, Danny makes sexual advances, but Sandy rebuffs him and leaves, insulted. Forlorn and sexually unfulfilled, Danny sings "Stranded at the Drive-In," while the advertisement for food on the outdoor screen behind him depicts hot dogs flipping into buns, a humorously and deliberately reflexive image of his unrealized desire. For the couple to get together, Danny must contain his desire, and so in the end the romance of pop wins out over the sexuality of rock. Danny earns a school letter, Sandy accepts him, and even though she appears to compromise by dressing more like the gang, the film concludes with their duet of "We'll Always Be Together" as they fly off into the sunset in their car—an image truly worthy of the Astaire-Rogers fantasies.

The strategy of validating rock, of making it acceptable, by defusing its sexual threat and asserting in some way its unifying power has been perhaps the major motif of rock movies. The eponymous hero melting the animosity of an all-black audience at Harlem's Apollo Theater in *The Buddy Holly Story* (1978)—an apocryphal event—serves the same function, as does the close-up of the white Carole King and black Frankie Lymon figures embracing in mutual admiration of rock in *American Hot Wax* (1978). The repeated image of the disc jockey at the disco in *Thank God It's Friday* (1978) in a booth that is a hollowed-out globe of the Earth suspended above the movie's disparate characters graphically literalizes the convention. One can see this impulse at work even in the rock concert films. *Woodstock* is the most obvious example, of course, but the idea is expressed in more subtle ways in other concert films as well. In *The TAMI Show* (1965), for instance, hosts Jan and Dean reassuringly refrain between acts, "Here they come from all over the world," and the most "threatening" act of the show, the Rolling Stones, conclude the film with what is for them a most uncharacteristic song, "Get Together," as all the performers mass on stage and dance together in a conventional that's-entertainment, show-biz finale reminiscent of Ethel Merman. (International benefit concerts such as Live Aid are a logical extension of this impulse.)

Rock musicals also reinforced a sense of community through the shaping of the male performer's image. Because of their overwhelming popularity, some rock stars have assumed iconographic significance of godlike propor-tions, a state of affairs that informs the basic metaphor of such rock musicals as *Jesus Christ, Superstar* (1973), *Godspell* (1973), and even Ken Russell's *Tommy* (1975), not only in the story of Tommy's rise to fame as prophet and pinball wizard, but also in the sequence where premier rock guitarist Eric Clapton appears as a priest who leads his flock with some mean guitar licks. Secular versions of the same theme can be found in both Peter Watkins's *Privilege* (1976), starring rock singer Paul Jones (former vocalist of Manfred Mann) as a rock star whose popularity is manipulated by church and state, and Hollywood's more reactionary *Wild in the Streets* (1968), which reverses the premise: here the enormously popular rock star succeeds in manipulating the political system to become president of the United States.

Lonely Boy (1962), the first rock documentary, was prescient in its examination of the constructed image of the male rock star. Made by Wolf Koenig and Roman Kroitor for the National Film Board (NFB) of Canada, the film shows Canadian-born singer Paul Anka being praised by fans of all ages and successfully performing in a variety of venues in the United States, from theme parks to swanky night clubs. At first glance, *Lonely Boy* seems a straightforward success story, a celebration of Anka's commercial breakthrough in the U.S. entertainment industry, but it is in fact a cogent examination of Anka's constructed teen idol image. It was made at a time when NFB filmmakers, along with a few others in France and the United States, were revolutionizing documentary film practice with the use of new, lightweight 16 mm cameras and portable sync-sound equipment, and it uses Anka to offer a candid examination of what the first words of the voice-over narration refers to as the more general "astonishing transformation of an entertainer into an idol."

Anka initially modeled himself on the generic type of the teen idol and rode the crest of a wave of teen idols that inundated American popular music from approximately 1959 to 1963, the age of the Frankies and Tommies and Johnnies and Bobbys. The teen idols carried on the process begun with pop covers of changing the image of male youth, in Richard Staehling's terms, from wild to mild,[15] by providing a cleaner, more wholesome image of masculinity than that of earlier rebellious rockabilly heroes like Eddie Cochran and Gene Vincent. Engineered by such Philadelphia labels as Cameo/Parkway, Chancellor and Swan, male rock stars became teen idols, with a safe and wholesome persona that would appeal to the largest possible number of female consumers.

Lonely Boy was made at the height of the teen idol craze, when Anka was nineteen, four years after his initial success and at that point in his career when, like Bobby Darin, he was consciously seeking to change his image to a more adult one. By 1960, Anka's repertoire began to change somewhat, as he recorded a number of standard Christmas tunes and a version of "Hello, Young

Lovers" from Rodgers and Hammerstein's *The King and I,* already recorded by the undisputed king of bland vocalists, Perry Como. Rock historians and cultural critics uniformly dismiss the teen idol as a corporate product, an inauthentic pseudo-artist manufactured by record companies to cash in on a trend. Steve Chapple and Reebee Garofalo, in their history of the popular music industry, *Rock 'n' Roll Is Here to Pay,* bluntly describe the music of the teen idols as "schlock rock: the death of rock n' roll."[16] Often, as in the case of Fabian, the teen idol was groomed (the very word Anka's manager Irvin Feld uses in the film to describe his preparation of Anka for appearing in New York's elegant supper clubs) and promoted because of his looks rather than for any innate talent.

An essential component in the marketing of teen idols was an emphasis on memorabilia, fetishistic objects fans might purchase and collect. *Lonely Boy* emphasizes this aspect of Anka's popularity when early on we see his fans collecting and displaying Anka buttons, postcards, and other items. One of his fans boasts that she has all his records as well as "555 pictures of Paul all over my room, and I have a Paul Anka sweater." Such memorabilia is central to what one critic refers to as "the apparatus of fetishism, a network of fantasy" that interpellates adolescent girls as consumers of the teen idol image of male sexuality.[17] This dynamic is nicely suggested in *Lonely Boy* in the shot of one teenage girl gazing longingly at the singing Anka through a haze of cigarette smoke, spellbound by the teen idol's image, which Simon Frith and Angela McRobbie describe as "an unformed sensuality, something sulky and unfinished in the mouth and jaw . . . a dreamy fantasy fulfillment."[18]

Perhaps the most important aspect of the teen idol image is its construction of heterosexuality. Although male, teen idols do not express an aggressive phallic sexuality; rather, they offer themselves to girls as heterosexual objects of desire without being overtly masculine or sexually threatening—"big fluffy candy-colored images of male niceness on which to focus their pubescent dreams."[19] In *Lonely Boy* Anka's fans describe him as "cute" and "sweet." His music, like that of teen idols generally, falls squarely within that category Frith and McRobbie, in their foundational essay on "Rock and Sexuality," call "teenybop." They identify the binary construction of masculine sexuality in popular music as comprising two distinct "rock genres"—"cockrock" and "teenybop." In opposition to the aggressive, boastful sexuality of "cock-rock," teenybop rock presents an image of "the young boy next door: sad,

In *Lonely Boy* (1962), Paul Anka is the archetype of the teen idol.

thoughtful, pretty and puppylike." Thus, the lyrics of teen idol songs tend to be "about being let down and stood up, about loneliness and frustration."[20] The teen idol, accordingly, is "soft, vulnerable, and caring"[21]—exactly the persona constructed by Anka in his songs: Anka is soft because he knows when it's time to cry; he is vulnerable in his loneliness, a lonely boy lonely and blue; and we know he cares because he supportively invites us to put our heads on his shoulder. For Frith and McRobbie, the teenybop fan should feel that her idol is addressing himself solely to her; "her experience should be as his partner."[22] Anka does exactly this with his "special material" at the Freedomland concert, as he pulls one lucky girl from the audience onto the stage and sings "Put Your Head on My Shoulder" to her as he gently nudges her head to rest on his arm.

The film shows nothing less than the construction and regulation of adolescent desire by the culture industry. At the Freedomland concert there is a montage of female faces all in paroxysms of desire; several shots of screaming girls fill the screen, and there are also a couple of shots of the muscular arms of male policemen gripping nightsticks, literally containing this effusion of female fantasy. At one point the screaming girls surge forward and one of the men attempting crowd control, a rather heavy-set fellow, is noticeably pushed backward by them. Early in the film we see two female Anka fans dressed the same with the same hairstyle equally breathless in the presence of Anka—the living proof, in Theodor Adorno's words, of "a system of response mechanisms wholly antagonistic to the ideal of individuality in a free, liberal society."[23]

Central to its investigation of the pop idol phenomenon, the film consistently emphasizes Anka's constructed image. Anka first appears in the film as a name on a billboard. His name moves across a pixilated marquee (its fleeting nature as it moves across the screen providing one of the film's comments on the ephemerality of pop fame), which is echoed subsequently in the graphic design of the title credit. When we finally do see Anka himself, he is in performance, singing the title tune (accompanied by female screams on the soundtrack), after which he exits the stage and returns for an encore, at which point the film's credits begin. By delaying the appearance of the credits in this manner, the film underscores its subject's performative aspect. As the film goes on, Anka becomes a multiplicity of images, like a hall of mirrors at the Atlantic City boardwalk along which he strolls. He appears on photo buttons worn by his adoring fans, the many photos they carry and affix to their purses, the covers of fanzines and concert programs. Dressing before a show, Anka is reflected in a mirror—an image of an image.

In *Lonely Boy,* Anka concedes that sex is the primary element of pop music success, but, consistent with his teen idol image, he dances around the word before finally saying it ("a word which we all know and which I'm not in accord to using but it's the only word which can sum up what I have to say which is sex") with a noticeable gulp of discomfort. The other rock stars who succeeded in establishing movie careers were inevitably fitted to the requirements of the genre and thus recast from wild to mild, their films similarly dancing around sex. Obviously, the image of a performer like Frankie Avalon did not need to change much for him to work into the beach movies, but Elvis Presley's image did for him to become an established movie star. In the early *Loving You* (1956) Presley's character is modeled on himself; he is "discovered" by Lizabeth Scott, a sort of female Colonel Parker, and in performance he surprises everyone with his sexual charisma. Of his performance in this movie the novelist Scott Spenser has written: "His last gyration—with the music slowing suddenly to a kind of sensual drawl—is one of his classic gestures, borrowed from strippers and preachers. He rotates his right arm around and around like a large, slow propeller and each time his hand passes his hip, his right knee turns inward at an excruciating 45 degree angle."[24] The movie's conventional climactic national TV broadcast becomes a forum for deciding whether Presley "should be allowed to sing anywhere he pleases." Reaction to his performance is likened to that at the premiere of Stravinsky's "Rite of Spring," but in the end everyone comes to appreciate his style and he is paired off with the wholesome Dolores Hart while older woman Scott gets together with the more appropriate Wendell Corey. *Jailhouse Rock* (1957) contains Presley's own energetic choreography, and *King Creole* (1958) is a gritty movie that opens with "Crawfish," perhaps his most sexually provocative song. But after his induction into the army and the public shearing of his distinctive hair, Elvis appears in *G. I. Blues* (1960) as a good boy who does things like babysit and sing to puppets. By the time of *Frankie and Johnny* (1966) his movements have been almost completely constrained, his musical numbers placed in such unlikely contexts as a conventional marching band. In his next to last film, *Change of Habit* (1969), Presley plays a crusading ghetto doctor and is now socially acceptable to the point that Mary Tyler Moore can consider leaving the nunnery for a secular marriage to him. His subsequent triumph in Las Vegas and the successful marketing of a variety of Elvis merchandise reduced Presley's image to the nostalgically sentimentalized figure of Henry Winkler's Fonzie on the television sitcom *Happy Days* (1974–84).

In a similar fashion, whatever sexuality may at first have been suggested by the Beatles and their music was effectively drained in their two movie collaborations with Richard Lester. It is true that *A Hard Day's Night* is one of the few rock films to find a stylistic equivalent to rock's energy in its narrative ruptures and fast editing rhythms, but it nevertheless subjugates the sexual aspect of the music in other ways. In contrast to the discord caused by Paul's grandfather, the seemingly asexual communal goodwill of the Beatles is more contagious and wins out in the end. When asked by a reporter whether he is a mod or a rocker, Ringo replies "a mocker"—a joke that literally brings the two opposing groups together through verbal conflation as well as points to the film's overall strategy of achieving harmony through comedy. Essential to this strategy is the depiction of the Beatles as sexually nonthreatening. Everyone

Elvis's image was tamed in a series of musical films culminating in *Change of Habit* (1969), with Mary Tyler Moore.

worries that "it'll be wine, women, and song" for Ringo, who has temporarily left the group, once he "gets the taste for it"; but, as we see, he can't even handle a drink in a pub by himself. Also, passing chorus girls in the close quarters of the TV studio corridor, the "boys," as the band is constantly referred to, begin to manifest some interest in the opposite sex, but their manager Norm (!) tells John to "put down those girls or I'll tell your mother." Even their music in the film seems carefully chosen for its lack of sexual implication; the tunes they sing either tend to use the conventional euphemisms of popular music ("I'm So Happy When I Dance with You") or to endorse its romantic, monogamistic vision ("If I Fell"). They may have sung "I Wanna Be Your Man" early in their career, but in the movie it's "This Boy" we hear.

Help! works in a similar manner, although here their fun-loving qualities are emphasized by their being placed within a thriller parody. Their opposition to the evil machinations of a death cult, which needs one of Ringo's rings to complete a sacrificial ritual, exaggerates the traditional rock movie's conflict between teenagers and the older generation's deathly antagonism to rock and anticipates the conflict between the Beatles' Sgt. Pepper personae and the Blue Meanies in the animated feature *Yellow Submarine* (1968), itself something of a parody of *The Sound of Music* (1965).

Black rock stars have not suffered this fate to the same degree since, because of their color, they were not as easily integratable into the established WASPish world of the Hollywood musical. Traditionally, if blacks were not segregated in their own musicals (*Hallelujah!* [1929], *Carmen Jones* [1954]), they had little place except in such lowly positions as shoeshine boys (*The Band Wagon*), boiler-room workers (*Shall We Dance*), special guests of the "massah" of the mansion (*High Society* [1956]), or simply replaced by whites in blackface (the Eddie Cantor musicals of the 1930s). In early rock movies, similarly, blacks were segregated from the narrative, since they tended to appear as featured performers rather than as characters with conflicts that motivated the plot. As in cover versions of black songs by white teen idols such as Pat Boone, racial difference was erased. The irony, of course, is that the black musical forms of blues and rhythm 'n' blues music were such crucial foundational influences on rock 'n' roll. Later musicals such as *What's Love Got to Do with It?* (1993), based on the life of Tina Turner; *Dreamgirls* (2006), about the tribulations of a trio of female soul singers; and *Cadillac Records* (2008), a somewhat revisionist history of bluesman Muddy Waters and his relationship with Chicago's pioneering R&B label, Chess Records, have, thankfully, changed this practice.

By the 1970s rock 'n' roll had become rock, the shortened term aptly connoting the degree to which the music had consolidated, hardened one might say, as an industry. Having successfully fit rock 'n' roll to its previously established system of conventions, rock musicals were a significant part of this process. Musical films successfully absorbed a new music that was both different in form and content from earlier popular music and that opposed the nature of the genre itself by defusing its aggressively phallic connotations as well as that of its performers. In Rick Altman's terms, the genre managed to incorporate a new semantic element into its previously established syntax. In so doing, it is a clear demonstration of Altman's thesis that "the Hollywood genres that have proven the most durable are precisely those that have established the most coherent syntax (the western, the musical)."[25]

Growing Up Absurd

Shtick Meets Teenpic in *The Delicate Delinquent*

Jean-Pierre Coursodon may not be entirely correct when he observes that Jerry Lewis "was the only Hollywood comedian to rise from mere performer to—in his own, quite accurate phrase—'total film maker' during the sound era," but despite the more respectable auteurist imprimatur of, say, Woody Allen, Lewis's involvement in the actual filmmaking process (he pioneered the video assist, for example) was greater and his achievements substantial, despite the entrenched antipathy of North American critics.[1] Clearly, there is a distinct and consistent vision animating Lewis's films that suggests, as Peter Lehman and Susan Hunt note in their discussion of Lewis's most well known film, *The Nutty Professor* (1963), that a "wavering opposition and oxymoron may be principal concerns, particularly regarding gender."[2] *The Delicate Delinquent* (1957) is, I would argue, an important, although hitherto largely neglected, film in the Jerry Lewis canon precisely for the way it addresses Lewis's "principal concern" and, by extension, larger questions about masculinity in the movies.

Despite its historical significance within the trajectory of Lewis's career, however, few scholars or critics discuss *The Delicate Delinquent* at any length or even mention the film at all. But it may be seen as an essential Lewis text to the extent that it expresses the contradictions that inform the cultural icon known as Jerry Lewis. Already in *The Delicate Delinquent* the fundamental clashes, both ideological and aesthetic, that characterize the mature Jerry Lewis (if one may speak thus) find full expression at every level. *The Delicate Delinquent* is neither a good nor even a particularly enjoyable Jerry Lewis movie—"an agreeable blend of sentiment and slapstick" is the kindest description one might offer[3]—yet an appreciation of it does speak directly to what Gerald Mast calls "The Problem of Jerry Lewis," that is, "whether he should be taken seriously at all."[4]

The very place of *The Delicate Delinquent* in Lewis's career is a pivotal one, for it sits on the cusp of the Great Divide, Lewis's breakup with Dean Martin. The film thus occupies a crucial transitional position for Lewis, marking a step forward in independence and assertion of creative control. Lewis produced the film, his first without Martin, but did not direct it. (He would wait until *The Bellboy* in 1960, three years and eight films later, before stepping behind the camera.) For *The Delicate Delinquent,* Lewis hired an old friend, Don McGuire, a writer who had just completed his first film as director, *Johnny Concho* (1956), an undistinguished western with Frank Sinatra.

McGuire, with a few routine pictures to his credit, merits no entries in any of the standard reference works on American filmmakers. He is unacknowledged, for example, in Andrew Sarris's comprehensive *The American Cinema* (1968), and indeed, in Sarris's entry for Lewis, *The Delicate Delinquent* is neither mentioned nor even italicized as important in the filmography. Familiar to Lewis as one of the group involved in making his amateur film parodies, McGuire is described by Lewis biographer Shawn Levy as "a former yes-man, someone he [Lewis] could control without argument."[5] Lacking the stylistic influence of a strong director like Frank Tashlin or even a very competent one like Norman Taurog, *The Delicate Delinquent* inevitably reveals much of its aspiring auteur, Jerry Lewis, newly liberated from Martin.

The screenplay, written by McGuire, was based on the story of Damon and Pythias, the Greek legend about two friends who switch places in prison, willing to die for each other. According to Levy, Lewis regarded the legend as a metaphor in some way of his relationship with Dean Martin,[6] so the story was personally important to the comedian. Levy sums up the plot of *The Delicate Delinquent* perfectly: "It's another schnook-makes-good story: a nebbishy apprentice janitor (Jerry) is mistaken for a young hoodlum by the cops, and a do-good patrolman (Darren McGavin) decides to take him under his wing and reform him. Jerry resists McGavin's help at first, but pretty soon he wants not only to reform but to join the police force . . . and, incredibly, he makes it (though not, of course, without the usual complications)."[7] Just as in the legend the tyrant Dionysius was so impressed by the pair's unwavering friendship and loyalty that he pardoned both of them, so in the film Pythias (Sydney L. Pythias) is rehabilitated by Damon (Mike Damon, the cop), and, in turn, Pythias's success at becoming a policeman redeems the comfortable liberalism of Damon. The slim plot serves as a pretext for a moral sermon, an argument for the redemptive value of niceness that would constitute an essential aspect of the Lewisian vision in later films.

The legend of two such intimate friends is an ideal narrative context for the Lewis persona, given its essentially split nature. As Dana Polan has noted, "There are two Jerry Lewises—the Id (short for Idiot but also suggesting the roots of comic idiocy in a primal unreason) and Jerry Lewis the Serious Man (with capital letters, si'l vous plait)."[8] Lewis's own conception of The Idiot is defined by a split: when Lewis acts as his own director, as he has flatly said, "the Idiot is another person."[9] Indeed, in his book, *The Total Film-Maker,* Lewis sounds almost schizophrenic about his dual role as director and actor: "There is no easy way to shake that schmuck you sleep with at night. No matter how you toss and turn, he's always there," he writes.[10] One of the reasons Lewis's films have not been well received in North America is because The Idiot is simultaneously silly and sentimental—although, for the French, Lewis's life and films "appear to combine the contradictory sides of America, the United States as a clash of attitudes and styles."[11] Damon and Pythias are individuals yet ideal soul mates; for each to be the other assumes a defined self either to become or to abandon. Their story assumes the kind of stability of identity that the Lewis persona is forever seeking.

Lewis's characteristic split between stupidity and seriousness is central to *The Delicate Delinquent.* The title of the film already suggests that this particular Idiot is an oxymoron. Sydney Pythias is both a good boy who embraces bourgeois values and a bad boy ready to rebel at whatever you've got. Sydney has a kind of Jekyll-Hyde personality split that anticipates Lewis's most important film, *The Nutty Professor,* in which he plays both the endearing nebbish Professor Kelp and the obnoxious lounge lizard Buddy Love. But where Lewis's personality split is given a narrative motivation in *The Nutty Professor* through the metaphor of a chemical potion, in *The Delicate Delinquent* the two types simply coexist in the same unbelievable character. Sydney's encounter with the theremin, improbably housed in the apartment of a mad scientist who lives in the building where Sydney works as a janitor, perfectly illustrates Lewis's split character in the film. According to Levy, "The idea of a gifted physical comic interacting with a musical device that is activated by the movement of human bodies in front of it is truly inspired"; but while Levy thinks that the scene is "primally satisfying, like watching a chimpanzee figure out a mirror,"[12] this bit of comic business is disappointingly brief and stands out as an anomaly in a film that is primarily preachy (compare, for instance, Lewis's more sustained physical comedy with the Buddy Rich band in the beatnik café in *Visit to a Small Planet* [1960]).

At the same time as Lewis's Sydney is The Idiot, he is also an idiot savant, the wisest character in the film. Even as Sydney is silly enough to become involved in the scientist's crackpot plan to evacuate all of Earth's frogs in tiny spaceships with little toilets, he frequently drops pearls of moral wisdom, like a Shakespearean fool. For example, despite his tongue-tied embarrassment in the presence of Patricia (Mary Webster), Sydney's obligatory love interest in whom the film is wholly uninterested as a character, he articulately explains his shyness to her by observing, "You got to find out what you are before you can know what you want to be." When Damon and Martha Henshaw (Martha Hyer), the prim, naive representative of the city council, argue over Sydney as a sociological "case" in his presence, Sydney has the sense to get up and leave. He protests, "You two think I'm a freak or something, or a guinea pig," and his indignation seems to us eminently sane and entirely justified. While Sydney's conceptual capacity limits him to forcing round pegs into square holes (as we see with one of the standard intelligence tests he has to take to become a policeman), it is also the case that, as Damon says in defense of him as a police candidate to the captain (Horace McMahon), "He's honest, he's got guts, and he's a decent human being."

Raymond Durgnat has described Lewis's "idiocy" as his ability to unleash "frenetic cadenzas" of emotional signifiers that do not "so much emote, as disintegrate into an emotional gamut."[13] Lewis's performance in *The Delicate*

Sydney Pythias (Jerry Lewis) with do-gooder Martha Henshaw (Martha Hyer) and policeman Mike Damon (Darren McGavin) in *The Delicate Delinquent* (1957).

Delinquent is a prime example. As Sydney walks out on Damon and Henshaw in anger, he says, "If you'll be good enough to excuse me, I'm going home"— Lewis's voice, with the last three words, suddenly and inexplicably changing in tone from The Idiot to The Serious Man. The radically altered "grain of the voice," in Roland Barthes' sense, gives these words a more emphatic symbolic connotation (home as one's proper place) but is impossibly inconsistent in terms of conventional realist character construction.[14]

At times in the film, Lewis's spastic physical humor, a barrage of emotional signifiers, suggests that Sydney is torn between the delicate and the delinquent. Initially deporting himself as a distrustful youth when approached by Damon, as soon as the policeman asks him about his school experience Sydney's body language changes and the sweet, vulnerable kid emerges; Lewis enfolds himself in his legs, his defensive caution melting away and the unself-conscious child blossoming before our eyes. Sydney's split character is literalized when Damon and Henshaw argue over him, standing on either side of him as he sits in a chair, like the proverbial angel and devil at his shoulders. When Martha describes Sydney as "a confused, unbalanced young man with only one thought in mind—self-destruction," Damon responds by asking Sydney if he would like to help him with the salad. Sydney, who had entered the scene wielding a switchblade knife with comic exaggeration, promptly switches both blades and modes, enthusiastically offering to lend a hand.

Lewis's particular inflection of The Idiot in *The Delicate Delinquent* cleverly mobilizes aspects of contemporary youth culture that parallel the Lewis character's own bifurcated construction between delicate and delinquent. As a delinquent, however delicate he may be, Sydney reflects the period's concerns over the development of postwar youth culture, the invention of the teenager, and the new phenomenon of juvenile delinquency. According to Thomas Doherty, the 1950s witnessed the first generation of bona fide teenagers, and throughout the decade the media exploited fears over rebellious youth, stereotypically fixing on "the image of the urban juvenile as a switchblade-brandishing menace."[15] Only four years before the release of *The Delicate Delinquent* a well-publicized Senate Judiciary Subcommittee led by Estes Kefauver was investigating juvenile delinquency and its causes. The year before the film's release, Frankie Lymon and the Teenagers sang "I'm Not a Juvenile Delinquent" in the rock 'n' roll musical *Rock, Rock, Rock* (1956).

Sociological and anthropological discourses were commonly invoked at the time to explain youth as a "subculture,"[16] and these discourses are referenced in a number of ways in *The Delicate Delinquent.* Most obviously, they inform the conflict between Damon and Henshaw over Sydney. Martha Henshaw, who spouts traditional social determinist theory (as she says, she has come "to investigate the deplorable situations in neighborhoods that are a breeding ground for crime"), is well intentioned but naive (she mistakes Sydney for "a perfect example of what juvenile delinquency represents") compared to Mike Damon, who, we discover, has experience in the field since he used to run with the pack himself. Ultimately, Martha is a caricature of the well-meaning but ineffective liberal do-gooder, an upper-class interloper, as signified by her clean white gloves. Damon describes her as "an emissary for would-be reformers who think that juvenile delinquency can be curtailed if we treat these hoodlums with kid gloves." Also, Sydney's dilemma of being caught between the world of the delinquents on the streets around him and his desire to find a better life for himself invokes David Riesman's contemporary and influential distinction between other-directed and inner-directed man in *The Lonely Crowd.*[17] And Sydney's conception of this better life ("There's an awful lot of nice people in the world, Monk, and I just wanna be one of them," he tells the leader of the gang when they come after him in the alley) marks him as the type of *Homo americanus* that William H. Whyte Jr., just the year before *The Delicate Delinquent,* had defined as "the organization man."[18]

Durgnat cites two main themes in Lewis's films, both of which are fully apparent in *The Delicate Delinquent:* "Jerry's desperate attempts to live up to his own ideals of 'benevolent toughness,' and his equally desperate search to find, be worthy of, and be accepted by a loving world."[19] As a comedy, *The Delicate Delinquent* seeks narrative closure, with Sydney successfully integrated into just such a "loving world" and his values valorized. The opening scene, to which I return shortly, shows the explosive presence of The Idiot when he suddenly bursts into view through a door, garbage flying out of his hands; but by the end of the film The Idiot all but disappears within The Serious Man (garbage, some have implied, replaced with rubbish).

The last scene shows Sydney in his new police uniform, embracing a suddenly proud Patricia, who describes him as "tall and handsome" and "respectable." Sydney then moves on to talk to Monk (Robert Ivers) and Artie (Richard Bakalyan), two of the neighborhood delinquents, as well as one younger boy flanking him. Thus, at the end of *The Delicate Delinquent* Sydney becomes the normative heterosexual lover and the father figure to some dead-end kids who ultimately are merely wayward, errant boys reclaimed by Sir Jerry, the knight-errant. In his police uniform and occupying a commanding position in the center of the final images, Sydney is now the embodiment of the Law of the Father rather than the butt of its humor, as he was early on when he was reduced to a sniveling crybaby after mistakenly being rounded up in a rumble bust and put into the police lineup. Tellingly, the last shot of the film is a close-up of Sydney touching his badge with reverence.

Sydney's transformation in the narrative is a perfect example of the frequent oedipal scenario operating in Lewis's films,[20] as suggested in the apparently irrelevant comic business about the threatening male voice asking for Zelda on Sydney's telephone, a voice that refuses to be stifled even when Jerry cuts and strangles the cord. Mr. Herman (Milton Frome), the bullying tenant whose aggressive masculinity is signified by his T-shirt, calls Sydney

Sydney begins to take his proper place in the patriarchal order (*The Delicate Delinquent*).

a "nothing," and when Sydney tries to stand up to the bullying Monk, who challenges him by asking what he is going to do about it, Sydney meekly backs down, saying, "nothin', not now," his own voice muted. Sydney is nothing because he hasn't yet acceded to his place within patriarchy; as he tells Patricia in their first meeting, "When I was a boy, I was jerky. And now, now I'm a man. And I'm empty. I'm nothing—but I would sure like to be something." In other words, Sydney is grown physically but not psychically.

And as the film moves toward its climax, Sydney becomes "something," now capable of standing up to Monk; when he and the other cops scuffle with the boys in the alley, Sydney is shown exchanging punches blow for blow, holding his own. A close-up at the end of the fight shows a dribble of blood at the side of Sydney's mouth, his red badge of masculine courage. Sydney's growth into manhood is metaphorically suggested when, a rookie on his first patrol, he has to help a pregnant woman deliver her baby. The film cuts from a shot of Sydney in panic when he realizes the situation to another of Sydney calmly and proudly holding the baby as the ambulance arrives. Contemplating Sydney's achievements in the penultimate scene, Damon asks of him admiringly, "Is that a boy? Is that a boy?"—an acknowledgment of Sydney's maturation as well as a reference to the earlier *That's My Boy* (1951), in which The Idiot similarly must grow up and take his place in the masculine order.

Sydney's metamorphosis from awkward and alienated youth to full male member of the symbolic order recalls the Charles Atlas bodybuilding ads familiar to all youth in the 1950s, which Lewis explicitly invokes as Clayton Poole in *Rock-a-Bye Baby,* made in 1958. The ads appeared with ritual regularity in comic books of the decade, elevating them to the level of teen myth. They tell a story, in comic-book panels, of the ninety-pound weakling who, bullied on the beach by a seemingly cool muscle-bound guy, loses his girl and is humiliated in public; but with the aid of Atlas's Dynamic Tension program, he gains both confidence and physical strength (along with visible musculature), returns to the scene of the trauma, defeats the bully, and wins back his girl. In the variant of the myth in *The Delicate Delinquent,* the nerd doesn't triumph by physical might but rather by bringing the delinquent boys who bully him around to his own values. Just when things look darkest for Sydney, accused of shooting one of the young hoodlums involved in the fight with police and therefore about to be suspended from the force, Monk appears and confesses that it was really an accident for which Sydney was being framed by one of Monk's buddies.

With a narrative built around Sydney's rite of passage, *The Delicate Delinquent* employs the central plot structure of the teen film. According to Doherty, in the 1950s "the teen years became a unique transitional phase between childhood and adulthood, in some sense an autonomous and in most cases a privileged period in an individual's life."[21] Teens, in other words, developed a distinct subculture, here taken literally, with Sydney's apartment located in the basement. Sydney says at one point that he "doesn't know what he wants to be when he grows up," and so the basement also represents his transitional status. On first entering Sydney's apartment (which requires a giant step from the doorway to the floor, emphasizing the initial gap between Sydney and "respectable" integration into society), Damon looks around and declares, "You're alone," to which Sydney replies, "You ain't kiddin'." Even the milkman and street cleaner avoid Sydney, obviously dubious beneficiaries of his "help" in the past. But as Sydney emerges into adulthood, the movie also fulfills the central ideological task of youth films: "the restoration of the adult culture informed rather than radicalized by youth."[22]

The Delicate Delinquent overlays the generic codes of the newly emergent teenpic genre in postwar American cinema onto the similarly emerging auteur Jerry Lewis. Riding the wave of teen exploitation movies that began with *Rock Around the Clock* in 1956, the film incorporates the teen film's tendency to represent teens as two opposing hyperbolic stereotypes: wild or mild. Richard Staehling describes these images as "the fantasy sociology of the 1950s":

> The wild-youth-kid stereotype was of a bum who rode around in his hot rod, half-crazed from drugs and liquor, looking for a chick to lay, a store to rob, or another car to drag; discourteous, greasy, irresponsible, and mean.
>
> . . . His mild youth counterpart was everybody's baby: clean, honest, moral and bright; everything a parent could hope for, incarnate. He was a little mixed up about love, and did silly things like playing the record player too loud and tying up the telephone, but he was all-American nonetheless, another clean-living member of the silent majority.[23]

Perhaps these two versions of youth in the 1950s, the delicate and the delinquent, represent the Lewis and Martin sides of Jerry Lewis, which Scott Bukatman sees as the juvenile and virile aspects of Lewis's personality, respectively.[24]

Staehling sees both mild and wild youth as defining distinct genres within the wider category of the youth exploitation film, but *The Delicate Delinquent* oscillates between both, tantalizing viewers with the latter's sensationalist possibilities but ultimately opting for the former's bland platitudes. Monk's expression of alienation in his debate with Sydney, wherein he cites Sydney's $60-a-week janitor's salary as class exploitation, hints at a potential social critique—always lurking as a possibility in crime films—that is never developed. Sydney responds simply that Monk looks at the world "sideways." Although the film elsewhere offers hints of such a critique—for example, in the caricatured depiction of Henshaw ("There's a beer in the icebox. I don't think you'll like it, though, it's domestic," says Damon insultingly) and in the references to inner-city ghettos—ultimately, *The Delicate Delinquent* may be one of the films Staehling had in mind "that masquerade as 'juve' movies but are really nothing more than mainstream Hollywood wearing leather jackets and saddle shoes."[25] When the press's interest in juvenile delinquency waned in 1958, the year after *The Delicate Delinquent,* the image of wild youth evolved into the tamer existentialist surfers of beach movies such as *Gidget* (1959) and *Where the Boys Are* (1960).[26] *The Delicate Delinquent* is at once a parody of wild youth movies and, infused with Lewis's characteristic *tendresse,* a harbinger of the mild youth cycle to come.

Within the larger generic landscape, the film occupies a contradictory position. On the one hand, *The Delicate Delinquent* is a movie in the venerable tradition of the postwar social problem film—movies such as *Gentleman's Agreement* (1947) and *Pinky* (1949) as filtered through *Blackboard Jungle* and *Rebel Without a Cause* (both 1955), films that present juvenile delinquency as a social problem. On the other hand, it is a comedy, and one, moreover, that often goes for cheap laughs. Treating serious issues with humor is always a difficult aesthetic balancing act, so given its confusing mixture of tones it is no surprise that contemporary reviews of *The Delicate Delinquent* described the film as confusing, "neither fish nor fowl."[27]

The film is Lewis's attempt at making socially conscious comedy in the tradition of Charles Chaplin. Indeed, several moments in *The Delicate Delinquent* seem deliberate references to Chaplin. Sydney's comic business with the Murphy bed in his apartment inevitably recalls Chaplin's short *One A.M.* (1916), in which, writes Gerald Mast, "the bed is one of the few inanimate objects in film history that could have been nominated as best supporting actor."[28] Sydney's being mistaken for one of the boys involved in the rumble and trundled off with them in the police wagon brings to mind the scene in *Modern Times* (1936) where poor Charlie is carted away as the leader of a Communist rally when he innocently picks up a red flag that has fallen off a beam on a passing truck, waving it to get the unaware driver's attention while, unbeknownst to him, a crowd has gathered behind him. Attempting a Chaplinesque combination of pathos and comedy, Sydney's lovelorn look through the banister bars in the hallway stairs at Patricia's apartment door, showing him a prisoner of his own emotions, evokes such images as the rebuffed Charlie looking in on the dancing Georgia in *The Gold Rush* (1925) or gazing upon the blind flower girl in *City Lights* (1931).

The film's motif of garbage as a physical emblem of human refuse and waste seems a particularly Chaplinesque attempt at pathos. When we first meet Sydney, he bursts into the alley in the middle of a gang fight, stumbling and spilling the garbage he's collected from the tenants in the building. Hauled

Sydney sings "By Myself" by himself in an alley (*The Delicate Delinquent*).

away with the other boys by the police, Sydney protests, "I was only taking out the garbage." When he meets Patricia at her apartment door and they are both too embarrassed and shy to speak, she gives him her garbage. At the conclusion of his musical number, "By Myself," Sydney moves two garbage cans from one side of the door to the other, a visual metaphor for the burden of his woes in the world. And when Monk confesses the truth about Artie's gunshot wound in the climax, he explains that there "ain't no reason for Sydney not to climb out of the garbage."

From scene to scene, *The Delicate Delinquent* veers clumsily between slapstick and social significance, just as Lewis lurches from stupid to smart. Where one scene is funny, the next is serious. The film's very tone and style pull in two different directions, mirroring the tension within Sydney, and are foregrounded immediately in the opening precredit scene. Beginning with shots of a city street complete with expressionist shadows and pools of water on the pavement, the film starts as film noir. Or this scene could be from a wild youth exploitation movie produced by AIP or Sam Katzman. Along with these images, jazzy percussion rises in volume on the soundtrack, the staccato rhythms connoting bohemianism, urban culture, and decadence.[29] But when the delinquents begin to appear, their actions are expressionistic, stylized, like the gangster choreography of "The Girl Hunt Ballet" in *The Band Wagon* (1953). When three of the youths confront three others in the alley, they take out their weapons sequentially—first chain, then knife, then brass knuckles—with dramatic flair and in perfect time with the nondiegetic musical accents. And when the cops arrive and surround the hapless Sydney, the images invoke at once the stark determinism of Fritz Lang's compositions and the surreal absurdity of Buster Keaton's.

Later in the film, when Damon and Pythias are riding in the prowl car and receive a call about the disturbance in the alley, we see two exterior location shots of a police car driving through the streets of New York that might well have come from *The Naked City* (1948), a Mark Hellinger–produced thriller recognized for its pioneering location photography. These are followed by studio shots of the two policemen inside the car, then a shot of the vehicle arriving at the alley, which is also a studio set. The fight that follows is clearly choreographed and not merely unconvincing realism. So in this single sequence we have abrupt joining of studio fabrication to realistic location shots, bleak noir sensibility to choreographic, almost musical, artificiality. I wouldn't agree that *The Delicate Delinquent* is "a minor work of American neorealism, a forgotten cousin of *On the Waterfront* (1954) or *Marty* (1955)",[30] but while the film is generally a studio-bound fantasy, there are moments in which reality suddenly and noticeably intrudes.

Shawn Levy criticizes the inconsistencies of *The Delicate Delinquent* as "sloppy" and dismisses the film because Lewis cannot stay in character. "And," he adds, "he's wearing the inevitable wedding band and pinky ring."[31] But the film, as I've suggested, is riven with inconsistencies at every level, and they are, in fact, part of what makes it so interesting. Lewis's unconvincing character challenges the typical representation of masculinity—here, delinquent adolescent masculinity—in Hollywood cinema, suggesting it is less monolithic than performative. As Bukatman notes, Lewis's presence in his films "demolishes any prospect of a coherent masculine subjectivity" because "the multiplicity of identities in the world of Jerry Lewis belies the existence of identity as anything other than a necessary but unworkable fiction."[32] This is certainly true of *The Delicate Delinquent,* in which Lewis's presentation of himself is marked as performance consistently within the film. When Martha, looking for a "typical" delinquent to bring to Damon's apartment, walks past Sydney in the alley, she sees him gesturing with the switchblade Monk had given him, exactly embodying "the urban juvenile as switchblade-brandishing menace"—and so mistakes him for the perfect example of juvenile delinquency. Sydney also imagines himself a policeman, addressing his own reflection in the mirror ("Good morning, Officer") like a mild Travis Bickle, and elsewhere imitates a sumo warrior for an audience of appreciative cadets during his police training. Lewis's performance of "By Myself" in the film is also emphasized as a performance when spotlighting from a nondiegetic source above illuminates him in the alley as he reaches the song's emotional climax.

Just as Sydney—as he himself tells Patricia—is a torn man, a nobody who wants to be a somebody, so Lewis is torn between the comic and the social critic in *The Delicate Delinquent.* The film is on one level about Lewis—without the anchor of straight-man Martin—looking for himself. Seeking to define himself as a solo performer after the departure of Dino, by film's end Lewis plays both partners of *Pardners* (1956), The Idiot and The Serious Man rolled into one New Man. It is no coincidence that the one song Lewis sings in *The Delicate Delinquent* is "By Myself," the Howard Dietz–Arthur Schwartz tune that Fred Astaire sang several years earlier in *The Band Wagon.* Lewis's allusion here is apt and very precise, for in Minnelli's musical Astaire's character, Tony Hunter, is a self-reflexive meditation on the evolving, maturing image of the star who is playing him, Astaire himself, just as the character of Sydney Pythias is for Jerry Lewis. Moreover, Astaire played Hunter, a performer whose career is at a turning point, at a turning point in his own career, just as *The Delicate Delinquent* inevitably constituted a turning point for Lewis. In Lewis's version the song begins and ends as a voice-over of Sydney thinking to himself, literalizing the idea of Lewis talking to himself ("I'll face the unknown, I'll build a world of my own," he sings).

Mast argues that the problem with Lewis is that he "simply does shtick. He contrives gags—many of them good ones. But the gags do not flow from any human or personal center."[33] But such a criticism is true only if we measure Lewis's characters by realist criteria. Lewis's films might more accurately be called "incoherent texts" in Robin Wood's sense. For Wood, in certain fragmented films the fragmentation "becomes a structuring principle, resulting in works that reveal themselves as perfectly coherent once one has mastered their rules."[34] Lewis's films, with all their inconsistencies of narrative, mise-en-scène, and style, speak to the difficulties of maintaining the kind of masculine ego ideal typically constructed by Hollywood movies and reveal it as constructed rather than natural. Thus it might be said that his films remain of interest precisely to the degree that they fail to fulfill the kind of seamless illusionism of classic cinema.

Andrew Sarris refuses to consider Lewis as an auteur because, he argues, there is a gap between Lewis's sentimentality and his sensibility. Unlike John Ford, to whom he compares Lewis, there is no "essential unity" to his personality.[35] But as *The Delicate Delinquent* demonstrates, it is precisely this lack of unity that is fundamental to Lewis's vision—indeed, the disunity is perhaps its most consistent, that is to say, unifying aspect. At war with itself—like adolescents in much of the discourse of the time—*The Delicate Delinquent* is fully representative of Lewis's cinema, built as it is on a number of tensions between auteur and genre, between style and content. Because of and not in spite of these tensions, *The Delicate Delinquent* emerges as an essential Jerry Lewis film, one that reveals the ongoing attempt by "Jerry Lewis" to negotiate his place in "the world," the Symbolic Order.

6

"Cussers Last Stan'"

Black Masculinity in *The Cool World*

Documentary filmmaker Frederick Wiseman has insisted that documentary films can be as complex as good novels, and, of course, his telling description of his work as "reality fictions" emphasizes the fictional aspects of their aesthetic construction. "My real interest is in trying to make good movies," he has stated.[1] In interviews Wiseman has often spoken of his wish to make a fiction feature using documentary techniques, citing Gillo Pontecorvo's *The Battle of Algiers* (1966) as a model.[2] He explains his interest in using documentary techniques in fiction as motivated largely by his view that a documentary "look" invests fiction with greater credibility and social impact, as in the case of Peter Watkins's films. Indeed, Pontecorvo's film has often been mistakenly perceived as a documentary because of its style, even though the film begins with credits and the claim that "not one foot of newsreel has been used in this reenactment of the battle of Algiers."

While Wiseman has dabbled in fiction filmmaking throughout his career,[3] in 1960, seven years before directing his first documentary, *Titicut Follies* (1967), he was already involved in bringing a documentary sensibility to fiction film as producer of *The Cool World,* directed by Shirley Clarke. Wiseman purchased the film rights to Warren Miller's 1959 novel of Harlem gang life, *The Cool World,* for five hundred dollars.[4] He invited Clarke, a New York filmmaker he had met as an investor in her previous film, *The Connection* (1960), to direct it, thinking that he lacked the necessary experience to do so himself. Clarke not only directed the film but also wrote the screenplay in collaboration with Carl Lee, who played Cowboy in both the film and the stage version of Jack Gelber's play, *The Connection. The Cool World* was completed in time to be shown at the 1963 Venice Film Festival (along with the official American entry, Martin Ritt's *Hud*), where it received generally favorable response as a powerful socially conscious film. Since then, however, the film has been unfairly neglected in histories of black American film, overshadowed by *One Potato, Two Potato, Nothing But a Man,* and *Black Like Me* (all 1964), released the following year, although *The Cool World*'s depiction of black male youth, and its uneasy collaboration between several artists and its resulting heterogeneous style, in fact anticipates aspects of black aesthetic theory by years.

The film maintains an uneasy but fascinating relationship to Hollywood cinema in its mixture of narrative and documentary elements. This is in large part a result of its play with the conventions of popular cinema, a technique Wiseman frequently employs in his documentaries.[5] In interviews Wiseman has stated his dislike of Hollywood fantasies and the failure of Hollywood movies to confront real social issues.[6] Hollywood's shameful history of racial representation, while by no means the only subject of avoidance, is a perfect example; the images of, for instance, African Americans in mainstream cinema have been a catalog of demeaning stereotypes. After World War II, a few films such as *Home of the Brave, Lost Boundaries, Pinky,* and *Intruder in the Dust* (all 1949) treated African Americans with a new awareness as, in Donald Bogle's apt phrase, "the problem people." In these movies, writes Bogle, black characters "had their color stamped indelibly upon them, and they suffered, struggled, bled, yet endured. But as Hollywood had it, they always won their battles."[7] *The Cool World,* like Miller's book, attempts to show without the usual sanctimoniousness and sentimentality characteristic of even Hollywood's more progressive movies about racial difference, some of the problems of contemporary American urban life, particularly that of young men.

The story concerns fourteen-year-old black youth Duke Custis (Hampton Clanton) and his struggle to survive in the hostile and violent ghetto environment of Harlem one summer. A member of a street gang named the Royal Pythons, Duke assumes leadership of the gang when the previous president, Blood (Clarence Williams), becomes a junky. He begins to establish a relationship with Luanne (Yolanda Rodriquez), a teenage prostitute who has taken up residence in the Pythons' apartment. Much of the story concerns Duke's ongoing attempts to raise fifty dollars to buy a gun from Priest (Lee), a local gangster, so that he can make a "rep" for himself during the coming rumble with a rival gang, the Wolves. The gang fight, followed by Duke's arrest, provides *The Cool World*'s strong climax. The author of *The Cool World*, Warren Miller, is white but makes a sincere attempt to get at the conditions of inner-city ghetto life without condescension. Interestingly, as early as 1949 Miller himself was championing the documentary approach over Hollywood illusionism in films.[8] The film is generally faithful to the novel's narrative and style—indeed, much of the dialogue is retained verbatim—although there are some minor changes in the plot. The book is narrated by Duke in dialect, in the tradition of Mark Twain's *Adventures of Huckleberry Finn,* although a closer parallel is Anthony Burgess's *A Clockwork Orange,* published only three years later.

In the novel, Duke's story occurred in the past (made apparent by remarks like "but at this time I tellin you about")[9] and is being recounted in some present but as yet unexplained situation. The reader cannot help but wonder about the circumstances of the narration and who it is addressing. Only at the end of the novel, in the final two-page chapter titled "Where I Am," is it revealed that Duke has been sent to reform school where he is being successfully rehabilitated, and that, in the narrative's present, he has recounted these events to a therapist, Doc Levine. This hardened boy from the violent ghetto, as we discover in the book's only serious lapse into sentimentality, is learning to read and write and now even enjoys tending the institution's flower beds. (*A Clockwork Orange* provides an ironic echo of this ending in the last sentence of the penultimate chapter, Alex's declaration that "I was cured all right."[10]) Immediately before this comforting conclusion, Duke is hauled away by police after the rumble with the Wolves.

The film, however, wisely ends at this point, with Duke's arrest, the patrol car whisking him off into the Harlem night. This ending is clearly more appropriate to the tone of both novel and film. It also justifies the cinema's tendency to narrate in the present tense, since there is nothing in the movie to suggest that this story has been, as it were, recollected in tranquility. Further, in refusing to provide narrative closure, the film not only anticipates the way Wiseman's subsequent documentaries frequently end by presenting the viewer either directly or implicitly with unresolved questions and issues, but also does not pretend to resolve the problems of poverty, racism, and juvenile delinquency as most of the Hollywood films do.

In its choice of subject *The Cool World* may be seen to have developed from the postwar movies of Hollywood directors like Elia Kazan who, inspired by Italian neorealism, looked at urban and working-class milieus. In particular it recalls Sidney Meyers's independent film *The Quiet One* (1948), also a fictional account of a troubled black youth shot on location in Harlem. Stylistically, though, *The Cool World* resembles observational cinema more than it does the classic narrative style. Yet rather than effacing its presence, the camera frequently calls attention to itself by its unorthodox (observational documentary style) movement, especially in some dialogue scenes done with a panning camera rather than conventional shot-reaction-shot figures. In one shot the camera follows the boys onto a school bus, the lens aperture adjusting for the extreme difference in available light (reminiscent of the famous shot following John F. Kennedy in *Primary* [1960]). The film was photographed by Baird Bryant entirely on location in Harlem, often with available lighting, a hand-held camera, muddy sound, and (with the exception of Carl Lee and Clarence Williams) nonprofessional actors.

According to Wiseman, none of the youths in the film had any prior professional acting experience.[11] Clarke's method of directing the actors was to outline a scene, and then allow them to improvise.[12] There is, consequently, a strong emphasis on the authenticity of the dialogue, an attempt to duplicate the slang and rhythms of black urban speech. (The only false note is the consistent use of the word "motherin'" as a euphemism for swearing.) Lee is listed in the credits for dialogue (according to Lauren Rabinovitz, he was denied credit as codirector),[13] a clear acknowledgment of the importance given to language in the film. Even though a few sequences seem to have been post-synced, in its use of improvised street talk the film recalls Louis Marcorelles's claim about the centrality of real speech in observational cinema,[14] also a dominant feature of Wiseman's documentaries.

The Cool World also makes use of found symbolism, an expressive device upon which observational documentary heavily relies. Once, when Duke leaves his tenement, for example, there follows a shot of a dog trotting freely in a street—a clear metaphor of Duke's "unleashed," rebellious personality. Several literal signs in the film resonate with meaning, such as the cinema marquee glimpsed while Duke sells reefers on the street. The marquee reads "Adventures of a Angry Young Man," a grammatically incorrect abbreviation for Ritt's *Hemingway's Adventures of a Young Man* (1962). The mistake is consistent with the ungrammatical speech of Duke and his friends as well as an appropriate description of his own story. When Duke and Luanne go to Coney Island, we see a "Lost Children" sign (like the "Missing Children" sign in Wiseman's *Deaf* [1986], about another group of marginalized youths) just before Luanne disappears. The sign, of course, serves as narrative foreshadowing, but also as editorial comment; in a sense, both youths are "lost" even before Luanne literally exits from the narrative.

Much of the credit for the film's authenticity must be given to director Shirley Clarke, and its style is clearly influenced by her as well. Clarke's work is consistently informed by a documentary approach (although later in her career much of her time was spent working in experimental video). She had been involved with a number of D. A. Pennebaker's early films, frequently as editor (*Brussels Film Loops,* 1958; *Opening Night in Moscow,* 1959), sometimes as camera operator (*Breaking It up at the Museum,* 1960). Some of Clarke's own early shorts, *In Paris Parks* (1954), *Bridges Go-Round* (1958), and *Skyscraper* (1959, on which Willard Van Dyke and Irving Jacoby, as well as Pennebaker, worked), are variations of the city symphony form of documentary. *The Connection,* her first feature, employs a mock cinema verité style; it even includes as characters the two-man documentary film crew supposedly filming the action. *Portrait of Jason* (1967), a two-hour monologue with a frustrated actor, is in its sparse "purity" of technique considered a classic of American cinema verité.

The use of music in *The Cool World* (both the diegetic rhythm and blues and the Mal Waldron score), likely reflects Clarke's interest in jazz. *Skyscraper* features a score by jazz composer and arranger Teo Macero; the music for *The Connection* was provided by jazz pianist Freddie Redd; and her last film, *Ornette: Made in America* (1978), is an experimental documentary about free jazz innovator, alto sax player Ornette Coleman. Most of the early shorts make use of rapid editing; as Clarke told Rabinovitz in an extensive interview conducted in 1981, there had been no sound, "and the one thing we couldn't do was jazz. So I made them all jazz."[15]

Reviewing *The Cool World* upon its initial release, Andrew Sarris acknowledged its sincerity but disliked Clarke's peripatetic camera, which he described as "visual hysteria blotting out intellectual contemplation." Similarly, both Gordon Hitchens and Dwight MacDonald faulted Clarke for her seemingly uncomfortable combination of fictional and documentary techniques.[16] But rather than being superfluous, the observational style is in fact quite appropriate. First, as suggested above, this style signals an opposition to the smooth flow of the classic Hollywood film, just as the subject is one that had been generally avoided in commercial American cinema. Second, it successfully captures the subjective perspective of the narrator, Duke. The film periodically allows us to hear Duke's thoughts (but no one else's) on the soundtrack, clearly marking the film's narration, like that of the novel, as first person. When Duke says, "I gotta keep movin'," the camera visually expresses his feeling; when he scrambles down the street after discovering Priest's body in the Pythons' clubhouse, the restless camera and swish pans visually capture his sudden panic.

The film and the novel emphasize that Duke is not an inexplicable social aberration but that his sensibility is to a large extent shaped by his environment. Hence the network of references to popular culture, and the film's use of genre conventions in particular. Duke's street name is itself inspired by the iconographical individualist hero established by John Wayne, largely in his western roles. The gun this Duke wants to obtain is a Colt, a weapon of central importance to the western genre. In the book one gang member identifies the Colt as the firearm used at "Cussers Last Stan." Also, Duke explains at length his admiration for the western hero of a movie he had seen titled *The Baron of New Mexico,* probably misremembering Samuel Fuller's *The Baron of Arizona* (1949). When Duke and Luanne go to Coney Island, he has a mock shootout with a mechanical gunfighter in an arcade; the machine's prerecorded voice echoes the word "draw" six times on the soundtrack, an expressionist use of sound that emphasizes the importance of western myth to Duke. For him, the perception of reality, and his sense of masculine identity, is informed to a significant extent by popular cinema.

"Stand up and shoot like a man," reads a sign on the mechanical gunslinger. Duke's obsession with being a "man," as he understands it, connects with

Duke (Hampton Clanton) and Luanne (Yvonne Rodriquez) before the showdown with the mechanical gunfighter in *The Cool World* (1964).

Wiseman's exploration of gender definition, particularly aggressive masculinity—seen most emphatically in *High School* (1968) and *Basic Training* (1971). Duke's fantasy of what people will say about him—"There goes Duke Custis. He's a cold killer"—echoes Howard Gilbert, the young black man arrested in *Law and Order* (1969), about the Kansas City police force, who boasts "I'm a killer," and more generally, D. H. Lawrence's description of the American male psyche ("cold, isolate, stoic and a killer"), already discussed in relation to John Wayne's Dunson in Howard Hawks's *Red River* (1948) in chapter 3. The pervasive presence of guns in American society and their totemic appeal is also seen in *Juvenile Court* (1973) and even *Deaf*, where the children are fascinated more by the deputy's pistol than anything else when they visit the county judicial building. Duke's overpowering desire to possess the gun is for him a way of defining his manhood. His thoughts about the Colt, "all black and oiled, just waiting to go," are infused with phallic aggression: "Man, a piece is the key. It's a screwdriver. You get yourself a piece, why, then, everything opens up for you." The close-up of Miss Dewpont's purse with the gun in it visually expresses the sexual potency he associates with the weapon.

Priest's black suit and white tie constitute familiar attire in the gangster film. His white moll, Miss Dewpont (Marilyn Cox), is a stock character of the genre. Hardy (Claude Cave), the black youth who plans to escape the neighborhood by playing basketball at an Ivy League college, and Douglas (Joe Dennis), Blood's freedom-rider brother, are like the gangster film's "Pat O'Brien" figures—representing "ballots not bullets." Blood's high-pitched, nervous laughter clearly recalls that of Richard Widmark's Tommy Udo in the noir crime drama *Kiss of Death* (1947). The shot of one of the Pythons leaving the gang's apartment and pausing at the entrance of the tenement building, shrugging his shoulders, and then being flanked by fellow gang members before descending the steps, is strikingly reminiscent of James Cagney's trademark body language in *Public Enemy* (1931) and other gangster movies, employing the genre's conventional triangular deployment of gangsters within the frame. Duke's fantasy of acquiring the gun and being "at the top of the heap" recapitulates the desire of virtually every American movie gangster— particularly as depicted in the famous conclusion of Raoul Walsh's *White Heat* (1949), when Cagney yells out "Top of the World, Ma," before immolating himself atop a huge gas tank. The overly stylized and choreographed scene in which the Wolves intimidate Hardy in the schoolyard recalls *West Side Story* (1961), while the later fight there on the jungle gym (a sly metaphor) appears to prefigure the stylized combat in Walter Hill's *The Warriors* (1979). (Clarke had been a dancer and choreographer before becoming a filmmaker, and was heavily influenced by the dance films of Maya Deren.)

Most of these references allude to dominant, white popular culture. In Richard Wright's novel *Native Son* (1940), when the impressionable and confused black youth Bigger Thomas goes to the movies, he sees lobby cards advertising two films: "One, The Gay Woman, was pictured on the posters in images of white men and white women lolling on beaches, swimming, and dancing in night clubs; the other, Trader Horn, was shown on the posters in terms of black men and black women dancing against a wild background of barbaric jungle."[17] Bigger, like Duke, is overwhelmed by the dominant white culture around him, presenting impossible alternatives as role models. On the one hand, he is offered a lifestyle of the rich and famous that he can never attain, and on the other, a debasing racist stereotype. In *The Cool World,*

Genre iconography is invoked throughout *The Cool World,* as in the gangster costume of Priest (Carl Lee).

black popular culture emerges only occasionally, as when gospel music plays or we see a poster advertising a James Brown show at the Apollo Theater. By contrast, white popular culture appears everywhere (as it does in Wiseman's *Canal Zone* [1977]): in the smiling face of a white woman on a large Canada Dry billboard, in the Mr. Freezee caricature, in the white doll held by black hands in one of the street shots. Duke, like Bigger, is attracted to but excluded from the fantasies of white culture, and both youths express their rage at cultural marginalization through violence.

In his influential 1962 article, "Notes on the New American Cinema," Jonas Mekas explicitly sets the work of several independent filmmakers, including Clarke, against the "'official' (Hollywood) cinema."[18] *The Cool World* sets itself apart by the unusual observational context in which it deploys genre conventions, a split that embodies aesthetically what W. E. B. Du Bois referred to as the "twoness" of the black American experience.[19] This twoness, as Addison Gayle points out, was necessarily reflected in artistic production: "The black artist of the past worked with the white public in mind. The guidelines by which he measured his production was its acceptance or rejection by white people."[20] Further, according to Henry Louis Gates Jr., black writing is marked by a revision of—or "signifying" upon—texts in the Western tradition. It is precisely in this play upon white texts, he argues, that black texts articulate their difference.[21] *The Cool World,* with its stylistic mix, is, like black writing and jazz, what Gates would call a "mulatto text." Thus, what Sarris sees as the film's inability to blend "the materials of stylized melodrama into the network of realistic cross-references" is actually a tension essential to the film's "counter-cinema" strategy and meaning.[22]

As several of Wiseman's documentaries (*Law and Order, Primate, Welfare* [1975]) so vividly illustrate, race is a burning issue informing all social relations in the United States. Racial tensions likewise surface throughout the narrative of *The Cool World,* beginning immediately in the opening scene with a Black Muslim's speech on the street about the white man being the devil. The accompanying montage of street shots shows that the only whites to be seen in the neighborhood are cops; there is no doubt as to who wields institutionalized power here. When the police arrest Duke at the end, they grab him, saying, "Get up, you little black bastard." The glaring presence of Miss Dewpont, the only important white character in the film, and Priest's abusive treatment of her, are inevitably charged with racial implications—as is the scene when the black man, Ben, slaps the white woman, Barbara, in *Night of the Living Dead* (1968) discussed in chapter 8.

Just as the film acknowledges a cultural split between black and mainstream America, so it emphasizes the physical separateness of Harlem. This sense of the ghetto as an oppressive, enclosed space is immediately established in the opening montage of Harlem street life. Other montage sequences, remarkably similar to Wiseman's street shots in his documentaries, appear regularly throughout the film. They frequently separate major sequences in the narrative, as they often do the major parts, what Bill Nichols calls the "tesserae," of Wiseman's mosaic structure.[23] The tracking shots of Harlem streets with their rows of tenement houses near the beginning of the film is strikingly similar to the openings of *High School* and *Law and Order,* early Wiseman documentaries separated from *The Cool World* by only a few years. The physically and emotionally sick people who endlessly file into New York's Metropolitan Hospital in *Hospital* (1970) might very well come from this neighborhood; the woman who has her purse snatched by Duke is, in a sense, the woman who is the victim of the same crime in *Law and Order*. The film's treatment of Harlem as both a distinct physical and social space and weltanschauung invites one to view the ghetto itself as an institution, the way institutions in Wiseman's later films become defined as much by constraints of ideology as by physical boundaries. Wiseman himself has made the connection, noting that "a hospital or a high school is as much a ghetto as central Harlem."[24]

The film not only explores life in the urban ghetto as a distinct world but also establishes at the outset that this environment exists in the context of, adjacent to, affluent America and capitalism. The poverty of Harlem—Michael Harrington's "Other America," as mentioned in *High School*—starkly contrasts with but is not inseparable from Wall Street or Central Park South, the route the school bus takes downtown. In a sense, Harlem is revealed as a gap between American ideology and its practice. References to business, profit, and purchasing power recur throughout the film. Priest, a gangster cum entrepreneur, refuses to do business on credit. As Duke is taken away in the patrol car at the end of the film, we hear a radio news broadcast; a report of gang warfare in Harlem comes between items about "a communist stronghold" (presumably in Southeast Asia) and lobbying to require the first astronauts on the moon to plant an American flag. Duke's fate is sandwiched between the forces of American capitalist imperialism, like that of the Panamanians in *Canal Zone*, outsiders in the middle of a world from which they are excluded.

The first major sequence of *The Cool World*, the school trip downtown, deserves particular mention in this context because it is crucial to the film and also suggestive in the context of Wiseman's documentary work. In her review of the film, Harriet Polt cited this sequence as one of its major flaws, describing it as "too blatantly ironic" and "extraneous to the body of the film."[25] In fact, quite the opposite is true. On the last day of school, before summer vacation, Duke's class is taken south by bus along Fifth Avenue to Wall Street in lower Manhattan. Most obviously, the trip demonstrates how very much these boys are out of place outside of Harlem. It is much like the scene where working-class boys are taken on a cricket trip to Mill Hill, a school for wealthy children, in Karel Reisz's Free Cinema documentary, *We Are the Lambeth Boys* (1959). The sequence further establishes the sense of the ghetto as a bounded space, one that the boys may leave but from which they can never really escape. "It ain't the Waldorf, but it'll do," says Priest's henchman, later surveying the Pythons' apartment. Their alienation is shown when they pause at the statue of Alexander Hamilton—"standing on the very ground where George Washington, the founder of this country, once actually was," the teacher observes—but are not the least interested or impressed. As they leave the site, the teacher reminds the boys to take a copy of a pamphlet titled "Own a Share of America," after which there is an abrupt cut to Duke back in Harlem stealing a purse. The editing here, which anticipates the ironic use of editing Wiseman often employs in his documentaries, serves as a comment on the disenfranchisement of these poor black youths.

Additionally, the school trip sequence, coming at the beginning of the film, brings Duke and his friends out of their element into what is probably a more familiar, less threatening environment for white viewers. As Donald Bogle notes, Harlem is a place largely unfamiliar to white viewers, even to most of the liberals among them.[26] This initial situation is then reversed; white viewers are placed in a similar position to the boys on the bus, as they are then taken on an excursion into the ghetto. David Eames observes that Wiseman would not be interested in a guided tour, that he prefers instead to get inside the institutions he shoots rather than perceive them from a distance.[27] Thus the appearance of the Japanese tourists with their inevitable cameras in *Meat* (1976) counterpoints Wiseman's more probing camera, just as *Canal Zone* opens with a voice-over explanation of the canal's operations by an official tour guide before the film goes on to penetrate the ideology masked by the cascade of official statistics. *The Cool World* works in a similar way; the shallow tour offered to the black youths is contrasted to the film's more thorough examination, below the physical surface, through the first-person narration. The film seeks to immerse the viewer in the Harlem environment, just as Wiseman would later claim that with *Titicut Follies* he "wanted to put the audience for the film in the state hospital."[28]

My reading of *The Cool World* foregrounds and seeks to make sense of the tensions and cracks that exist in the film on both the thematic and stylistic levels. The questions raised by the issues of genre and authorship in this collaboration of three different artists (Wiseman, Clarke, and Lee; two male, one female; two white, one black) reflect the more important tensions in the film that may be understood as articulating part of the black experience in America. It also anticipated by almost three decades the cycle of hood films, beginning with *Do the Right Thing* (1989) and including *Boyz N the Hood* (1991),

Juice (1992), *American Me* (1992), *Menace II Society* (1993), and *Dead Presidents* (1995), that sought to capture the harsh realities of inner-city life by updating conventions of the classic gangster and crime film. Duke Custis in *The Cool World* is uncompromising in a way that Sidney Poitier's "sexual neutralization" was not; and he constituted an important step toward the type of black masculinity embodied by later black actors such as Jim Brown, the "black buck hero for a separatist age."[29]

Upon the film's release, Wiseman declared, "I intend to make sure that *The Cool World* is not exploited as just another picture about juvenile delinquency."[30] The subject had been popular in the 1930s, in such movies as *Wild Boys of the Road* (1933), *Dead End* (1937), and *Angels with Dirty Faces* (1938), and, as discussed in the previous chapter, reemerged in the postwar youth culture of the 1950s in such films as *The Wild One* (1954), *Blackboard Jungle* (1955), and *Rebel without a Cause* (1955). But the issue was trivialized in short order by the flood of formula teen exploitation quickies released by American International Pictures, independent producers Albert Zugsmith and Sam Katzman, and Jerry Lewis's *The Delicate Delinquent* (1957). By the early 1960s Gidget and the Annette Funicello/Frankie Avalon cycle of beach movies were washing over real problems of youth. It is in this context that *The Cool World* stands out as a healthy antidote. Nobody is reformed by film's end, unlike, say, Sidney Poitier's character, Gregory Miller, in *Blackboard Jungle.* In Hollywood it is possible that the kids in *Angels Wash Their Faces* (1939) become the likeable Bowery Boys, and even go on to save America from a Fifth Column spy ring. By contrast, the Royal Pythons might wash their faces, but the blackness of their skin will never come off.

Of Men and Monoliths

Science Fiction, Gender, and *2001: A Space Odyssey*

The general impression that viewers tend to bring away from Stanley Kubrick's *2001: A Space Odyssey* (1968) is an overall feeling of "coldness," not just of the physical cold of outer space but of the film's sense of humanity. As has often been observed, the computer HAL seems a more complex character with greater emotional depth than any of the people in the film. And while the computer's death is a scene of wrenching pathos, the three hibernating scientists expire in what is perhaps the most antiseptic depiction of death in all of cinema, a bland-looking monitor indicating "Life Functions Terminated." *2001*'s relative dearth of dialogue, wooden characters, slow pace, and sleek production design, which depicts the environments of space travel as thoroughly antiseptic and ordinary, all contribute to the film's cold tone.

These aspects of *2001* have been much commented upon by other critics, sometimes positively, sometimes not, but what has gone largely unnoticed is how many of the film's stylistic elements work in relation to one of its primary themes, the gendered implications of space exploration. The coldness of the film's characters, most of whom are men, is part of the film's overall view of the relationships among science, technology, violence, and patriarchal masculinity, a view consistent with other Kubrick films. This perspective is surprisingly similar to that of feminist philosophers of science who have critiqued traditional science as informed by a masculinist bias at least since Francis Bacon employed metaphors of rape and seduction to describe men's mastery over a feminized Nature.[1] Baconian science, based on rational empiricism, induction, and a masculine culture of objectivity and nonsensuality, is "a science leading to the sovereignty, dominion, and mastery of man over nature," as Evelyn Fox Keller puts it.[2] I want to suggest that this sensibility of masculine mastery, as conveyed in popular culture's representations of space travel, is purposefully undermined by 2001. That is to say, Kubrick's space epic explores a discursive space as much as a physical space in that it seeks for a stylistic alternative to the science fiction film's conventional depiction of space exploration as an act of phallic masculinity, of penetration and possession—or, to borrow the title of one of the first Hollywood movies on the subject, *The Conquest of Space* (1955).

2001 makes clear immediately in the opening section, titled "The Dawn of Man," that it will explore these issues. Kubrick depicts the landscape here as harsh and hostile, a man's world where only the fittest survive. Warring bands of apes contest with one another and with other animals for control of the crucial natural resource, a water hole; the blanched skeletons of dead apes mingle with the rocks and dust, a reminder of the stakes of survival, like the grave markers in *Red River*. The balance of power tips decidedly when one ape (Moon-Watcher in the script) takes the human race's first technological step by turning a bone into both a tool for killing prey and a weapon for bludgeoning enemies. Only now do the apes seem to walk more upright for, the film suggests, it is the very point when men begin to harness technology for the purposes of extending their inherent aggression that they truly become men. This opening section of *2001* plays out in brief this theme, which preoccupied Kubrick over the course of his career even as it is central to the science fiction genre.

According to science fiction writer and critic Damon Knight, the genre's appeal resides in what he calls "a sense of wonder." As Knight explains: "Some widening of the mind's horizons, no matter in what direction—the landscape of another planet, or a corpuscle's eye-view of an artery, or what it feels like to be in rapport with a cat . . . any new sensory experience, impossible to the reader in his [*sic*] own person, is grist for the mill, and what the activity of science fiction writing is all about."[3]

Science fiction offers us worlds clearly discontinuous from our own, fantastic worlds that inevitably return us to the known world for comparison.[4] If this dynamic of "cognitive estrangement"[5] is central to science fiction, then theoretically it is an ideal genre for exploring the ideology of gender, for questioning our culture's constrained thinking regarding gender. Yet science fiction has been overwhelmingly masculine and patriarchal, and truly alternate visions of gender have been few. While some progress has been made in literature, this state of affairs remains overwhelmingly the case in film.

Mary Shelley's *Frankenstein,* published in 1816 and generally considered to be the first true science fiction novel, offered a critique of masculine scientific presumption in its story of a masturbatory male scientist who chooses to create life on his own rather than with his new bride.[6] Yet by the time of Jules Verne fifty years later, the genre was taken over and shaped by men, and women writers retreated from the expansive vistas of science fiction to the more domestic spaces of Gothic melodrama and the novel of manners. Nathaniel Hawthorne, himself a writer of science fiction tales in the 1840s, famously dismissed women writers as "d—d female scribblers."[7] Verne's popular *voyages extraordinaires,* such as *Journey to the Center of the Earth* (1864), *From the Earth to the Moon* (1865), and *20,000 Leagues under the Sea* (1870), are colonialist tales about male explorers going where no man had gone before, adventure stories wherein, in the words of Robert Scholes, "boyish men played with new toys created by science."[8] At the turn of the twentieth century, H. G. Wells became the founder of modern science fiction with his series of "scientific romances" beginning with *The Time Machine* in 1895. Wells himself was a champion of women's rights, among other social causes, but his novels are "romances" only in the literary sense—that is, as a fictional mode. In fact, Wells's major science fiction novels contain no significant female characters, with the one possible exception of Weena, the childlike, helpless woman in the distant future of *The Time Machine.* But she is less a rounded character than a tabula rasa on which Wells's heroic but patriarchal Time Traveller, retreating from the rapid social changes at the dawn of the twentieth century, including the growing independence of women, can reinscribe his Victorian values.

Several decades later, during the so-called golden age of science fiction literature of the 1930s through the 1950s, the popular pulp magazines assumed a male readership with their typical stories of BEMs (bug-eyed monsters) to be destroyed and BBBs (big-breasted babes) to be enjoyed. The promise of both pleasures often was featured prominently in their sensational cover illustrations. These images carried over into science fiction film in the 1950s, when the abrupt arrival of the atomic era suddenly made the genre one of the most popular. *Gog* (1954), for example, is atypical only to the degree to which its imagery is embarrassingly explicit in linking masculinity with power, potency, and technology, all coming to a head, so to speak, in the deliriously libidinous climax wherein the scientist hero (the staunchly reassuring Richard Egan) asserts his phallic dominance by destroying rampaging robots that have been reprogrammed by a Soviet ship in space. The robots are themselves excessively phallicized, their defeat by the hero indicating that American science is more potent than that of godless communists. Amply demonstrating his masculine potency, the hero wins the hand (and presumably the body) of the sexualized woman scientist, a damsel in distress dressed in a provocatively tight lab suit and high heels.

The rationale behind *Gog*'s typical conflation of space exploration as masculine potency and Cold War propaganda (the "space race") is emphatically clear in the scientist's explanation in *Invaders from Mars* (1953), another science fiction movie of the period, for why conquering space is so important: "If anybody dared attack us, we could push a few buttons and destroy them in a matter of minutes." *Destination Moon* (1950), the film that launched the decade's spate of science fiction movies, takes the position, as one of the characters explains, that "whoever controls the moon will control the Earth." When the astronauts land on the lunar surface, they claim the moon "by the grace of God" and (adeptly anticipating Neil Armstrong) "for the benefit of mankind" in the name of the United States.

The intertwined issues of technology and patriarchal masculinity are central to stories of space travel, which constitute such a significant part of science fiction that they have their own subgeneric designation—the space opera (a type, we might note, to which *2001*, with its soundtrack of classical music by Johann and Richard Strauss rather than the more typical theremin-inspired electronic score, has a special relation). Space stories usually involve an emphasis on technology and gadgetry since both elements are required by

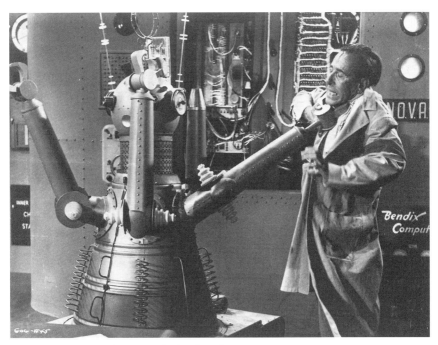

Technology as masculine power in *Gog* (1954).

the premise of interstellar travel. Outer space, like the frontier in the western genre, is a dangerous place that requires the fortitude of men to traverse it.[9] (It is worth noting that, according to the generic discourse of science fiction and mirroring the operative distinction in the real sciences, stories of space are deemed, appropriately, "hard" SF, as opposed to stories more concerned with social extrapolation, which are called "soft" SF.) Space stories have conventionally depicted interstellar travel as the penetration by men of the dark, womblike vastness of space in phallic-shaped rockets. In the standard iconography of the genre, while aliens frequently float in rounded spacecraft (flying saucers), earthlings tend to take their giant steps for mankind in protruding, pointed ships.

Once rocket technology became imaginable in the early twentieth century, science fiction literature quickly dispensed with such patently impractical means of interstellar travel as Cyrano de Bergerac's bottles of dew, Poe's balloon, Verne's giant gun, and Edgar Rice Burroughs's astral projection, and seized upon spaceships, which were quickly streamlined and masculinized. The hyperbolic covers of the pulps typically emphasized the piercing and penetrating power of human spacecraft through such graphic techniques as the exaggerated foreshortening of rocket nose cones. With the aim of settling other worlds, astronauts often are depicted as piercing and impregnating the universe, spreading the seed of human civilization. In movies, the phallic power of human spaceships was emphasized with the first science fiction movie ever made, *Une voyage dans la lune* (*A Trip to the Moon,* 1902), in which French filmmaker Georges Méliès envisioned a giant cannon that discharges a space capsule moonward with an eruptive force powerful enough to achieve escape velocity. As if to demonstrate the masculine triumph of this technology, the cannon ejaculates to the incongruous accompaniment of a group of dancing women—in effect, the first chorus line of "Rockettes"—in the mise-en-scène literally below the powerful phallus. Méliès borrowed the idea of a giant space gun from Verne's *From the Earth to the Moon,* in which the cannon is erected by the members of the all-male Baltimore Gun Club, and it appears again as late as 1936 in *The Shape of Things to Come,* where it protrudes, so to speak, as a strikingly unscientific anomaly in H. G. Wells's tale of the future, which otherwise strives for scientific accuracy.

Polish science fiction writer Stanislaw Lem parodies the phallic discourse of space fiction in his 1961 novel *Solaris* (an element entirely missing from both film adaptations). The novel opens with Lem's narrator, a male scientist named Kelvin, describing his journey through space in a small rocket shell:

> My body rigid, sealed in its pneumatic envelope, I was knifing through space with the impression of standing still in the void, my only distraction the steadily mounting heat. . . . The capsule was shaken by a sudden jolt, then another. The whole vehicle began to vibrate. Filtered through the insulating layers of the outer skins, penetrating my pneumatic cocoon, the vibration reached me, and ran through my entire body. The image of the dial shivered and multiplied, and its phosphorescence spread out in all directions. I felt no fear. I had not undertaken this long voyage only to overshoot my target!
>
> . . . A sharp jolt, and the capsule righted itself. Through the porthole, I could see the ocean once more, the waves like crests of glittering quicksilver. The hoops of the parachute, their cords snapped, flapped furiously over the waves, carried on the wind. The capsule gently descended.

Chorines help launch the space capsule in *Une voyage dans la lune* (*A Trip to the Moon,* 1902).

> . . . With the clang of steel rebounding against steel, the capsule came to a stop. A hatch opened, and with a long, harsh sigh, the metal shell which imprisoned me reached the end of its voyage.[10]

Kelvin has traveled through space to investigate a distant planet that is one large sentient ocean. Earth scientists have been studying this ocean planet for generations, producing exhaustive volumes of data and theoretical tomes about it, but thus far have been unsuccessful in the attempt to make contact with it. In his opening description of Kelvin's space flight, Lem establishes his character's phallic stance toward the universe while, in contrast, the ocean planet represents a kind of feminine mystery, pliant yet impenetrable in its difference, seemingly beyond the scientific comprehension of men.

While the planet Solaris may never explain itself, in the 1970s feminist voices in science fiction began to speak, beginning with the publication of Ursula K. Le Guin's *The Left Hand of Darkness* in 1969, just one year after *2001.* Earlier, a few women writers had ventured into the masculine territory of space fiction, including Thea von Harbou, who wrote the screenplay for her husband Fritz Lang's *Metropolis* (1927) and *Frau im Mond* (*Woman in the Moon,* 1929), which introduced the concept of the countdown adapted by NASA; and Kate Wilhelm, whose 1961 story "The Ship Who Sang" is about a physically deformed girl who is hardwired into a spaceship as its computer. But Le Guin's novel opened the stargates for women to write about space travel. Described by science fiction critic Carl Freedman as "the book with which sf most decisively lost its innocence on matters of sex and gender,"[11] *The Left Hand of Darkness* imagines an alien race, the Gethenians, who are normally genderless except during the fertility season, known as kemmer, when they may become either male or female depending partly upon the gender of others near them. The plot isolates a Gethenian politician and a human male ambassador from the planetary federation on an epic adventure, like Hawkeye and Chingachgook, Ishmael and Queequeg, or Captain Kirk and Mr. Spock. But while the classic American fiction of Cooper, Melville, and Twain, as Leslie Fiedler and D. H. Lawrence have pointed out, represses the dread of femininity and homoerotic desire within stories of male adventure,[12] Le Guin foregrounds these tensions with a character who is at once both genders and neither. As the two protagonists, initially alien to each other, begin to overcome their distrust and become intimate friends on their arduous journey together, the earthman, like the terrestrial reader, is prompted to rethink his rigidly conceived, heterosexist categories of gender and sexuality.

The influence of Le Guin's novel was enormous, and on its heels came a wave of feminist science fiction from such writers as Joanna Russ, Marge Piercy, Pamela Sargent, Connie Willis, Kit Reed, and Octavia Butler. Sargent's three anthologies of feminist science fiction, the *Women of Wonder* series, published between 1974 and 1978, provided solid evidence of a feminist "movement" within the genre. Earlier, women science fiction writers such as C. L. Moore (Catherine Moore), Idris Seabright (Margaret St. Clair), and James Tiptree Jr. (Alice Sheldon) used masculine or gender-indeterminate noms de plume in order to get published, to "pass" with editors and readers. But by the 1970s, women science fiction writers could boldly go where few had gone before, announcing their gender difference and writing science fiction that in various ways challenged the genre's traditionally masculinist bias. Novels such as Russ's *The Female Man* (1974) and Piercy's *Woman on the Edge of Time* (1976) targeted the very language of science fiction as a masculine discourse, not only by featuring female protagonists but also by experimenting with unconventional narrative structures and multiple points of view in order to provide alternatives to the masculine way of looking at things. These works provided science fiction's sense of wonder, but one consciously rooted in gender difference.

To take a particularly relevant example, Tiptree's story, "The Women Men Don't See" (published in 1973, four years before the author revealed herself as a woman), deconstructs the masculinist assumptions and ideology of male adventure fiction by undermining the misogynist clichés of the genre's characteristic hard-boiled style. The story involves a stereotypical macho adventurer, Don Fenton, who becomes stranded with two women when the small charter plane on which the three are passengers crashes in an isolated, rugged part of Mexico. Fenton promptly takes charge, assuming the responsibility of providing for the women's survival and seeking a way of making contact with the outside world while, at the same time, the women stumble upon and make contact with aliens who have landed in the seclusion of the jungle for a pit stop. In the end, the women decide to leave Earth with the aliens rather than stay with the intolerably sexist Fenton, who would kill the aliens in order to "protect" the women, which he assumes without question is his masculine duty. The narrative is told from Fenton's decidedly male point of view, and although he uses all of the stereotypical clichés of male adventure fiction in his narrow attempt to understand the women, Tiptree makes clear that they are more complex people who could never be fixed by Fenton's formulaic phrases. Ultimately, the two women are as alien to Fenton as the undulating extraterrestrials he automatically fears, while the women are so alienated by Fenton's patriarchal limitations that they would just as soon pull up terrestrial stakes and, like so many male adventurers before them, light out for the territory. Trying to explain their decision to Fenton, one of the women tells him that Earth is a patriarchal world and that women are like opossums: "What women do," she says, "is survive. We live by ones and twos in the chinks of your world-machine."[13] The story's prose style, which appropriates but subverts the masculine hard-boiled style typical of its genre, is an example of a guerrilla aesthetic striking a blow at the patriarchal world machine.

In film, however, the genre has advanced little since the 1950s, when male anxieties about women's postwar independence were given expression in the form, on the one hand, of monstrous wasp women, she-creatures, and fifty-foot-tall dominatrixes, and on the other hand, of passive lab assistants and scientists' virginal daughters, who must be rescued by men, as in *Gog*. A few later science fiction films, such as the *Terminator* and *Lara Croft* movies, switch the gender of the traditional male hero, but this is an illusory form of "empowerment" that simply reinscribes rather than questions the patriarchal values of such narratives. Apart from only two films, Rachel Talaley's *Tank Girl* (1995) and Kathryn Bigelow's *Strange Days* (1995, discussed in chapter 10)—both of which critique masculinity and the pleasures of masculinist representations, and both of which, not coincidentally, were box-office failures—science fiction films have held onto the conventions of cinematic style and representation that have characterized popular cinema generally.

Laura Mulvey and other feminist film scholars have argued that one of the defining qualities of mainstream narrative cinema is that the gaze of the camera tends to be gendered as masculine. According to Mulvey, classical film construction positions male characters as subjects, as the bearers of the camera's gaze, authorizing its look, while women are consequently rendered as objects, possessed and fetishized by the camera.[14] In science fiction, the patriarchal gaze and objectification of the female body is clearest in campy space operas like *Fire Maidens of Outer Space* (1955) or *Barbarella* (released the same year as *2001*), but other movies are only slightly more subtle. *Alien* (1979), for example, is progressive in its representation of gender insofar as it shows female characters working alongside men in space and as it makes one of them, Ripley (Sigourney Weaver), its hero, in fact, the only crew member of the Nostromo to survive and defeat the eponymous extraterrestrial. Yet precisely when Ripley is at her most heroic, the film stylistically reinscribes a masculine perspective during the climactic battle between Ripley and the creature by displaying her as an erotic sight, the object of masculine desire. The camera's position and angle emphasize Ripley's gender in a provocative "crotch shot"—a shot motivated not by the requirements of the story but by the apparent necessity of reminding viewers of her gender difference.[15] Thus, if science fiction films like *Alien* present a more active and heroic female protagonist, on the discursive level they tend to remain traditional in their gender politics by containing women within a sexualized and controlling masculine gaze.

Given this generic context, *2001: A Space Odyssey* may be seen as especially progressive and innovative in ways far more profound than simply its convincing, then state-of-the-art special effects, although these elements of the film certainly contribute to its wider rewriting of the science fiction genre. In taking science fiction in new directions, in truly unexplored territory (to "Jupiter and beyond the infinite"), *2001* anticipated the wave of revisionist genre movies that characterized the New Hollywood of the 1970s. The way in which *2001* treats science fiction's depiction of space exploration turns the genre on its ear, like Kubrick's depiction of zero gravity in the film, and aims, as John Cawelti said, to "set the elements of a conventional popular genre in an altered context, thereby making us perceive these traditional forms and images in a new way."[16] Instead of rewriting the myths of the western frontier, as did films like *Little Big Man* (1970) and *McCabe and Mrs. Miller* (1971), *2001* deconstructs the myths of the final frontier.

An avid reader, Stanley Kubrick professed a particular fondness for science fiction. Three of the director's thirteen films—*Dr. Strangelove* (1964), *2001,* and *A Clockwork Orange* (1971)—are generally recognized as important contributions to the genre. The fact that Kubrick made three science fiction films in a row indicates the extent to which he was interested in the genre. (A fourth science fiction film, *A.I.,* was begun by Kubrick but completed by Steven Spielberg in, appropriately enough, 2001.) Indeed, Kubrick claimed that by the time he began work on *2001,* the middle film of the series, he had seen virtually every science fiction film ever made.[17] Robert Kolker argues that *2001* differs from earlier science fiction movies by deliberately employing elements of the genre's conventional streamlined production design, which equates progress with orderliness, neatness, and efficiency—but not to celebrate these values so much as to question them by showing how such progress "equals emotional and intellectual death" in a world where "perfect order and perfect function decrease the need for human interference."[18] This is true enough, but the film also differs from most earlier science fiction films in its focus on masculinity and technology as major themes rather than simply containing these values as unexamined or naturalized ideology.

Kubrick was drawn to science fiction for the same reason he was attracted by the war film: both genres are fundamentally concerned with these themes, which were prominent in the director's work. Masculinity and violence are central to *The Shining* (1980), which chronicles the descent of a family patriarch into violent madness. In *Dr. Strangelove,* satirizing the Cold War paranoia of the previous decade's science fiction films, the nuclear apocalypse is initiated when General Jack D. Ripper (Sterling Hayden) overcompensates for his sexual impotence by talking loudly and carrying several big sticks: a cigar clamped in the side of his mouth, a machine gun at his hip, and a wing of nuclear bombers, which he unleashes on the Soviet Union to prevent the communists from sapping his "precious bodily fluids." The marine recruits in *Full Metal Jacket* (1987) are trained to think of their weapons as synonymous with their penises. One of the platoon's marching mantras, as they parade holding their rifles in one hand and their genitals in the other, is "this is my rifle, this is my gun / this is for fighting, this is for fun." Grammatically, the antecedents of the couplet's pronouns are ambiguous, so it's unclear which tool is for which job. The film's very title, which refers to a type of bullet with a hard metal casing surrounding a lead core, also evokes the image of the male body armed and armored against the world.

The aggressive power of the phallus in Kubrick's world is made literal when Major Kong (Slim Pickens) straddles the nuclear bomb he drops on a Russian target in *Dr. Strangelove,* and in *A Clockwork Orange* when droogie Alex (Malcolm McDowell) attacks the Cat Lady with a sculpture of a giant penis. Kubrick's adaptation of Anthony Burgess's novel about urban life in the near future shows that sexual aggression is an essential part of masculine identity because when Alex is conditioned to be sickened by violence, he becomes a whimpering, helpless victim of the violence inflicted on him by other men. Women in Kubrick's films tend to be dominated within a patriarchal world, as metaphorically visualized by the tables in the shape of nude women in the Korova Milkbar in *A Clockwork Orange,* or living in the cracks of the male world machine, like the female sniper in *Full Metal Jacket.* The masculine world machine in *Dr. Strangelove* is ultimately the Doomsday Machine, which at the film's end destroys all life on Earth. In *2001,* Kubrick's view of the destructive, phallic nature of technology is expressed beautifully in the celebrated cut from the ape's bone, at once man's first tool and first weapon, to a space station; in this one magnificent edit, Kubrick summarizes 4 million years of human history as a continuation of phallic territoriality and conquest. This is perhaps the film's most memorable moment, but other aspects of *2001* also may be understood in relation to this critique of traditional masculinity.

Most obvious perhaps is the film's casting and detached treatment of its characters, to which I alluded at the outset. Accounts of classical film narrative argue that the reliance on heroic and virtuous characters with whom spectators can easily identify is the central device for involving viewers in the cinematic story.[19] But *2001* denies viewers any such easy figure of identification. William Sylvester gives a low-key performance as Dr. Heywood Floyd, who serves as the audience's escort to the moon and then disappears from the narrative except for the recorded message that plays when the *Discovery 1* ship reaches Jupiter. Both Gary Lockwood and Keir Dullea, who play astronauts Frank Poole and Dave Bowman, are inexpressive actors cast in similarly inexpressive roles. Lockwood had only a few undistinguished roles before *2001*—perhaps his most notable being, ironically, his appearance on the *Star Trek* episode "Where No Man Has Gone Before" in 1966, in which some crew members of the *Enterprise* develop powers of ESP when they journey to the edge of the galaxy. Dullea's previous credits included *David and Lisa* (1962), his debut, and *Bunny Lake Is Missing* (1965), two films in which he played psychologically disturbed characters repressing their real feelings.

Vivian Sobchack has noted that in science fiction movies the combination of rationality and strength needed to "conquer" space means that emotion and sexuality are displaced onto the iconography of space technology. Almost always at the helm, in control, are men, astronauts who are typically cool, rational, even sexless. In Sobchack's words, "whether named Buzz or Armstrong, Buck, Flash or Bowman," they are typically "as libidinally interesting as a Ken doll; like Barbie's companion, they are all jaw and no genitals."[20] Kubrick's astronauts in *2001* are perhaps the most sexless and undemonstrative of the lot, their libidinous impulses completely sublimated by the technology that envelops them. The images of the semi-nude yet laconic Lockwood supine on his tanning bed have nothing of the corporeal, eroticized charge of Sigourney Weaver in her improbably flimsy space underwear in *Alien.* After the star-studded casts of *Paths of Glory* (1957), *Lolita* (1962), and *Dr. Strangelove,* the avoidance of big-name actors in a blockbuster production like *2001* seems a deliberate attempt to avoid the larger-than-life quality of movie stars in deference to the grandness of the celestial stars. If *2001* has a "hero" it is, as in Olaf Stapledon's novel *Last and First Men* (1930), Wells's *The Shape of Things to Come,* or other science fiction narratives with similarly epic scope, the human race itself, not a particular individual.

David Bordwell describes the classical narrative style as "an excessively obvious cinema" because it always aims at orientation, which he refers to as "a larger principle of perspective": "not the adherence to a particular spatial composition but a general 'placing' of the spectator in an ideal position of intelligibility."[21] Yet *2001* consistently works to thwart or make problematic such a privileged spectatorial position. For example, the film's motif of spiraling imagery denotes the weightlessness and absence of directional orientation in space but also refuses to orient spectators with fixed reference points, unlike classic narrative construction. Such images appear, for example, in the cockpit console of the shuttle to the Clavius moonbase, with its spinning telemetry; when the flight attendant on the shuttle turns "upside down" to enter the cockpit with refreshments; and in the spinning cylindrical drum that Poole and Bowman enter before leaving the *Discovery 1* to repair the AE35 unit. When Dr. Floyd is in the Bell photophone booth at the space station talking to his daughter, through the window we see the Earth seeming to spin around outside the porthole ("Daddy's traveling," Floyd says tellingly to his daughter), a sight repeated during his discussion with the Russian scientists. Although this use of sustained rotating imagery has since been absorbed into the mainstream, appearing, for example, in *Star Trek: The Motion Picture* (1979) and in Brian de Palma's *Mission to Mars* (2000), the technique was radical when Kubrick introduced it in *2001*. Further, *2001* employs this imagery in more complex ways than these other films, playing off spectators' perceived spatial orientation with seemingly contradictory movement within the frame. So, for example, when Bowman is tumbling and spinning toward the *Discovery 1* from the repair pod—at the point, that is, when he is finally taking action, being most "heroic"—he looks upside down in the image. Back in the ship, as Bowman descends a ladder, he seems to be moving sideways within the frame, given the camera's position in relation to him. And when he proceeds with determination to disconnect HAL, Bowman goes up a ladder, although in the shot it looks as if he is going down head first. A similar trompe l'oeil effect occurs while Bowman floats in HAL's memory logic center. The famous first shot inside the *Discovery 1* shows Frank Poole jogging in the rotating centrifuge, which immediately challenges our spatial orientation in the ship. As this is the first shot inside the *Discovery 1*, it is an ironic "establishing" shot because it establishes only our disorientation, an effect entirely apposite in the context of a journey into the unknown.

According to Bordwell, classical mise-en-scène relies on balanced compositions and the centering of protagonists in individual shots.[22] But in *2001*, emphasizing the vastness of space and humanity's relatively humble place within it, Kubrick's characters are often depicted as tiny creatures in

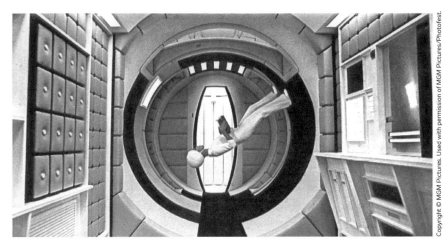

2001: A Space Odyssey (1968) frequently challenges conventional means of orienting the viewer in cinematic space.

big wide-screen images, sometimes placed off to the side of the frame, as when Poole spins off into the void. The film's long takes use time to convey the immensity of space, as do the periods of silence on the soundtrack ("In space no one can hear you scream," as the advertising tagline for *Alien* put it). While Dr. Floyd may be utterly certain of his central place in the universe ("moon/American/ Floyd" is the way he identifies himself at the computerized security check), Kubrick's mise-en-scène in the space sequences undermines conventional ways of regarding the universe and our place in it.

The spatially disorienting images are echoed by the ambiguities Kubrick builds into the film even at the level of the soundtrack. Every time we see a monolith, it is accompanied by the choral music of György Ligeti. But while Ligeti's music may sound, in the words of Norman Kagan, "like a frantic collage of all the religious themes in the world,"[23] its diegetic status, hence its meaning, is unclear. The apes do not seem to respond to the music, and the scientists looking at the monolith in the Tycho moon crater respond to its signal, not to the music. How, then, are we to understand the music? Are Ligeti's voices emanating from the monolith, the music of the spheres that modern man is incapable of hearing? Or is the music the stylistic embellishment of a filmmaker who is known for the careful and striking choices of music in his films?

Unlike classical film narrative, *2001* is excessively opaque rather than excessively obvious. Just as Stanislaw Lem wisely never reveals the motives or meanings for the humanoid manifestations created by the entity Solaris, so *2001* contains numerous enigmas that remain unresolved at the film's end. It is never clear, for example, whether the monoliths represent alien technology, a supernatural force, or the presence of God. Nor is it clear whether the monoliths actually determine human evolution and history, or merely inspire, or just observe us. And the film never explains what happens to Bowman once the *Discovery 1* reaches its destination and the final "Jupiter and Beyond the Infinite" sequence begins. Alexander Walker notes that when Bowman listens to Dr. Floyd's recorded message after disconnecting HAL—when, that is, the film is almost over—Floyd's comments are at once "the first audible and unmistakable clue to the audience of what the film is narratively 'about'" and, amazingly, "also the last utterance in the film."[24] And Floyd's brief briefing, which does not really explain very much (he notes in his recorded message that only HAL knows the details of their mission), is itself somewhat ambiguous. Is its playback, as would appear to be the case, pretimed to begin when the *Discovery 1* reaches Jupiter? Does the recorded message engage automatically when Bowman disconnects HAL? Or does HAL initialize it as his dying gesture? In the end, the film's story seems to remain a "total mystery" like the monoliths as described by Dr. Floyd in his recorded message. Just as we should not master the universe, we are unable to master this film's narrative.

What slim narrative *2001* possesses falls away completely when Bowman enters the Stargate where, along with the astronaut, we are showered with an awesome display of distorted landscapes and abstract, swirling colors, more like a nonrepresentational experimental film than a mainstream movie. The very length of the sequence seems motivated by a desire to immerse us in a visual experience rather than to convey narrative information and advance the story, the primary goal of classical narration. After the Stargate, Bowman appears in a room that looks at once old and new, an odd combination of Louis XVI and modern styles, where the astronaut confusingly watches himself age and die. It is never clear whether what we are seeing is a trip through outer space or the inner space of the astronaut's mind. In a detailed formalist analysis of this sequence, Mario Falsetto has shown how Kubrick's editing consistently subverts the viewer's understanding of narrative space and time by violating such normally inviolable techniques as the conventional shot-reaction-shot in order to convey a sense of Bowman's transcendent experience.[25] Each time Bowman sees another, more-aged version of himself, we first see the newer yet older Bowman from the physical point of view of the older but younger Bowman; but then the next shot reveals that the earlier Bowman is no longer there. Thus these apparent point-of-view shots cease to be point-of-view shots, and their perspective—and ours as viewers—becomes "disembodied," just as Bowman will lose his male body when he transforms into the star child.

As we travel through the Stargate, Kubrick inserts periodic close-ups of a human eye, presumably Bowman's, which each time it blinks changes to the same hues that color the Stargate images. Whatever these images might "mean," we see them through Bowman's eyes, which begin to merge with what he beholds. This sense of extreme sensitivity to the point of merging with nature rather than conquering its secrets is what Evelyn Fox Keller describes as "a feeling for the organism" demonstrated by, for example, the intimate and empathic relationship that geneticist Barbara McClintock established with the maize seedlings with which she was working.[26]

In Kubrick's cinema, eyes figure prominently as images of vision and perception, or the lack of it. *A Clockwork Orange* features numerous close-ups of Alex's eye, first in his droogie garb with eye make-up and the eyeball cufflinks, and later when his eyes are propped open during the Ludovico treatment. Kubrick's last film, completed just before his death, shows people blinded by the quotidian world, entrapped within the confines of their individual egos and living with their "eyes wide shut." But *2001* suggests that we learn to be more open to nature, to perceive beyond the armored confines of traditional masculinity. Significantly, the star child at the end of *2001* is not only naked, ungirded, vulnerable to the universe, but its eyes are already wide open, not shut. Orbiting the Earth in the film's last shot, the star child can see beyond our terrestrial limitations, perceiving with a new, widened consciousness even while still encapsulated within the enclosed but transparent cosmic womb.

Twice we see close-ups of Bowman's face as he experiences the Stargate, bright colors reflecting off the glass visor of his helmet almost as if they were radiating from within. These shots recall the famous moment in experimental filmmaker Stan Brakhage's *Reflections on Black* (1955), in which he scratched the emulsion off the image of a man's eyes to suggest his metaphorical blindness. But where Brakhage's blindness is represented as a gaping absence within

Bowman (Keir Dullea) in the Stargate in *2001: A Space Odyssey.*

the image, Kubrick's astronaut experiences a transcendent vision that seems to flood his eyes with a riot of color. Brakhage was a filmmaker whose great subject was vision and the possibilities of expanding perception. He once challenged spectators to free their vision from the blinkered constraints of culture: "Imagine an eye unruled by man-made laws of perspective, an eye unprejudiced by compositional logic, an eye which does not respond to the name of everything but which must know each object encountered in life through an adventure in perception."[27] In *2001* Kubrick similarly asks us to look at the world out there in just this way, as an adventure in perception, as experience rather than expropriation. Kubrick himself refused to explain the ending of *2001,* saying that "its meaning has to be found on a sort of visceral, psychological level rather than in a specific literal explanation."[28]

Arthur C. Clarke's initial script for *2001* was based largely on his 1948 short story, "The Sentinel," which concerns the future discovery of an alien artifact on the moon. The artifact, a crystal pyramid, acts as a beacon, presumably signaling its makers that the human race had, in Clarke's words, "proved our fitness to survive—by crossing space and escaping from the Earth, our cradle."[29] Although the conclusion of the story seems carefully constructed to avoid using any masculine terms, such as "mankind," after working with Kubrick on *2001* Clarke said that from the outset the director "had a very clear idea of his ultimate goal. . . . He wanted to make a movie about Man's relation to the universe."[30] His words are well chosen, for Kubrick was talking about exploring a perceptual space that has been left largely uncharted by men.

In Kubrick's 1960 epic, *Spartacus,* there is a telling scene in which Kirk Douglas as the rebellious slave, inspired by his sudden freedom, tells his love, Varinia (Jean Simmons), of the new horizons he envisions. Spartacus crouches on the ground, just as Kubrick's man-apes would do several years later in *2001,* and says he wants to know everything (including, significantly, where the sun goes at night and why the moon changes shape). When he concludes that as yet he knows nothing, Varinia responds by reminding him, and the audience, that in fact he knows important things, things that cannot be taught, deeper truths than mere scientific facts. Spartacus is a true hero for Kubrick because he seeks a higher wisdom, to understand without possessing, the very opposite of the decadent Romans in the film, who know only material wealth and power. Ina Rae Hark argues that in searching for a subjectivity other than the two choices offered to Spartacus, animal or Roman, Spartacus asks the question: "Is there a non-phallic human subjectivity?"[31] Within the context of science fiction rather than the biblical epic, *2001* asks the same question. In the film's final shots, the star child's gender is indeterminate; the first glimpse of it is a quick long shot that shows no visible genitalia, while subsequent shots do not show it below the chest. The star child is a new human who, in its openness to creation, has transcended patriarchy's characteristic binary thinking about gender. If Bowman begins his journey to Jupiter and beyond the infinite in a spermlike ship, one more astronaut out to conquer and impregnate the universe, he comes to possess nothing from his previous being but the spherical, womblike repair pod before he is reborn, the aspiring sire becoming the sired.

Kolker suggests that instead of regarding the monoliths as literal artifacts of a higher alien intelligence, they be read as metaphorical "markers of humanity's evolution," perhaps a symbolic "obstacle, a perceptual block that must be transcended."[32] This obstacle, I would suggest, is phallic masculinity. The monoliths have a firm and solid presence and are seemingly everywhere, like the Law of the Father. In "The Dawn of Man" section, when the first monolith appears, the apes gather around it, touching it provocatively, at once wary and worshipful. At the end of the film, the aged, dying Bowman also reaches for it, but his gesture, like so much else in the film, is ambiguous. Is he reaching out, like Moon-Watcher in the opening sequence, to touch the monolith, or is he raising his arm in a gesture of farewell as he completes the process of dying to an old consciousness and being reborn into a new? The ending would seem to suggest the latter, for, as I have argued, *2001* seeks to restore to us a sense of wonder that modern man has forgotten in embracing a masculine quest for scientific mastery.

Of course, it might be argued that *2001*'s reliance on special effects is a fetishization of cinematic technology and a betrayal of its theme. Given the resources available for the film's production, one is reminded of the young Orson Welles's remark upon finding RKO's studio resources available to him for making *Citizen Kane* (1941), that he felt like a boy with the world's largest train set. Filmed in Super Panavision and presented during its first run in Cinerama, with state-of-the-art special effects costing more than half of the film's total budget of $10.5 million and all supervised or created personally by Kubrick, *2001* is a convincing display of technological mastery by a master director entirely in charge of his production. That majestic cut from the bone to the space station not only cuts to the bone of cinema's unique ability to conquer time and space through editing,[33] but also points to the pervasive and potent presence of the auteur.

There is no escaping the fact that the cinema is an inherently technological medium, and *2001* marshals cinema's technological possibilities to invite us to experience the world rather than to master it—not unlike Bowman, who needs technology to reach Jupiter, but who then abandons it to journey beyond the infinite. If the film's astronauts initially privilege the values of reason and control, in the end Bowman must turn off his ship's computer in order to let the Force be with him. But this is not to suggest that George Lucas's space opera is anything like *2001,* for the *Star Wars* saga is a juvenile oedipal drama that embraces the very patriarchal myths of space adventure fiction ("I am your father," in the immortal words of Darth Vader) that Kubrick seeks to go beyond. Where Luke must grow up and take his place within the patriarchal order, Bowman grows into a new being with a new perspective.

2001: A Space Odyssey ends with the star child back in the view of Earth, not only looking at the Earth in a different way but also rotating to face the camera, returning our gaze as spectators as if challenging us to meet it, that is, to see better, to attain its higher plane of being. Here Kubrick, usually regarded, and rightly so, as a pessimist and determinist, offers us a remarkable gesture of hope and faith for an artist who elsewhere sees violence and death. The kind of sensual, open spectators whom Kubrick's film encourages us to be recalls Stapledon's description of the sexual nature of the next human order in his similarly visionary *Last and First Men:*

> Around the ancient core of delight in physical and mental contact with the opposite sex there now appeared a kind of innately sublimated, and no less poignant, appreciation of the unique physical and mental forms of all kinds of live things. It is difficult for less ample natures to imagine this expansion of the innate sexual interest; for to them it is not apparent that the lusty admiration which at first directs itself solely on the opposite sex is the appropriate attitude to all the beauties of flesh and spirit in beast and bird and plant.[34]

Simultaneously one of the most scientific of science fiction films and an anti–science fiction film, *2001* suggests that with such an open, nonmasculinist perspective, we can leave the cradle and truly take a giant step for humankind.

Taking Back the
Night of the Living Dead

George Romero, Feminism, and the Horror Film

Near the beginning of George Romero's original *Night of the Living Dead* (1968), Barbara, one of the film's three female characters, sinks into near-catatonic helplessness to become a burden on the other living characters. She remains this way until near the end, when she attempts to help free another woman from the clutches of the zombies, only to be dragged out the window by her now undead brother. In the remake of *Night of the Living Dead* (1990), written by Romero, no longer can it be said that the character of Barbara, as Gregory A. Waller aptly puts it, "would seem to support certain sexist assumptions about female passivity, irrationality, and emotional vulnerability."[1] Indeed, in the remake, Barbara is the only one of seven characters in the farmhouse to survive the night, and she is an active, assertive character, not only within the diegesis but as a narrative agent as well. This revision warrants closer examination, for it is at once simple yet stunning in its implications.

Romero's broad knowledge of the genre in which he has most often worked is signaled in his films by numerous references to other horror movies, both in dialogue and visual style.[2] In the afterword to his novelization of *Martin* (1978), he explicitly writes that his intention was to "re-vamp" the vampire story.[3] The film's treatment of the vampire makes it clear that, as the pseudo-vampire himself says, "There's no magic"—but there is ideology. And clearly, Romero has been particularly concerned about the ideology of gender representation in the horror film, attempting to "revamp" that tradition of the genre as well. Many of his films address this issue, especially the living dead series.

As has often been noted, movies such as Wes Craven's *The Hills Have Eyes* (1977), John Carpenter's *Halloween* (1978), the sequels to both these films, and the seemingly endless *Friday the 13th* and *Nightmare on Elm Street* series—all those horror shows Robin Wood describes as "a single interminable chronicle of bloodletting"[4]—owe much to the original *Night of the Living Dead*. The film inaugurated a cycle of zombie movies that eventually turned what Herschell Gordon Lewis, director of *Blood Feast* (1963) and *2000 Maniacs* (1964), once called the "gore film" into the more ominous-sounding "meat movie" or "splatter film." Romero himself is credited with having coined the term *splatter cinema* to describe those films that revel in physical violence and maiming to the extent that such spectacle becomes their sole raison d'être.[5] And it is no secret that such movies concentrate their violence upon women.

Night of the Living Dead has had astounding commercial success: made for a paltry $114,000, the film has grossed over $30 million worldwide and become a cult classic.[6] But if it was such a critical and commercial success, the immediate and obvious question is, why should Romero bother to remake it? The cynical view would be that the director is exploiting his own past success, feeding on himself like an ironic variation of his own horrible creatures in a calculated attempt to bolster a sagging career. (None of his other films—particularly those outside the horror genre—have been commercially successful.) But as certain auteurs have returned to their fictional worlds and, over time, deepened their characters and themes—Truffaut with Antoine Doinel, Lang with Mabuse, Coppola with Michael Corleone—so here Romero has retuned to his original zombie narrative and fashioned a more politically progressive view than in the original, particularly in terms of the feminist issues raised by the first *Night's* influence on the subsequent development of the genre.

It is this unfortunate heritage—his own monstrous offspring, so to speak—that Romero increasingly attempts to confront in his living dead

The zombies attack the farmhouse in the original *Night of the Living Dead* (1968).

movies. In the living dead tetralogy—*Night of the Living Dead, Dawn of the Dead* (1978), *Day of the Dead* (1985), and *Land of the Dead* (2005)—the zombie becomes as crucial a metaphor of social relations for Romero as the prostitute for Godard.[7] *Night,* which David Pirie calls "probably the only truly modernist reading of the vampire myth," has been read variously as a critique of the Nixonian "silent majority," of American involvement in Vietnam, and of the family under capitalism. *Dawn* self-consciously uses the zombie as a conceit for macho masculinism and conspicuous capitalist consumption, "the whole dead weight of patriarchal consumer capitalism," as Robin Wood puts it. (Romero's own description of the film as "a satirical bite at American consumerism" is equally apt.)[8] *Day* shows the extent to which society has collapsed five years later, concentrating the political connotations of zombiedom on the issue of sexual politics. Men in the film are consistently shown to be as much of a threat to life as the zombies that are forever surrounding the band of human survivors.

Romero wrote the screenplay for the new version of *Night,* which was directed by Tom Savini (makeup chief on *Martin, Dawn, Day, Creepshow* [1982] and leading player in *Knightriders* [1981]—all directed by Romero). The original was certainly a "personal" film: Romero co-wrote it based on his original story, and he directed, photographed, and edited it as well. His low-budget horror films that followed the first *Night*—*Jack's Wife* (a.k.a. *Hungry Wives/Season of the Witch* [19731]), *The Crazies* (a.k.a. *Code Name: Trixie* [1973]), and *Martin*—all approach the genre from a similarly subversive perspective, clearly revealing Romero as an auteur before he was officially so dubbed in *Film Comment* by Dan Yakir in 1979.[9] So even though he did not direct the remake of *Night,* Romero's authorship is evident throughout the film.

Surprisingly—especially given Savini's reputation for physically gruesome special effects—the new *Night* downplays graphic violence. Rather, following the trajectory of the tetralogy, it consistently foregrounds the dramatic implications of the first version, concentrating on social tensions embodied in relations between living characters. For example, the bickering of the bourgeois couple, Harry and Helen Cooper, is now more pronounced, and unambiguously involves physical abuse; and the racial tension raised by the presence of the black hero, Ben, whose racial difference is never mentioned by the other characters, is now more explicit.

But I want to focus here on the rewriting of the character of Barbara. Like her predecessor, the new Barbara initially seems "mousy," as conventionally coded by her tightly buttoned high-neckline blouse, brooch and neckerchief, and the inevitable eyeglasses. She, too, is frightened at the beginning of the film by her brother Johnny's scary stories, and it initially seems as if she, like the first Barbara, will quickly fall into a catatonic stupor. But when implored by Ben to maintain her composure, she quickly rallies herself. Confronted with some approaching zombies, she and Ben dispatch them at the same time, Barbara in fact disposing of the larger of the two with a poker. "I'm not panicking," she coolly tells Ben afterward. "You told me to fight, so I'm fighting." In the course of the narrative, she exchanges her traditional female attire for clothing found in the farmhouse resembling fatigues and combat boots. She emerges as the fittest to survive and is the only one of the group in the farmhouse alive at the end of the film. Interestingly, according to the original script, Barbara was to have survived in the 1968 film as well—albeit reduced to catatonic paralysis.[10] In the remake, she not only survives but also does so by deducing the correct strategy in response to the zombie attacks: neither to defend the house (Ben) nor to retreat to the cellar (Harry), but to flee, since the zombies can easily be outrun. She acts more effectively, in other words, free of the territoriality associated in the film with masculinism.

This change in the character of Barbara should not be surprising, for, although it seems to have gone largely unnoticed, a crucial aspect of Romero's vision almost from the beginning has been his generally positive treatment of women, even a striking empathy with them. Romero's third film, *Jack's Wife*—which he wrote, photographed, edited, and directed—is unambiguously sympathetic toward its female protagonist, a bored housewife experiencing growing dissatisfaction with her patriarchal husband and prescribed lifestyle. Like Fellini's Giulietta, Joan escapes into her imagination, and her fantasies and dreams, to which the viewer is privileged, become indistinguishable from reality. She becomes interested in witchcraft, its appeal for her obviously a fantasy inversion of her real disempowerment. In one of her dreams, Joan imagines her husband, Jack, leading her around with a dog collar and leash, attacking her in her car, and slapping a newspaper on the window in a deliberate reference to the zombie with the brick who attacks Barbara in the opening scene of *Night*.

Indeed, if there is an agent of horror in the film, it is not the witch Joan but her husband, who here and in several other scenes is visually coded as the monster. The film thus demythifies witchcraft as supernatural, its ideological project perfectly summed up by the image of Joan buying her witchcraft paraphernalia in a trendy shop and paying for it with a credit card. Her official induction as a witch near the end of the film shows her again being led about on a leash around her neck—witchcraft, that is to say, is just another oppressive ideology (superstition) that prevents this woman from being herself. Romero explicitly describes the film as "feminist," saying of Joan that "she's got everything she could possibly want, except a life."[11]

The clearheaded, unsentimental resourcefulness of the new Barbara in response to the crucible of the undead follows from the treatment of Fran in *Dawn* and Sarah in *Day,* and calls to mind another central aspect of Romero's zombie films: their striking similarity to the adventure films of Howard Hawks and the code of professionalism these films explore (see chapter 3). Waller has shown how stories of the undead are about humanity's fitness for survival, although he nowhere links this to the Hawksian theme.[12] Romero himself has explicitly acknowledged the influence of Hawks on his work, and of the 1951 Hawks-produced science fiction/horror film *The Thing from Another World* (direction credited to Christian Nyby) in particular.[13] The Hawksian influence on Romero is pronounced both in his films' plots—the familiar narrative situation wherein a small group is cut off from society and must accomplish a certain dangerous task—and in their mise-en-scène, particularly in the kinds of gesture so crucial to the Hawksian universe. Roger's lighting of Peter's tiparillo in *Dawn,* for example, is clearly indebted to similar gestures in Hawks's work: Clift's lighting of Wayne's cigarettes in *Red River* (1948), for instance, or the similar interplay between Bogart and Bacall in *To Have and Have Not* (1944).

The much-underrated *Knightriders*—which Romero describes as a personal film and, after *Martin,* his own favorite[14]—is an unabashed homage to the Hawksian code of professionalism. *Knightriders* is about a traveling band of performers who go from town to town engaging in jousting tournaments on motorcycles. The troupe adheres to a rigid moral code that determines both their actions and their social position, the feudal chain of being by which they abide serving as a perfect metaphor for the world of Hawksian professionalism, which is defined in large part by knowing one's limits and abilities. King Billy (Ed Harris), the troupe's leader, fights to uphold the code and prevent its corruption by commercialism and egotism. Both temptations are lures to which the unprofessional rebels, led by Sir Morgan (Savini), succumb. Personal grudges and partisan politics rather than the code begin to influence the jousts, and King Billy ultimately keeps the troupe together through his martyrdom, sacrificing himself on the chrome altar of the front grille of an oncoming commercial semi. (This is, of course, corny and melodramatic stuff—the very words Robin Wood uses to describe the comparable work in Hawks's oeuvre, that "completely achieved masterpiece," *Only Angels Have Wings.*[15])

The world of the living dead films is a brutally Hawksian one in which the primary task is survival itself. Being able to survive in this world requires a philosophical detachment and existential determination in order to cope with the zombies physically, psychologically, and spiritually. As with, say, the cowboys on the Chisholm Trail in *Red River* or the men in the Arctic in *The Thing,* the characters in the living dead films are cut off from established codes of ethics, forced to survive on an "existential precipice" even steeper than the mountains surrounding the flyers in *Only Angels Have Wings.*[16] Dr. Grimes's remark on TV in the first *Night* that "the bereaved will have to forego

The armored professional male: Sir Morgan (Tom Savini) in *Knightriders* (1981).

the dubious comforts that a funeral service can give" explicitly establishes this theme, and the films go on to explore both the failure and inappropriateness of such institutions as family, religion, even traditional humanism, to defeat the legions of the undead. This total collapse is shown most powerfully in the opening sequence of *Dawn,* in which a tenement roomful of dying people sequestered by a priest for the giving of last rites becomes a hellish pit of ghoulish violence, and in *Day,* when Sarah unhesitatingly cuts off her lover's arm after he is bitten by a zombie to prevent the infection from spreading.

In the new *Night* Romero clearly has recast Barbara as the film's one true Hawksian professional. The others in the farmhouse are unable to deal with the zombies in a professional manner because of egotism and sentimentality. Tom admits that he could never have shot the first zombie dispatched by Barbara because he was "Uncle Rege," and soon after, as she kills another, Judy screams hysterically, "You shot Mr. Magruder." Barbara coolly demonstrates the necessity of so doing (despite the invitation to sentiment in the shot of a granny zombie) by proving to them that these attackers are already dead: as

The foundations of civilization collapse in a tenement basement in *Dawn of the Dead* (1978).

a zombie comes through the door, she calmly shoots it several times in the chest first, allowing it to keep coming at them as vivid empirical proof of her rational assessment of the phenomenon before hitting it between the eyes. Ben accuses Barbara of "losing it," but she emphatically denies this as she blows away another zombie with the shotgun. "Whatever I lost I lost a long time ago. I'm not planning on losing anything else," she retorts, and then turns the accusation around by telling Ben and Harry that they seem like squabbling children. In the film's dramatic climax, Harry, like Tom and Judy earlier, cannot bring himself to shoot his daughter once she becomes undead even though he knows he must—it is a job that only the true professional can accomplish, and again it falls to Barbara to perform the unpleasant but necessary task.

Romero's treatment of gender in relation to the philosophy of professionalism seeks to resolve the thorny problem for feminism of assessing the value of the Hawksian worldview. Feminist critics have been divided in their opinion of Hawks. Peter Wollen and Robin Wood (even in his later, more politically conscious criticism) clearly articulate the classic auteurist understanding of the relation between Hawks's comedies and adventure films as a dialectic between the "feminine" and "masculine" principles of human nature. The comedies, according to this orthodox view, privilege the emotional life of female characters who are shown to provide a healthy balance to the professionalism of male characters in the adventures.[17] Thus Molly Haskell and other early feminist critics also value Hawks's work. As Naomi Wise puts it, "While the men in Hawks's adventure films are professionally skilled . . . Hawksian women are professional human beings."[18] Nonetheless, critics as diverse as Claire Johnston and Raymond Durgnat disapprove of these films for the very same reason, finding unacceptable the fact that Hawks's women must constantly prove themselves within a masculine world according to masculine standards. As Johnston notes, the problem with Hawks is that for him "there is only the male and the non-male: in order to be accepted into the male universe, the woman must *become* a man . . . she is a traumatic presence which must be negated."[19]

By contrast, Romero is considerably more progressive. *Knightriders* shows that it is unnecessary for women to struggle throughout a narrative to demonstrate their professionalism, for it is a fait accompli, a given: after a victorious joust in the troupe's first performance, Sir Rocky (Cynthia Adler) removes "his" helmet to reveal that the knight is a woman. Further, nowhere is she shown to have a heterosexual attachment ("I know who I am," she declares at one point, in contrast to Jack's wife); she is simply there, one of the group. Romero is also willing to allow homosexuals into his professional group, as when Pippen, the troupe's master of ceremonies, is unintentionally brought out of the closet and no one thinks twice about it, since his sexual preferences are irrelevant to his professional function within the group. And if Hawks can be seen as an apologist for capitalism by equating it with manliness (most clearly in *Red River,* as explored in chapter 3),[20] then Romero's films attack capitalism as consistently as they do the ideology of masculinity. The shots of cash registers in the mall in *Dawn* filled with now useless money, and of bills blowing in the bank entranceway in the zombie-filled streets of Fort Meyers in *Day* are clear comments about the irrelevance of capitalism and materialism to the new morality contemplated by the zombie films.

In fact, it is more often the men in Romero's horror films who fail to prove themselves professionally. In *The Crazies,* the first person to become insane is a father who kills his wife and sets fire to the family house. And in *Creepshow,* the comic-book morality tales of monstrous revenge and poetic justice can be read as the unleashed imagination of a boy against his patriarchal and repressive father in the movie's frame story. This depiction of men as insane oppressors is consistent in the zombie movies. In *Dawn,* Roger becomes so taken with the sporting pleasure of killing zombies that he acts recklessly and, as a result, is fatally bitten. The internecine conflict among the living in *Day* is obviously motivated by the threat to phallic control represented by the professional woman—she is, in Johnston's words, a "traumatic presence," but significantly, Romero refuses to allow her to be "negated." And in the new *Night,* as before, Harry and Ben lock horns, so to speak ("playing rooster" is how Judy describes it), in a struggle for masculine dominance and territorial control.

Social order quickly collapses—"It doesn't take long for the world to fall apart, does it?" Ben remarks when the farmhouse telephone goes dead—because of the inability of Romero's male characters to work together. Threatened with violence and dissolution, masculine power oppressively asserts itself in attempts to impose order through authorial control rather than group cooperation. Waller aptly describes the scene in *Dawn* in which the men arm themselves: "The fetishistic objects flash by: high-powered rifles, derringers, revolvers, western-style handguns and holsters, cartridge belts, shotgun shells, and more . . . the central icons in the so-called male action genres."[21] Social organization and law revert merely to physical power, like Freud's primal horde. The roving band of bikers in *Dawn* is Romero's most explicit image of this masculine power principle, although this is also clear in the new ending he has provided for *Night.*

The territorial battle between Harry and Ben in the farmhouse is a microcosm of the larger social breakdown, as we see toward the end of the film. Radically unlike the first *Night,* Barbara escapes from the farmhouse and, after wandering in the dark wary of approaching zombies, comes upon the local paramilitary unit scouring the countryside for zombies. In the original film, the group appears the next morning and brutally shoots Ben, who has survived the night alone in the cellar but whom they assume (?) is just another zombie. In the remake, these men are presented at first like zombies: in a sudden, startling close-up, the first man is shown wide-eyed, his arm threateningly stiff around Barbara's neck. "What in the name of Jupiter's balls are you doing out here alone, little lady?" he asks. The next morning she awakes (physically and politically) to this barbarism fully institutionalized: some of the men taunt zombies in a pen, treating them like animals for sport; other zombies are hung for the spectacle of watching them wriggle before they are shot.

Barbara (Patricia Tallman, right) is recast as a professional fighting against male culture in the remake of *Night of the Living Dead* (1990).

This is the debasement of professionalism, its requisite lack of sentiment souring into callousness. Barbara acts as a corrective to the narrowness of "masculine" professionalism, rather than, as in Hawks, having to be measured by it (in that key Hawksian phrase, to be as "good enough" as men). The image of a truck selling hot sausages and pork roasted on a spit to hungry participants of the spectacle makes clear the link between zombies and patriarchy, its own monstrousness; like the customers ordering fried chicken in the diner in Hitchcock's *The Birds* (1963), it is an ironic sign of a brutish, insensitive culture.

Crucially, we see the sudden appearance of the zombie hunters and the society they represent from Barbara's horrified perspective. Indeed, the new *Night* adopts the same strategy of narrative viewpoint as the earlier *Jack's Wife*, in which all but a very few shots are motivated from Joan's physical or psychological perspective. Initially the camera adopts Barbara's physical point of view; thus, when the first zombie attacks her in the car in the opening cemetery scene we are inside, with her, looking out. But then, more importantly, from the moment when she begins to assert her professionalism, we see from her perceptual, or moral, perspective. As soon as Barbara asserts herself, the film dispenses with shots of her frightened looks at the monsters—that crucial moment in horror films when, as Linda Williams has argued, the aspiring independent woman is punished for attempting to assert her own gaze.[22] So when the now zombified Uncle Rege approaches her from behind, Barbara experiences no horrified discovery; rather, at the last possible moment—and without any indication that she was aware of his presence, so that, perhaps, we are encouraged to expect her to respond with fear and surprise—she wheels about and promptly dispatches him. The viewer is thus prevented from delighting in the voyeuristic spectacle of a frightened and helpless woman.

Yet Barbara *does* look horrified after being "rescued" when, seeing the zombies being hung from a tree and then shot, she says, "We're them and they're us" (a line also heard in both *Dawn* and *Day*). Seen from her point of view, patriarchy is made exceedingly strange, becoming, in fact, repugnant and monstrous. Significantly, the film provides no opportunity to view Barbara undressed before she dons her Rambette costume—as is the case in *Alien* (1979), where it can be argued that the Ripley (Sigourney Weaver) character is recuperated for male pleasure in the unmotivated shots of her wearing implausibly flimsy underwear as she is about to do battle with the creature. In refusing to provide the viewer with the dominant male gaze typical of the horror film generally and of the slasher cycle—with its conventional alignment of camera viewpoint and the monster victimizing women—in particular, the second version of *Night* subverts the form's characteristic sexual politics.[23]

Robin Wood's observation that horror films are progressive to the extent that they refuse to depict the monster as simply evil seems clearly borne out by these films,[24] for even as Romero progressively downplays the Otherness of the zombies, he depicts patriarchy as increasingly monstrous. If the zombies are indeed "nothing but pure motorized instinct," as they are described in *Day*, then the automatic relegation of Sarah to a subordinate role by the men makes them very much "undead." By contrast, the literal living dead are depicted with increasing sympathy in the series. Beginning as an undifferentiated mass of murderous machines in the first *Night*, they become the pathetic victims of the bikers' crude violence in *Dawn*. *Day* features Bub, described by Romero as a "zombie with a soul," who in the end uses a gun to kill the macho army captain with at least partial moral approval by both filmmaker and audience. In *Land of the Dead*, one zombie kills another out of mercy, to spare him pain, a more humane gesture than is shown by the living characters. According to Romero, "You have to be empathetic with the creatures because they ain't doin' nothin'. They're like sharks: they can't help behaving the way they do."[25]

The new *Night* encapsulates the series' depiction of patriarchy. At the beginning of the film the zombies are the monstrous threat, but at the end it is hysterical masculinity that is truly horrifying. In the conclusion, Barbara returns to the farmhouse the next morning to rescue Ben, followed by some of the men. They let Ben out of the basement to find that, unlike in the original, he has indeed become a zombie, and they shoot him. Barbara, having wandered off alone, discovers Harry, who, wounded but still alive, has crawled into the attic (ironically, given his earlier unyielding commitment to the basement). Perceiving Harry as a horrible patriarch, she shoots him in the head at point-blank range without hesitation. When the men come into the room, she says, "There's another one for the fire," correctly guessing that they will assume Harry also had been a zombie. In the original, Barbara's concluding line belongs to the redneck sheriff instructing his men what to do with Ben's corpse; in the remake, it accompanies a woman's response to patriarchy as defiant as the killing of the salesman in Marleen Gorris's militantly feminist *A Question of Silence* (1982). The new *Night* endorses Harry's fate no less than that of the macho Captain Rhodes in *Day,* who lives just long enough to see his lower body torn off and dragged away by zombies.

The new *Night,* then, attempts to reclaim the horror genre for feminism, for all those female victims in such movies who attempt to resist patriarchal containment. Where, say, R. H. W. Dillard finds the original *Night* to be so effectively frightening because it articulates a fundamental nihilism and negation of human dignity,[26] it is more accurate to say that all of Romero's zombie films are so powerful because his undead demand the suspension of normal (bourgeois) values, particularly those of patriarchy. Wood is, I think, exactly right about the apocalyptic yet progressive politics of Romero's zombie films.[27] Indeed, they offer a perfect instance of the exploitation film's potential, as noted by such critics as Pam Cook and Barbara Klinger, for incorporating progressive ideas.[28] When the search team at the beginning of *Day* lands in Fort Meyers, which has become populated entirely by zombies, it is significant that they are shown in front of an empty, now meaningless cinema; Romero, as an independent regional filmmaker, has managed to make several progressive and commercially viable features while remaining on the margins of the mainstream. (In this sense, *Knightriders* gains additional significance as an autobiographical work about the attempt of a filmmaker to maintain integrity and avoid ideological compromise for commercial reasons.)

"Have we conjured up creatures and given them mystical properties so as not to admit that they are actually of our own race?" Romero has asked.[29] The remake of *Night of the Living Dead* shows that Romero has put this question to himself, and even if, ultimately, he falls into the trap of defining women in terms that one could argue are still masculinist, he has nevertheless provided one of the most significant feminist perspectives in the history of the horror film.

Rich and Strange

Economic Performance Anxiety and the Yuppie Horror Film

Some genre critics deny that the genre of horror is particularly flexible and adaptable. For example, Andrew Tudor claims that horror is a particularly "limited" film category because "its conventions are unidimensional and straightforward."[1] Such an assessment, however, relies in large part on how one defines the genre—the problem of definition always being a thorny one for genre theory and criticism. In this chapter I discuss a cycle of popular American films that presents a distinct variation of the horror film, revealing a striking example of its protean adaptability. This group includes, among others, *After Hours* (1985), *Desperately Seeking Susan* (1985), *Something Wild* (1986), *Fatal Attraction* (1987), *Bad Influence* (1991), *Pacific Heights* (1990), *The Hand That Rocks the Cradle* (1992), *Poison Ivy* (1992), *Single White Female* (1992), and *The Temp* (1993). Some of these films, to be sure, reveal affinities to other genres: both *Something Wild* and *Desperately Seeking Susan,* for example, possess elements of screwball comedy (a classification that shares with horror the irruption of the irrational into the workaday world). Yet, to a significant extent, all these films retain much of the style and syntax of the horror genre while substituting a new set of semantic elements, or what Rick Altman calls "building blocks,"[2] to address the fears and anxieties of the contemporaneous yuppie subculture. In these movies, the concerns of the yuppie demographic, which has been estimated to include anywhere from 4 to 20 million people,[3] tilts the transformation of "evil" from the classic horror film's otherworldly supernatural to the material and economic pressures of this world that is too much with us.

Although it may be argued that some of these movies exhibit only minimal relation to the horror film, together they form a distinct generic cycle that, instead of expressing the repression and contradictions of bourgeois society generally, as many critics agree is central to the ideology of the genre, specifically addresses the anxieties of an affluent culture in an era of prolonged recession and the consequent perceived threats especially to masculinity incited by changing gender relations in the same period. These challenges to masculinity are perhaps most explicit in *Falling Down* (1993), in which "D-Fens" (Michael Douglas), as his name suggests, feels overwhelmingly besieged as a male breadwinner. Having already lost his white-collar job, he drives to work through rush hour every day, following his old routine, in denial of reality—although he snaps mentally as the film opens. D-Fens becomes monstrously violent, using aggression and an assortment of weapons to assert his masculine identity as he marches across Los Angeles.

Defining Yuppie Horror

The term *yuppie* was coined in 1983 to describe an emergent and seemingly distinct class of young urban professionals that embraced values of conspicuous consumption and technology as unambiguously positive.[4] Yuppiedom thus combined the "me-generation" philosophy of the Carter era with Reaganomics, becoming a convenient icon of the era's zeitgeist. More precisely, according to Marissa Piesman and Marilee Hartley's *The Yuppie Handbook,* the term "would include a person of either gender who meets the following criteria: (1) resides in or near one of the major cities; (2) claims to be between the ages of 25 and 45; and (3) lives on aspirations of glory, prestige, recognition, fame, social status, power, money or any and all combinations of the above."[5] These values coalesced into a lifestyle, a veritable weltanschauung that embraced what one observer has called a "religion of Transcendental Acquisitions."[6] This is nicely expressed in *Bad Influence* when the yuppie Michael (James Spader), asked whether he needs his elaborate new video system, says, "That's not the point." With his hair slicked back and braces on his trousers, Michael Douglas's Gordon Gekko in *Wall Street* (1987) became the perfect icon of the high-powered businessman—and the patron saint for yuppies, for whom "greed is good" because "money means choices."[7]

The term caught hold of the popular imagination, generating much media hype and spawning a gaggle of other demographic acronyms. In short order, there were, among others, DINKs (Double Income No Kids), WOOFs (Well Off Older Folks), and SWELLs (Single Women Earning Lots and Lots).[8] The trend is nicely satirized in the instant group identified in the Jane Austen–like comedy of manners *Metropolitan* (1990): the indelicate and cumbersome UHBs, or Urban Haute Bourgeoisie, a term that by the end of the film shows signs of catching on despite its apparent awkwardness. Commercial cinema, with its antennae sharply attuned to popular taste, mobilized the tested appeal and contemporary popularity of the horror film to address this new cultural force.

Yuppie horror is a subgenre that employs—but modifies—the codes and conventions of the classic horror film. "A good horror film," notes Bruce Kawin, "takes you down into the depths and shows you something about the landscape; it might be compared to Charon, and the horror experience to a visit to the land of the dead."[9] In *After Hours,* Paul Hackett's (Griffin Dunne) taxi ride to the different, bohemian world of Soho in lower Manhattan is shot in fast motion—a joke about New York cab drivers, to be sure, but also a suggestion of crossing over into another place, like Jonathan Harker's coach ride through the Borgo Pass in F. W. Murnau's classic *Nosferatu* (1922). Other instances of the use of this narrative convention include Michael's descent into the underground bar in *Bad Influence,* site of alternative sexual practices (the passwords include "gay white male" and "fun-loving couple"), and the movement in *Desperately Seeking Susan* from the rational materialism of Fort Lee, New Jersey, to the dark and magical world of Manhattan, as if New York were across the River Styx rather than the more mundane (but perhaps equally dead) Hudson.

In an economy characterized by increasing economic polarization and spreading poverty, these scenes of crossing into the netherworld of urban decay "exude the Manichaean, middle-class paranoia . . . that once you leave bourgeois life, you're immediately prey to crime, madness, squalor, poverty."[10] Hence in *Bonfire of the Vanities* (1990) wannabe Gekko Sherman McCoy (Tom Hanks), a self-described "master of the universe" with a "$6 million apartment," quickly plummets from his usual upscale haunts into the dark underpass of a highway ramp in the Fort Apache wilderness of the South Bronx. So, too, in *Pacific Heights,* the reddish bulbs of a "Loan" sign flash behind Patty Palmer (Melanie Griffith) as if in warning to abandon all hope ye who enter here.

This fear informs the premise of the descent by middle-class characters into the hell of the inner city, as in *Trespass* and *Judgment Night* (both 1993)— the latter employing the metaphor of the mobile home to signify a lack of bourgeois stability, an idea used earlier in the supernatural horror film *Race with the Devil* (1975). Like the return of the oppressed, this nightmarish world threatens always to erupt, as in *Grand Canyon* (1992) when the yuppie entrepreneur (Steve Martin) is hospitalized after a mugger takes his Rolex. To use the terms of another of these movies, one must always be on guard against the temp who aspires to become permanent.[11]

Within this dark underworld of bankruptcy and property divestiture, several of the films offer upscale variations on the horror film's old dark house, what Robin Wood calls the terrible house and Carol J. Clover the terrible place, making them into gothic, horrifying "workspaces" or "living spaces."[12] Indeed, the eponymous upscale high-rise in *Sliver* (1993) is explicitly referred to several times by some of its inhabitants as a "haunted house." The New York apartment building in which the two women in *Single White Female* live is visually reminiscent of the spooky Dakota in *Rosemary's Baby* (1968)—a deliberately resonant reference, as Roman Polanski's film may be seen as an early instance of yuppie horror in which Satan's manifestation functions as the unrepressed return of Guy's real desire to further his career over commitment to raising a family.[13] In *Unlawful Entry* (1992), the installation of the warning system and the periodic spotlight from the police car put the white family in the position of South Central Los Angeles blacks, making their home seem more like a prison, a horrifying representation of the couple's anxiety about whether they can afford their house. Michael's place in *Bad Influence* becomes frightening mostly after Alex (Rob Lowe) has stripped it clean of all the yuppie toys—an ironic inversion of the conventionally cluttered Gothic mansion.

This seeming oxymoron of the terrible luxury home is explicitly the subject of *Pacific Heights*. The plot concerns a couple's efforts to gentrify an old Victorian house, a popular yuppie pastime.[14] Initially, the yuppie couple, Patty Palmer and Drake Goodman (Matthew Modine), conceive of their home as little more than a profitable investment, as a financial arrangement not unlike their cohabitational agreement. But the home soaks up renovation money like an insatiable sponge, a money pit—a scenario presented not with the blithe spirit of *Mr. Blandings Builds His Dream House* (1948) but with the ominous foreboding of *Amityville Horror* (1979), perhaps the first real estate horror film. (Stephen King perceptively described it as the generic "horror movie as economic nightmare."[15]) Drake and Patty inexorably fall from the beatific heights of potential profit to the lower depths of looming insolvency.

An essential visual difference between horror and science fiction films is one of vision. In science fiction, the outlook is characteristically bright and directed upward and out; in horror films, vision—that of the characters, the text, and the spectator—tends to be directed down and inward and to be darkened and obscured.[16] A similar visual design tends to inform yuppie horror films. In *Poison Ivy*, for example, both the mother and the deadly outsider contemplate sinking downward into the big sleep of reason, creating a vertiginous gloom that pervades the entire film from the opening giddy bird's-eye shots of Ivy (Drew Barrymore) swinging out over a steep cliff. The sleek black car driven by Carter Hayes (Michael Keaton) in *Pacific Heights* appears ominously over the crests of hilly San Francisco streets as if surfacing from the underworld. Carter, Peyton (Rebecca De Mornay) in *The Hand That Rocks the Cradle,* and the deadly roommate Ellen (Jennifer Jason Leigh) in *Single White Female* are all associated with the basement and darkness. *Pacific Heights* uses a swirling 360-degree camera movement at crucial moments to comment on Patty and Drake's crumbling finances, both to visualize their sinking deeper and deeper into debt and to lend their descent into the fiscal maelstrom metaphysical weight, as if their very worldview had been pulled out from under them, à la *Vertigo* (1958). Not coincidentally, this Hitchcock film is one among several referred to diegetically on the television in the smartly intertextual *Single White Female.*

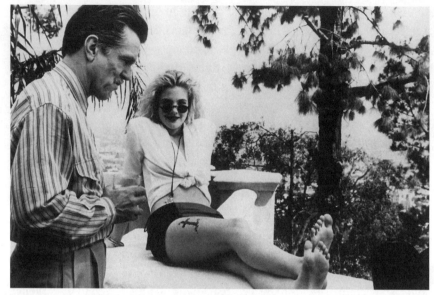

Ivy (Drew Barrymore) disturbs the family patriarch Darryl Cooper (Tom Skerritt) in *Poison Ivy* (1992).

Monstrous Others and Material Fears

An essential element of the horror film is the presence of a monster. In yuppie horror films, the villains are commonly coded as such. Alex's face in *Bad Influence* is frequently streaked by the noirish shadows of trendy Levelor blinds, and the male killer's face in *Desperately Seeking Susan* is often bathed in a hellish red light. When Carter Hayes successfully installs himself in the apartment of the yuppie couple's home in *Pacific Heights,* he is said by their lawyer to have "taken possession"; and in the climax, Carter is impaled, a fitting demise for a bloodsucking vampire, financially speaking. In the climaxes of *Fatal Attraction* and *Something Wild,* both Alex Forrest (Glenn Close) and Ray Sinclair (Ray Liotta) seem implausibly unstoppable, like their supernatural counterparts Jason, Michael Meyers, and Freddie Krueger. And in *The Hand That Rocks the Cradle,* the tension established between the seeming girlish innocence of nanny Peyton and her fiendish malevolence is firmly rooted in the tradition of such "possessed child" horror films as *The Exorcist* (1973) and *The Omen* (1976), and, further back, *The Bad Seed* (1956).

Furthermore, much like the traditional monsters, the evil characters in yuppie horror movies function as the Other, as an external, disavowed projection of something repressed or denied within the individual psyche or collective culture. These films tend to depict the monstrous Other as the protagonist's doppelgänger or double, a convention Wood calls "the privileged form" of the horror film.[17] Roland Barthes writes that "the petit-bourgeois is a man unable to imagine the Other" and so makes him over into the image of himself, a point that would seem especially true for yuppies, who, according to sociologist Jerry Savells, "assume control of their lives and their fate, without question."[18]

Pam Cook has suggested that Max Cady in Scorsese's remake of *Cape Fear* (1992) offers a "distorted picture" of the Bowden family's "rage and pain, and of their desire for revenge," called forth from within the family by the daughter, Danielle. Cook argues that the film has to be understood as Danielle's subjective vision, what Kawin would call her mindscreen, because it is marked by her voice-over in the form of recollection.[19] Cook's reading may be applied equally to several other of these films, among them *Pacific Heights, Bad Influence,* and *Poison Ivy.* In the latter, for example, the bad girl who seduces the father is clearly the incarnation of the rebellious daughter who considers herself to be unfeminine and unloved and, as in *Cape Fear,* the film's narrative is framed by the daughter's voice-over remembrances.

In Michael Cimino's remake of *The Desperate Hours* (1991), the fleeing criminal Michael Bosworth (Mickey Rourke), threatening the upscale family he has taken hostage in their home, suggests that he represents a "reproach" to what he refers to as the "mendacity" of the family patriarch (Anthony Hopkins), who is having an extramarital affair, as if Bosworth were the return of the man's repressed self—the father confronted by Big Daddy, as it were—a relation wholly absent from the original drama. Similarly, in *Something Wild,* Charlie (Jeff Daniels) begins as what "Lulu" (Melanie Griffith) calls a "closet rebel," but the "something wild" within him is brought out by his passion for Lulu/Audrey and his struggle against Ray. During the climax, Charlie and Ray seem to embrace even as they fight, like twin Stanley Kowalskis in their T-shirts. Lulu says to Charlie in the end, "What are you going to do now that you've seen how the other half lives . . . the other half of you?" A similar reading is invited by *Desperately Seeking Susan,* in which the bland Roberta (Rosanna Arquette) learns to be more self-assured, like the extroverted Susan (Madonna), whom she encounters, significantly, through the personal want ads.

In *Single White Female,* in a way the inverse of *Poison Ivy,* Ellen is the plain Other of Allie Jones (Bridget Fonda), the unattractive woman whose career would proceed unimpeded by sexual entanglements. The shots of the two women in mirrors, posed in positions reminiscent of the famous mirror shot of Liv Ullman and Bibi Andersson in Ingmar Bergman's *Persona* (1966), makes their psychological interdependence clear. In *Pacific Heights,* Drake Goodman grows increasingly violent in response to the "bad influence" of Carter Hayes. At first glibly willing to commit white-collar crime by, as he says, "fudging the numbers a bit," Drake later viciously beats Carter and is about to strike him a murderous blow with a tire iron when he is finally restrained by Patty's screaming plea. But like Nathaniel Hawthorne's Goodman before him, Drake has glimpsed the underlying moral ambiguity of human nature.

In *Bad Influence,* Alex is the incarnation of what Michael calls the "voice that tells you what to do some time," a therapeutic materialization of Michael's much-needed assertiveness training. Like Bruno Anthony to Guy Haines in Hitchcock's *Strangers on a Train* (1951), Alex is Michael's unrestrained id, the embodiment of Michelob's yuppie admonition that "you can have it all." As Alex shows Michael how to be more competitive and assertive, Michael's hair, like his personality, becomes increasingly Gekko-like. In the end, before going over the edge himself, Michael shoots Alex, who falls heavily from a pier, the water closing over him as he sinks back into the murky depths from which he had emerged, the creature from the black lagoon of Michael's mind now vanquished.

Even *Fatal Attraction,* which has almost uniformly been condemned for its scapegoating of the professional female, may be read in this way. It is possible to view the narrative as the horrifying mindscreen or psychodrama of Dan Gallagher (Michael Douglas), wherein the result of his affair with Alex Forrest is, on one level, the return of his repressed dissatisfaction with his marriage.[20] Dan feels trapped by domesticity, his discontent imaged forth in the family's cramped apartment. He is clearly disappointed about the evening's prospects when he returns from walking the dog to find their daughter sleeping in his bed with his wife, Beth (Anne Archer). So he fantasizes a relationship with no distracting responsibilities in the form of Alex.

Alex (Rob Lowe) represents the unrestrained desires of Michael (James Spader) in *Bad Influence* (1990).

But then, like a networking party turned nightmare, to assuage his guilt, Dan projects the blame onto her—at one point he calls her "sick"—making her a monstrous Other because she does not recognize what he calls "the rules" for such affairs. Alex will not be "reasonable," will not be treated like the sides of beef that hang outside her apartment building. She refuses to allow the removal of her voice, an ideological operation of the text that feminist critics such as Kaja Silverman and Mary Ann Doane have argued happens so often in Hollywood film.[21] Alex telephones Dan insistently and leaves an audio cassette in his car that questions his masculinity—both instances of an assertive female voice that seems beyond his masculine control. Indeed, it is not Alex but Dan who is silenced, as her adamant refusal to have an abortion leaves him, as he admits, "no say."

Many commentators on yuppiedom have noted that yuppies are always threatened by the looming specter of "burnout" because they are "workaholic[s] whose main identity and sense of self-worth is often supplied by [professional] success."[22] Burnout is thus a fearful possibility that, like the portrait of Dorian Gray, haunts the yuppie's prized public image. It is no coincidence that Michael in *Bad Influence,* Drake Goodman in *Pacific Heights,* and Allie in *Single White Female* all show clear evidence of work-related stress. As an article in *Newsweek* put it, "You can, after all, stay on the fast track only so long, even in a $125 pair of running shoes."[23] The important distinction is that the visage of Dorian Gray in yuppie horror films is handsome rather than grotesque. Here the craggy ugliness of a Rondo Hatton is replaced by the smooth charm of a Rob Lowe, for the ethical horrors of cupidity supersede the physical revulsion of the classic horror film. The fact that so many of these characters are at once ethically monstrous and physically attractive befits an age in which, as someone observes in *The Temp,* "They still stab you in the back as much as in the '80s, only now they smile when they do it."

Indeed, it is exactly this view that animates the worldly narrative of *Ghost* (1990), a film that, while in fact marginal as horror, is nevertheless strongly informed by yuppie angst, and Brett Easton Ellis's remarkable 1991 novel *American Psycho,* a book that perhaps stands in relation to yuppie horror as *Psycho* (1960)—to which its title obviously refers—does to the modern horror film. If yuppie consciousness and values fetishize appearances—"Surface surface surface was all anyone found meaning in," observes Patrick Bateman, Ellis's handsome Wall Street mass murderer—then yuppie horror films show how frightening such surfaces can really be. "I have a knife with a serrated blade in the pocket of my Valentino jacket," Bateman matter-of-factly observes at one point, like that sage observer in *The Temp.*[24] It is perhaps no accident that Ellis's narrator often describes his perceptions in terms of movie techniques such as pans, dissolves, and slow motion.[25] Narrated with the same kind of dark humor as pervades *Psycho,* it is as if Norman has grown up and moved from a remote place off the main highway to life in the fast lane in the big city. Master Bates has become BateMAN, but, ironically, the onanism only suggested in the Hitchcock film is chillingly literal in the novel.

Because of the valorization of conspicuous wealth in the yuppie worldview (and one of the great jokes of Ellis's style in *American Psycho*), the monsters in yuppie horror films tend to threaten materiality more than mortality. For yuppies, in the words of the portrait in *Newsweek,* "The perfection of their possessions enables them to rise above the messy turmoil of their emotional lives."[26] Thus, yuppie horror films exploit the subculture's aspiration for material comfort, and the material success the characters so covet becomes frighteningly vulnerable and fragile, like the close-up of the splintering scale model of Patty and Drake's home in *Pacific Heights.*

The vindictive Cady sums it up well in *Cape Fear* when he says, "That house, that car, that wife and kid, they mean nothing to you now." The Puritan-like material emblems of election come to seem suddenly damned, the appurtenances of an expensive lifestyle often turned deadly, like Claire's (Annabella Sciorra) greenhouse in *The Hand That Rocks the Cradle,* which becomes an elaborate weapon hailing lethal shards on her best friend, Marlene. The husband (Kurt Russell) in *Unlawful Entry,* fetching a golf club to ward off a possible intruder in their home, jokes to his wife (Madeleine Stowe) that if it turns out to be dangerous, he'll come back for his driver. This yuppie joke is realized in *Something Wild* when Audrey uses one of Charlie's clubs to whack the attacking Ray, and in *Bad Influence,* in which one of Michael's clubs (he owns a set although he doesn't play) serves as the murder weapon for Alex. *The Hand That Rocks the Cradle* devotes much of its time to chronicling objects that become "unruly." In an upscale yuppie home fitted with, as Elayne Rapping notes, tasteful "houseware 'touches' out of L. L. Bean and Bloomingdale's," Peyton is like a yuppie gremlin, relocating icons of status (such as a gold cigarette lighter) and thus encouraging a "misreading" of their subcultural signification.[27]

Perhaps, then, the quintessential moment of fright in the yuppie horror film is the image in *After Hours*—emphasized by director Martin Scorsese in slow motion—of aspiring yuppie Paul's lone $20 bill flying out of the cab window. In yuppie horror films, it would seem that to be broke is more frightening than being undead or mutilated. So Charlie desperately clutches at his wallet in *Something Wild,* although he allows himself to be handcuffed to the bed by Lulu, whom he has just met, with barely a protest. Because yuppies are already "possessed," these films suggest, they are more frightened by the sight of acid eating into the smooth finish of Dan's Volvo in *Fatal Attraction* than by, say, Uncle Ira no longer quite being Uncle Ira in *Invasion of the Body Snatchers* (1956).

Ideology of Yuppie Horror

While this yuppie cycle tends to rely primarily on the visual and narrative conventions of the classic horror film, on occasion their very discursive structure is also similar, employing what Tzvetan Todorov has called the Fantastic, and which critics have found to inform traditional horror films. According to Todorov, the fantastic is characterized by a "hesitation" that eludes either a realist explanation (the "uncanny") or a supernatural one (the "marvellous").[28]

Such hesitation is found in those yuppie horror films that can be read as mindscreens, as already discussed, but perhaps the most interesting in this regard is *The Temp*. Narrated from the viewpoint of the male protagonist, Peter Derns (Timothy Hutton), the film begins with his finishing a therapy session, and we soon learn that he has suffered from paranoid delusions in the past. Since we never see the temporary secretary (Lara Flynn Boyle) actually do anything ominous until the end, we can't be sure whether Peter's interpretation of events is correct or if the woman is merely a terrific secretary and the protagonist is experiencing a series of unhappy coincidences. This intriguing ambiguity is clearly resolved in the climax, where the patriarchal power of the narrator/male boss is forcefully reinstated with the defeat of the infernal secretary who has refused to stay in her allotted place in the corporate hierarchy. But until the film reaches for such predictable generic and ideological closure, it insistently questions patriarchal assumptions.

Fredric Jameson's observation that *Something Wild* is about patriarchy applies to many of these movies that on another level, as my reading of *Fatal Attraction* suggests, are about masculine fears.[29] This is hardly surprising, given that yuppie horror films necessarily question (by expressing an unease about) capitalist ideology. Indeed, to the very substantial extent to which yuppie horror films are about masculine panic, they are simply the most overt articulation of a theme that dominates contemporary Hollywood cinema, most obviously in the hyperbolic hybrid of the science fiction action movie, with its excessive display of masculine "hardbodies" (discussed further in the following chapter on the action films of Kathryn Bigelow).

This is not to suggest, however, that all yuppie horror endorses the ideological status quo. For if we were to examine this subgenre according to Wood's "basic formula for the horror film"—the way the texts define

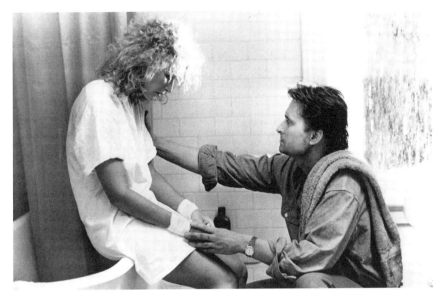

Dan Gallagher (Michael Douglas) attends the overwrought Alex Forrest (Glenn Close) in *Fatal Attraction* (1987).

normality, the monster, and the relation between these two terms—we would find they range from the reactionary to the progressive, as with any genre.[30] In *Pacific Heights,* for example, all's well that ends well: Patty reconciles with Drake, sells the house for a tidy profit, and defeats Carter Hayes while adding further to her income, tax-free yet. The film thus endorses yuppie capitalist values and neutralizes any potential threat in the fact that Patty, as Carter says, has "crossed the line" of acceptable behavior. *Pacific Heights* is no Hitchcockian text.

By contrast, the ending of *Fatal Attraction* may be seen as more subversive. It is Beth who kills Alex, after which she and Dan embrace, reunited because she has submitted to the patriarchal imaginary; only then can their marriage be "happy." The final shot is thus heavy with Sirkian irony, worthy of the famous ending of *All That Heaven Allows* (1955): the camera pans to the fireplace mantle, the hearth of the family home, showing a photograph of the married couple—a still image—and a pair of bronzed baby shoes. Both objects undercut the notion that anything has changed in Dan and Beth's marriage; rather, the objects connote immobility and stasis and are a comment on their embrace of traditional values. Similar is the ending of *After Hours,* when Paul returns from his descent to the netherworld and arrives at the entrance to his midtown office. No longer what poet Andrew Marvell would call the iron gates of strife, these heavenly portals open of their own accord and, transformed by the golden light of dawn, seem to beckon Paul into the comfy haven of his low-level executive job.

In their articulation of lurking dread, even the most conservative of these films are more interesting than bland yuppie melodramas like *Rain Man* (1988), wherein the yuppie is humanized and learns that there are more important things in life than imported sports cars, or *Grand Canyon,* in which the economic gap is dwarfed by the geographical one.[31] Jameson is right to call *Something Wild* and other such movies modern gothic tales, although he incorrectly, I think, chooses to emphasize their reliance on nostalgia.[32] These movies are emphatically about now.

Certainly the fact that mainstream cinema has turned more to horror and the thriller than to, say, comedy and the musical (as it did in the past), to address fears about America's affluent but now struggling economy—as well as the very nature of contemporary relationships—tells us how very deeply these anxieties are rooted. Indeed, these films tend to locate these larger cultural concerns at a more basic, personal level, within the dynamic of intimate personal relationships—the perfect adaptation of the horror genre to the troubled narcissism of the post-me generation. In yuppie horror films, monsters do not roam the countryside, killing indiscriminately; instead, we find ourselves sleeping with the enemy, often literally.

One can discern a decided evolution within the cycle. In the early yuppie horror films, the nightmarish situations were as often as not the result of recklessness rather than fiendishness. But as the recession deepened, the monsters tended to become increasingly malevolent: the Big Chill became a wind from hell. (One might view the chronologically overlapping cycle of films based on old TV series—*The Addams Family* [1992], *The Beverly Hillbillies* [1993], *The Flintstones* [1994], and *Car 54, Where Are You?* [1994]—as the flip side of yuppie anxiety. Truly based on nostalgic appeal, they recall both the historical "better time" of the affluent 1960s, when the shows were first broadcast, and the ahistorical once-upon-a-time fantasy world of TV-land.)

Certainly, as I've already suggested, there are examples of earlier horror films, like *Rosemary's Baby* and *Race with the Devil,* that anticipated the yuppie cycle. *The Exorcist* is similar to Polanski's film in that it suggests that the demonic possession of the daughter is the result of the mother's putting her career before family. But of the several examples one might cite as precursors of the modern horror cycle, only *Strangers on a Train,* in typical Hitchcock fashion, steadfastly refuses to locate or "explain" the monstrous as supernatural. And although there are earlier films that we might identify as examples of Stephen King's notion of economic horror, the yuppie horror cycle truly begins to appear around the time of the publication in 1985 of an article titled "Second Thoughts on Having It All" in *New York* magazine, described by one observer as an "epochal event."[33]

Whether the yuppie protagonists are contained within their personal space in the movies of besiegement (*Fatal Attraction, Pacific Heights, The Hand That Rocks the Cradle*) or removed from it in the "road movies" (*Something Wild, After Hours*), they share a frightening sense of alienation from a comfortable, privileged routine. Films that combine elements of both subclassifications (*Trespass, Judgment Night*) emphatically demonstrate that you can't take it with you, even if you have yuppie buying power.

Significantly, yuppie horror films exhibit minimal interest in gore and splatter effects. They avoid the kind of body horror characteristic of, say, George Romero or David Cronenberg, even though, as one writer puts it, "The body is the yuppie's most prized possession."[34] In these movies, it is less life than "lifestyle" that is threatened. *Disclosure* (1994) is filled with trendy dialogue about the dilemmas of contemporary sexual politics, and it suggests throughout a wish to avoid, rather than a fear of, the body that culminates, in the climactic scene in which Michael Douglas is pursued by a virtual reality Demi Moore, in its rejection altogether. The greater concern with lifestyle in yuppie horror films is perhaps nowhere more clear than in such movies as *The Firm* and *The Fugitive* (both 1993): the former is an upscale variation on such demonic cult horror films as Val Lewton's *The Seventh Victim* (1943); the latter is little more than the hoary mechanics of the chase, situated within a yuppie context. At the same time, graphic body horror, by contrast, became increasingly characteristic of more mainstream horror and science fiction films in which the body literally is a material thing, as in *Robocop* (1987), *The Terminator* (1984), and such less distinguished clones as *Universal Soldier* (1992).

For similar reasons, fear of racial difference is not particularly important in yuppie horror movies. As in yuppie ideology, race is subsumed by economic difference. Hence, *Judgment Night* is careful to include a black among the group of four suburban men who carelessly venture, in a state-of-the-art mobile home, into the monstrous violence of inner-city Detroit. By contrast, race, an issue in such earlier horror films as *White Zombie* (1932) and *I Walked with a Zombie* (1943), returned in such mainstream horror movies as *The People under the Stairs* (1991), *Candyman* (1992), and *Candyman II* (1995). But whether the monstrous Other in yuppie horror films is seemingly aristocratic (as in *Bad Influence*) or strictly blue collar (as in *Poison Ivy*), the fear exploited may be understood as the nightmarish result of the yuppie's typical narcissistic self-absorption.

Conclusion

If, as some would argue, yuppies are nothing more than a "media mirage,"[35] an imaginative creation of the culture industry, they nevertheless have had a powerful effect on advertising and marketing. Moreover, since yuppies come from the "baby-boomer" generation that constituted the teenagers to whom horror films were directed in the 1950s and '60s, they share an already established bond with the genre. Thus, it is not surprising that Hollywood would seek to incorporate into its rhetoric these viewers who, in the words of one advertising executive, are themselves "like a Hollywood movie, not real life."[36]

Curiously, Rick Altman does not include horror in his examples of durable genres that have established a particularly coherent syntax, although the genre has been around since almost the beginning of cinema and, of course, before that in literature and folklore.[37] Surely, the yuppie horror film is a particularly vivid contemporary instance of a genre's semantic modification within its existing syntax to accommodate a newly defined potential audience. Horror, it would seem, is a more flexible genre than such critics as Tudor and Altman have claimed. Rather, I would agree with Stephen King's assertion in *Danse Macabre* that the horror genre is "extremely limber, extremely adaptable, extremely useful."[38] In fact, the yuppie horror film would seem a vivid demonstration of Altman's thesis that the "relationship between the semantic and syntactic constitutes the very site of negotiation between Hollywood and its audience."[39] And if this cycle of the horror film demonstrates the protean adaptability of genre, it also reveals the inevitable anxiety generated by the biggest monster of all, late capitalism, particularly for men as the traditional "breadwinner." To paraphrase William Carlos Williams, yuppie horror films depict the pure products of America gone crazy.

Man's Favorite Sport?

The Action Films of Kathryn Bigelow

Introduction

With only a few features to her credit—*The Loveless* (1983, codirected with Monty Montgomery), *Near Dark* (1987), *Blue Steel* (1990), *Point Break* (1991), and *Strange Days* (1995)—writer/director Kathryn Bigelow succeeded in establishing herself as the only female filmmaker specializing in action films who, at least to this point, can claim the status of auteur. Bigelow's films employ, in the words of Anna Powell, "stunning and expressionistic visuals, rapid narrative pacing, thrilling and visceral scenes of eroticized violence and physical action,"[1] providing all the expected pleasures of action films. Yet at the same time they also work within the various genres that fall within the category of action cinema—cop films, buddy and road movies, westerns, horror films, and war films—to question their traditional and shared ideological assumptions about gender and violence.

Some critics have hesitated to call Bigelow an auteur because of her personal and professional association with James Cameron, the creator of such muscular action movies as *Terminator* (1984) and *Terminator 2: Judgment Day* (1991), who also produced *Point Break* and wrote and produced *Strange Days*. Certainly her biological status as a woman has entered into the discourse surrounding Bigelow, with critics and reviewers often referring not only to her gender but also to her physical attractiveness—hardly the kind of discourse that generally surrounds male directors.[2] Yet close analysis of her films reveals a remarkable consistency of style and theme that, as with most canonical male auteurs, works in relation to the parameters of genre.

The action film is perfectly suited to Bigelow's themes. The representation of violence is of course central to the genre, and as Steve Neale notes, the ideology of masculinity that it traditionally has worked so hard to inscribe centers on "notions and attitudes to do with aggression, power, and control."[3] Bigelow's first film, the short *Set-Up* (1978), which shows two men fighting in an alley while on the soundtrack two theorists interpret the violence, is in a sense a paradigm for her features to follow. All explore the nature of masculinity and its relation to violence, especially within the context of spectatorship, largely by playing on the look of the viewer as conditioned by the generic expectations and conventions of traditional action films. The "false" beginnings of both *Blue Steel* and *Near Dark,* which are tests of perception for Bigelow's protagonists as well as for the viewer, are only the most obvious instances of the importance of looking and the look in her films.

Critics have duly noted the thematic and stylistic importance of vision in Bigelow's films—her "cinema is essentially a discourse on vision," writes one[4]—a theme that likely has its roots in her days as a film studies student at Columbia University in New York City, at a time when the influence of feminist gaze theory was at its height. Much as Douglas Sirk and R. W. Fassbinder had approached the genre of melodrama or "the woman's film," providing their pleasures while critiquing the ideology that underpinned them ("bending," in Sirk's phrase), so Bigelow works within the action film. Her music video for the pop band New Order's "Touched by the Hand of God" is indicative of her approach: just as in the video she incongruously films the new wave band with the iconography of costume and the conventions of performance associated with heavy metal, thus foregrounding and questioning their masculine coding, so Bigelow's films mobilize a range of the genres traditionally regarded as "male" precisely to interrogate that term specifically, as well as the politics and pleasures of gendered representations in genre films more generally. Gavin Smith is thus absolutely correct in describing her work as "metacinema of the first rank"[5]

Men with Guns

While action in film has been popular ever since the Lumières' train entered the Ciotat Station, the action film as a recognizable genre for the definition and display of male power and prowess was clearly established with the rousing swashbucklers of Douglas Fairbanks (*The Mark of Zorro,* 1920; *The Black Pirate,* 1922) and Errol Flynn (*Captain Blood,* 1935; *The Adventures of Robin Hood,* 1940). The depth of the genre's masculine perspective is painfully clear in a movie like *True Lies* (1994, written and directed, ironically, by Bigelow's former husband, James Cameron). At one point in the narrative Jamie Lee Curtis is forced to succumb to the humiliating process of visual objectification in a scene that exceeds any narrative requirement: thinking she must do so to save her husband's life, she is made to enter a hotel room and strip for the pleasure of an unknown male spectator sitting in the shadows. The apparent joke is on her, since she does not realize (but we do) that the mysterious man is in fact her husband, whom she does not know is a spy. The husband is played by Arnold Schwarzenegger—"an anthropomorphized phallus, a phallus with muscles," in the apt words of Barbara Creed[6]—the actor who more than any other embodies the action film in the 1980s and 1990s and who, in this scene, explicitly functions as the ego ideal of the male viewer.

It is stating the obvious to say that successful action stars often rely on anatomy rather than acting. Male action stars such as Schwarzenegger, Sylvester Stallone, Jean-Claude Van Damme, Steven Seagal, Chuck Norris, and Bruce Willis offer impressively muscular bodies for visual display and as the site of ordeals they must undergo in order to triumph at narrative's end. Critics such as Yvonne Tasker and Susan Jeffords have discussed the contemporary action film's exaggerated masculinity as an expression of patriarchal ideology, the reassertion of male power and privilege during and after the Reagan administration and in an era of eroding hegemony.[7] It is no accident that the hyperbolically masculine action film gained popularity roughly at the same time that other genres, traditionally regarded as "male," were beginning to be opened up to revisionist readings.

Into the 1980s, genres and genre movies remained almost exclusively the cultural property of a white male consciousness, the center from which any difference regarding race, gender, and sexuality was defined and marginalized. In all the action genres, it was white men who had to get the job done, whether driving the cattle, solving the crime, capturing the spies, or defeating the aliens. Movies such as *Westward the Women* (1951), in which a wagon train of women successfully makes the cross-country trek to California, were only the exceptions that proved the rule. In every type of action film, women and visible minorities assumed subsidiary and stereotyped roles, serving as hindrances, helpers, or rewards for the white male's doing. With the ghettoized exceptions of musicals and melodramas—at one time referred to in the industry as "women's films"—most genre movies addressed an assumed viewer who was, like almost all of the filmmakers who made them, white, male, and heterosexual. But by the next decade many contemporary genre movies sought to grapple with and redress the implications of traditional generic representations of race and gender, often deliberately acknowledging and giving voice to groups previously marginalized by mainstream cinema, including women, blacks, and gays.

The film that more than any other provided the impetus for this new generic transformation was, undoubtedly, *Thelma and Louise.* One of the most popular movies in North America in 1991, *Thelma and Louise* is a generic hybrid of the western, the buddy film, and the road movie—three of those genres traditionally regarded as male—and the outlaw couple movie, the protagonists of which had always been romantically involved heterosexual couples. *Thelma and Louise* reversed Hollywood's conventional definition of woman's place as the domestic sphere and reimagined the buddy movie as female adventure. The acts of rebellion on the part of the two women, like blowing up the tanker truck of a driver who makes obscene gestures at them, come to seem nothing less than imaginative acts of retribution for all women, transcending their personal plight. As Peter Chumo observes, "what Bonnie and Clyde do for Depression evils, Thelma and Louise do for the evil of sexual violence."[8]

In the film's controversial ending, Thelma and Louise drive over the edge of the Grand Canyon rather than capitulate to the police. The last image is a freeze frame of the car in midair, just beyond the apogee of its arching flight, followed by a fade to white. This ending is, of course, a direct reference to one of the most famous of buddy movies, *Butch Cassidy and the Sundance Kid* (1969), and it sparked considerable debate regarding *Thelma and Louise*'s political value. Did it signify suicidal defeatism or triumphant transcendence? This debate in itself was significant for, as Rebecca Bell-Metereau noted, "Critics did not concern themselves with the outcome of *Butch Cassidy and the Sundance Kid* [or] *Easy Rider* [1969], because a male death in the conclusion is sacrificial, symbolic, and Christ-like. A female death at the end of the story rarely receives such a heroic interpretation, from feminists or non-feminists."[9] The contentious but popular reception of *Thelma and Louise*'s ending suggests how novel the film was at the time.

Regardless of how one reads the film's ending, the fact that it was the subject of such heated debate suggests both the complexities of gendered representations in popular cinema generally and the difficulty of finding a place for women in the action film specifically. Many recent genre films are content merely to borrow *Thelma and Louise*'s gender "gimmick," simply plugging others into roles traditionally reserved for white men. But in reversing conventional representations, they are prone to fall into the trap of repeating the same objectionable values. The question of whether female action heroes such as Sigourney Weaver's Ripley in *Alien* (1979) and its sequels or Linda Hamilton's Sarah Connor in *Terminator 2: Judgment Day* are progressive representations of women or merely contain them within a masculine sensibility has been a matter of considerable debate. It is just here that Bigelow's films constitute a site of intervention, for while they often reverse generic expectation (the female cop in *Blue Steel,* for example, or the black female bodyguard and feminized male protagonist in *Strange Days*), they also employ a variety of stylistic means to question the gendered values that animate action film genres.

The Children of Eisenhower and Coca-Cola

The Loveless, Bigelow's first feature film, remains her most avant-garde or experimental. Set in the 1950s, the film is a generic amalgam of mainstream biker movies of the period, particularly *The Wild One* (1954), and the celebration of gay iconography in Kenneth Anger's experimental film *Scorpio Rising* (1963). As such, *The Loveless* might more accurately be described as an anti-action film because of its stylized compositions and deliberately slow pace—especially curious given the kinetic potential of a movie about guys on motorcycles. The main character, Vance (Willem Dafoe), accurately describes the film's style when he tells the other bikers "we're going nowhere . . . fast."

The minimal plot involves a group of bikers (all men, with the notable exception of the bleach-blond Debbie Sportster) who converge on a small southern town on their way to the drag races at Daytona, waiting while one of them does some necessary repairs to his motorcycle. Their presence catalyses the townspeople, who respond to them either with desire or fear, these extreme and polar reactions coming together in a violent climax featuring a shoot-out in a roadside bar and the suicide of a local girl. The bikers function like the monstrous other of the horror film (in fact, there are a number of correspondences between them and the vampire clan in the later *Near Dark*), a graphic representation of the return of the repressed. And like the more sympathetic monsters of some progressive horror films, they are less evil than merely different in their bohemian lifestyle.

The Loveless works toward its violent climax not so much as a necessary dramatic resolution, but more because, like Michel and Patricia in Jean-Luc Godard's *À bout de souffle* (*Breathless*, 1959), the characters are trapped within the constraints of genre. A tragic outcome seems inevitable, a given, the kind of ending we expect when free-spirited bikers are confronted by rednecks in movies like *Easy Rider.* But the specific form this violent climax takes in *The Loveless,* turning in on the town and making the townspeople the victims, is a more subtle critique. Appropriately, *The Loveless* contains many references to Godard's work—most obviously in the shots of Vance driving in the open convertible with Telena (Marin Kanter), the local jailbait. The sense of buoyant freedom as they drive, the way Kanter turns her head away from the camera, and her short, boyish haircut, all deliberately echo Jean Seberg in *À bout de souffle. The Loveless*'s bold color palette, use of deliberately choreographed tracking shots (a central element of what Brian Henderson calls Godard's "non-bourgeois camera style"),[10] and vivid deployment of consumer iconography (the brilliant red Coke machine in the filling station) all invoke Godard's distinctive style of political filmmaking.

The actors are often filmed doing nothing, even being completely motion-less, in Brechtian tableaux. Vance tellingly says in the opening scene, when the woman with the flat tire asks him what he does for a living, "not a whole

The Loveless (1982) displays the bikers in Brechtian tableau.

lot." These shots are frequently held longer than the time required for narrative comprehension, encouraging us to examine their studied composition. As a result, the characters—male and female—become objects of aesthetic contemplation for the spectator. The images are often composed so that the actors are decentered in the frame, emphasizing the iconographical import of gesture (smoking a cigarette, drinking a Coke) or costume (motorcycle jacket, boots). In the roadside diner—Bigelow's equivalent to the Parisian cafe for Godard—when they wonder where one of their group is, Debbie comments that he must be outside "fine-tuning his sideburns." The film's first image is of Vance laconically combing his hair before heading out on the highway. Bigelow thus subverts the traditionally masculine gaze of the camera, fetishizing, as in Anger's more experimental work, the accoutrements of the biker subculture. The languorous shots of the bikers ultimately reveal them as poised, posed, performing, so that any sense of a monolithic or essential masculinity is called into question. This subversion is literalized in the climax, and the violence precipitated, when Telena's abusive and belligerent father discovers one of the bikers wearing women's undergarments beneath his leather in, significantly, the bar's men's room.

Terror in a Texas Town

Bigelow's second feature, *Near Dark,* is a generic hybrid of the western and the vampire film in the venerable tradition of such unassuming genre fare as *Curse of the Undead* (1959), *Billy the Kid vs. Dracula* (1965), and *Jesse James Meets Frankenstein's Daughter* (1966), but with considerably more serious ambitions. As Christina Lane points out, both genres "have traditionally been used to work through ambivalent feelings toward nature and civilization, and both usually tell stories in which threatening natural forces are purged for the sake of society."[11] Both genres are structured by binary oppositions that at root reflect the ongoing tension between individual desire and social responsibility—civilization and its discontents, in Freud's terms—in the western, as a topographical mapping onto the frontier and in the horror film, as a psycho-social projection.[12] *Near Dark* mixes elements of both genres, revealing their common conventional gendered assumptions.

A midwestern farm boy, Caleb (Adrian Pasdar), seemingly falls in love at first sight with an attractive female vampire named Mae (Jenny Wright) after a romantic evening together. Mae bites Caleb, who turns almost immediately into a vampire and is snatched away by the vampire clan, a terrible family reminiscent of those in horror movies like *The Texas Chain Saw Massacre* (1974) and *The Hills Have Eyes* (1977) and westerns like *My Darling Clementine* (1946) and *Wagon Master* (1950). But Caleb, like the classic western hero, refuses to kill except in self-defense, allowing Mae to do it instead and then drinking her blood. In a final showdown at high midnight on Main Street, Caleb, now cured by a blood transfusion performed by his father, destroys the vampire clan, literally earning his spurs.

In the denouement, Caleb administers the same cure to Mae, who, in the film's final shot, can now step into the sunlit promise of domesticity, the place typically reserved for women in the western—see, for example, *High Noon* (1952) or *Shane* (1953)—and a gaping void in Caleb's family, given the unexplained absence of a mother. (This absence, unmentioned by the characters, is addressed by the film in the scene of the three family members having dinner, the fourth chair at the table noticeably empty.) This ending recalls that of numerous horror films, particularly Tod Browning's *Dracula* (1931), which concludes with the romantic couple ascending a long flight of stairs in the vampire's dark crypt to the security of sunny daylight and church bells on the soundtrack after the staking of the vampire.

Near Dark's narrative closure thus seems emphatically to restore patriarchal gender politics, as do both the classic horror film, when the monster is destroyed and civilization made safe, and the western, when the bad men or Indians are defeated and the frontier tamed for settler families. But given the rest of the film, this ending rings hollow, like the apparently happy ending of Sirk's *All That Heaven Allows* (1955) in which the heroine, seeking to define herself as a desiring subject, can be reunited with her lover only when she is summarily forced into the position of nurturer after he is seriously injured while hunting. In both cases the apparent happy ending fulfills generic convention but lacks thematic conviction.

Bigelow suggests that the happy ending of *Near Dark* is intended to be read as similarly perfunctory and ironic, given the sexual meanings of vampirism both within generic tradition and in *Near Dark* specifically. The sexual basis of the vampires' allure is shown when, during a typical night of feeding, we see Severen (Bill Paxton) use his charm as a hitchhiker to attract two women who pick him up in their truck hoping for a good time. The attractive Mae, a seemingly archetypical blue jean baby, arouses such strong desire in Caleb that it threatens to destroy his traditional family by luring him away from home and the daytime world. Further, this desire threatens to erupt and destroy bourgeois stability at any moment, as we see when Mae comes back, a literal return of the repressed, after Caleb is cured of his vampirism. Unhesitatingly, Caleb rushes to hug Mae, noticeably exposing his neck to her as they embrace. Like the popular song, the film asks, "How are you gonna keep 'em down on the farm after they've seen Paree?"—a question that directly acknowledges the necessity of repression for maintaining traditional social values. Like Bohemian Paris, Mae represents the siren song of desire, so in the course of the narrative she must be literally defanged and thrust into the glaring sunlight of normalcy. Now saved by her man, no longer feminized, she will likely take her place in that empty chair, adopting the kind of maternal role Caleb had tried to impose on her when they were vampires and he fed from her blood like a helpless, hungry infant suckling at its mother's breast.

The film consistently contrasts Caleb's normal, good family with the undead, evil family of the vampires. The vampires are capable of terrible violence, as we see several times in the film and especially in its memorable set piece, their decimation of a roadhouse and its occupants. This violence is tinged with eroticism throughout, and it intoxicates even as it repels, a perfect expression of Susan Sontag's description of the appeal of monster movies as "the aesthetics of destruction, with the peculiar beauties to be found in wreaking havoc, making a mess."[13] During the massacre, Caleb, like the spectator, watches mesmerized, even finding himself participating against his will when he sends a tough-looking biker flying through the air with one punch ("Did I do that?" he asks with bemusement). Christopher Sharrett complains that the vampire clan is "wholly repugnant and destructive," so that, in contrast to the kinds of horror films Robin Wood calls progressive, there is no sympathy generated toward them.[14] He views the vampires as unproblematically Other, but I would suggest that *Near Dark* does indeed problematize the relation of the normal and monstrous once we accept the seductive and violent pleasures the film offers. Their inherent appeal is underscored by the fact that the monstrous patriarch Jesse (Lance Henrickson) is associated with American history (he claims to have fought for the Confederacy), and that the clan travel across middle America, the center of what poet Allen Ginsberg called the "heart of the vortex" out of which American violence emanates.[15] Despite the film's apparent rigid contrast between the daytime world of the farm family and the nighttime world of the vampire clan, we are implicated in the latter, all of us near dark.

Sleeping with the Enemy

Blue Steel is a stylish police thriller that exploits to the fullest the action film's conventional association of the gun with the phallus, exploring the representation of the gun as a totem of masculine power. From the opening credit sequence in which the camera penetrates the interior of a Smith and Wesson handgun, *Blue Steel* (according to one critic, the term is American slang for an erection[16]) explores the genre's iconographical fetishization of the pistol. By making possession and control of the gun a contest between a policewoman and a male criminal, the film foregrounds the metaphorical and gendered implications of one of the primary icons of the action film.

The plot involves a rookie female cop, Megan Turner (Jamie Lee Curtis),

Megan (Jamie Lee Curtis) usurps control of the phallus in *Blue Steel* (1989).

whose gender troubles all the men in the film once she dons her uniform. Intervening in a supermarket robbery, Turner shoots and kills the hold-up man, while one of the cowering bystanders in the store, Eugene Hunt (Ron Silver), secretly pockets the thief's handgun. As the film progresses, Eugene becomes increasingly psychotic, obsessed with the image of Turner wielding her weapon and usurping phallic power. In the final violent confrontation, Turner manages to kill the seemingly unstoppable Eugene.

Some have read the film as empowering for women. Megan is like the hero of a rape revenge film, an example of Carol Clover's "final girl." In this sense, the casting of Curtis, protagonist of the prototypical slasher film *Halloween* (1978), is particularly resonant.[17] After all, it is Megan who defeats Eugene in battle, not her superior, the suitably named Detective Nick Mann (Clancy Brown), who is "disarmed" when Megan handcuffs him to their car door during her penultimate confrontation with Eugene. Nevertheless, *Blue Steel* suggests that the triumph of Megan and the femininity she represents can only be limited because of the entrenched power of patriarchy since the film contextualizes the male world of Eugene as a monstrous extension of normative masculinity.

Employing a standard motif of the horror film, Eugene is doubled with Megan's abusive father (Philip Bosco), emphasizing a continuity between apparently masculine norms and the horribly psychotic. Also, like Patrick Bateman in Brett Easton Ellis's controversial novel *American Psycho* (1991), published the year after the release of the film, Eugene is a stockbroker, his position of economic privilege apparently allowing him the power to commit horrible criminal acts, including murder, with impunity. Both works link their central male character's craziness to capitalism, competition, masculine identity, and violence. Eugene hears voices in his head and so expresses a desire for quietude—an understandable wish given his profession; on two occasions we see him screaming and wildly gesticulating in a sea of commodity traders, all male, on the floor of the stock exchange. (It is in this same space that Eugene first fantasizes shooting the gun he has picked up at the supermarket.) When Mann asks Megan why she became a cop, she ambiguously replies, "Him," which, as Tasker notes, may refer to her abusive father specifically or more generally to "the man," to men, to the many potential Eugenes.[18]

The film employs other conventions of the horror film, particularly the werewolf film. Eugene is hirsute, with a dark beard, and associated with the night; at one point we see him digging for his gun like an animal under the full moon in New York's Central Park (Eugene's last name, remember, is Hunt). These associations of masculinity with violence and animality appear throughout Bigelow's films: hothead biker Davis (Robert Gordon) in *The Loveless* literally barks at his friends and yelps wildly as he fires his gun in the violent climax in the bar, while in *Near Dark,* when Caleb thinks he has killed Severen by running over him with a diesel truck, another icon of phallic power (see Sam Peckinpah's *Convoy* [1978]), he similarly howls with satisfaction. Violence is associated with male animality in Bigelow's films because violence is seen as an inherently masculine quality. *Blue Steel* demonstrates this idea visually, in its painterly images combined with careful foley work that emphasize the physical and sensual qualities of the gun. Frequently the film emphasizes the texture and tactility of guns—the way hands caressingly grip them, how they slide across a table or are provocatively unbuttoned from a holster—as well as the sounds they make. Viewers are seduced, within the context of the action film, by the power of the phallus, like the men in the film in their more extreme ways.

Megan's desire to be a cop thus becomes a desire to enter into the phallic domain, literalized in her struggle with Eugene over possession of the gun. Her uniform is a sign of transgression as Megan encroaches on a traditionally male world, an idea made clear at the beginning of the film in the montage of Megan suiting up for graduation. Individual shots fetishize parts of her uniform, reminiscent of the shots of the bikers' costumes in *The Loveless.* The character's gender is initially indeterminate, but then, as she buttons her shirt, we glimpse her lace bra underneath. Viewers are likely taken aback for a moment, "disarmed" like the several men in the film when they see her in uniform the first time or learn what her job is. Megan's wearing of a traditionally male uniform also suggests the extent to which, apart from the masculine propensity toward violence, gender is a constructed performance, dependent upon the semiotics of style for meaning.

Imitation of Life

If *The Loveless* deconstructs the action, *Point Break* is a thoroughly successful reconstruction. As the story unfolds, viewers are treated to some terrific action sequences, the most memorable of which is an extended chase, effectively photographed through alleys, houses, and backyards with a modified Steadicam that adeptly places us squarely within the action. (Bigelow uses the same strategy more trenchantly in the opening of *Strange Days.*) A combination of buddy and caper movie, it nevertheless has the same objective of subverting the power of masculinist generic myth by challenging our sense of the conventions of "realism" characteristic of classic Hollywood cinema. In Sirkian fashion, Bigelow treats the action excessively in *Point Break,* pushing the macho mysticism into overblown spectacle. As Tyler (Lori Petty), the lone woman in the film's hypermasculine world of skydiving, surfing, and bank robbing, disgustedly opines at one point while the men are busy bonding on a beach, "There's too much testosterone here for me."

The film's plot concerns a band of bank robbers who commit heists because they are devoted surfers who need to maintain their cash flow as they travel around the world in search of the perfect wave. The gang is known as the Ex-Presidents because they wear masks of former U.S. presidents while committing their robberies. The case is being investigated by a pair of FBI agents, seasoned Angelo Pappas (Gary Busey) and hotshot rookie Johnny

Johnny Utah (Keanu Reeves) and Bodhi (Patrick Swayze) bond in action in *Point Break* (1991).

Utah (Keanu Reeves). Undercover, Utah infiltrates the gang and experiences a conflict between his duty as agent of the law and the spiritual bond he has developed with the gang's leader, Bodhi (Patrick Swayze).

The film, it is true, offers some direct (and humorous) social criticism with its band of presidential bank robbers—particularly when "Nixon" jumps up on a counter to declare "I am not a crook!" and when Bodhi, wearing his Reagan mask, waves a gas pump in the air and ignites a filling station into a flaming fireball.[19] But for the most part *Point Break* is more sly in its subversion of the masculine myths of action cinema, frequently reminding us that it is only a movie, a generic construction. The male characters are clearly types rather than rounded individuals. Keanu Reeves's typically flat performance style ironically works well here, emphasizing Johnny Utah's lack of psychological depth. His name is itself something of a mythic amalgam, at once evoking the American West and the western, as well as legendary athleticism in the masculine world of football (Utah was a college football star; his name recalls that of both Johnny Unitas and Joe Montana, two legendary NFL quarterbacks), and the fact that he is a fictional character in the tradition of *Johnny Guitar* (1954) and *Johnny Handsome* (1989).[20]

If action movies exhibit a masculine homosocial hysteria mapped onto the excessive display of the male body,[21] then *Point Break* is a paradigmatic action movie. The male characters are on constant display, even to the point that the gang members are identified by the tan lines on their buttocks when they "moon" for the security cameras at one of the banks they rob. The film emphasizes Swayze's body and long blond tresses and pushes its representation of the surfer gang's macho camaraderie to the point of parody. This excessive treatment comes to a head, as it were, in the climax when Utah jumps out of an airplane without a parachute in a determined attempt to catch Bodhi, who had jumped moments before with the last one. The sequence of Utah's windy free fall toward Bodhi and clasping of him in midair becomes a hysterical visualization of the repressed homoerotic subtext of the buddy movie. The two men embrace as they grapple, their windswept faces together in intimate close-up as they tussle for either the gun or the pull cord ("Pull it, pull it," Bodhi cries). And as we see in the subjective zoom shot of the ground rapidly coming nearer, for both men it is an experience in which the earth has moved. The sequence ends with them rolling in the dust, the parachute flapping gently to the ground in postcoital calm.

Back to the Future

Strange Days is set just slightly in the future of the film's release, in Los Angeles on the day before New Year's Eve, 1999. Lenny (Ralph Fiennes), a black market dealer in "clips," an outlawed form of total cinema produced by a new technology that taps directly into the cerebral cortex for both recording and playback, must learn to abandon the simulated memories of his former girlfriend (Juliette Lewis), however realistic, and embrace a new life in the real world with Mace (Angela Bassett). Through this metacinematic metaphor, violent action and eroticism are critiqued as voyeuristic, sadistic, and decidedly masculine. It is not surprising that Bigelow has called *Strange Days* her most personal film.[22]

The film begins by positioning us as viewers of one of these clips, although it is only in retrospect that we realize this, since no exposition precedes it.

On the soundtrack we hear someone say, "Boot it," and the image seems to form as pixels, but the meaning of this is unclear. Once the clip boots, there is no apparent difference, such as a frame within a frame or disparity in image resolution, to mark these images as a film within the film rather than as images within the world of the film. For all intents and purposes, what we are seeing is the film—and by extension, any action film. We are thrust immediately into the viewing dynamic, our identification fully mobilized, despite the fact that as yet we do not know who "we" are. Like clip users within the world of the film, we are fooled by the reality status of the sequence.

As in *Point Break,* we are immersed in the action, a part of it, featuring Bigelow's tour-de-force use of the subjective camera. In what seems like one lengthy, technically breathtaking shot (there are actually a couple of disguised cuts) on a par with the opening shot of Orson Welles's *Touch of Evil* (1958) or Robert Altman's *The Player* (1992), the viewer is put into the perspective of one of the participants. "We" drive up to an Asian restaurant with a group of robbers, sitting in the back seat; commit robbery, intimidating staff and patrons in the process; frantically flee from the arriving police in a confusing shootout; attempt to escape across a series of rooftops, police in hot pursuit; and finally, plunge to "our" death in the street below when we fail to make the leap from one rooftop to another. In this opening sequence we know only that we are male, as indicated by the dialogue, and by the hands we see from "our" physical point of view, à la *Lady in the Lake* (1946). But the individual man here is in fact irrelevant—we are, the film immediately suggests, masculinity itself. The apparent long take maintains a consistent point of view and thus heightens our sense of presence throughout the action, the appeal of which is marked as racist and sexist since the victims of our abuse are "fucking chinks" and "bitches," as our invisible surrogate calls them.

This astonishing opening sequence exposes the subjective camera common to such genres as action and slasher movies as nothing less than a tool of naked male aggression. Many of the violent action sequences that follow in *Strange Days* involve the victimization of women with the SQUID (superconducting quantum interference devices) technology, in the infamous manner of Mark Lewis (Karl Bohm) in Michael Powell's *Peeping Tom* (1960). It is no coincidence that (with the exception of Mace's one reluctant SQUID trip for Lenny's sake) the only users we see in the film are male. (The extent to which women are involved in the production or consumption of SQUID clips may be read as an indication of their moral corruption, as in the case of Faith.) Thus the subsequent scenes of violent action in the film cannot be viewed with the same kind of "innocent" pleasure we may have brought to the opening sequence, for we have been made aware of the gendered dynamics involved in such pleasure.

But strangely—or perhaps not strangely, since this is, after all, a Hollywood movie—*Strange Days* builds to a climax that denies what has come previously, that seems to recuperate its own ideological critique. In the climax, Lenny, his friend, Mace, and a female bodyguard (Angela Bassett) try to give to the police commissioner a clip that has recorded the truth about the killing of a popular militant black rock star by two racist white cops. The two policemen confront Mace during the wild celebration on the eve of the millennium and begin to assault her with their nightsticks. The scene obviously invokes the infamous tape of the Rodney King beating, which also occurred in Los Angeles, but in the movie, unlike the real world, the crowd of onlookers responds by actively banding together to fight this act of racial oppression. Finally, the honest white male commissioner, brandishing the evidence in his raised hand, parts the suddenly compliant crowd like the archetypal patriarch Moses parting the Red Sea and calls for the arrest of the two rogue cops. Power, ultimately, is retained in the (literal) hands of the white male, who now supersedes the once-capable and independent black woman.

Conclusion

Robin Wood has angrily dismissed *Strange Days* as "a tease and a cheat" because of the emphatic way it compromises its own premises.[23] But this response may be somewhat ungenerous, for it is no more an ideological cheat than the majority of mainstream American movies are. Perhaps it seems more disappointing because of how radical its initial premise is. Wood more accurately might have called *Strange Days,* in his own terms, "an incoherent text." As discussed in relation to Jerry Lewis's *The Delicate Delinquent* in chapter 5, such texts, for Wood, are fractured but have a "consciously motivated incoherence [that] becomes a structuring principle, resulting in works that reveal themselves as perfectly coherent once one has mastered their rules."[24] Bigelow herself has described *Strange Days* as "at war with itself."[25] From this perspective, the film's ideological contradictions speak quite eloquently of the tensions inherent in the situation of a woman making action movies about the traditionally male genre of action movies. Indeed, this position seems as fraught with difficulties as Megan Turner seeking phallic power in the male world of the police force, only with the penetrating, affective power of the motion picture camera instead of a gun. *Strange Days* does collapse at the end—an ending, significantly, that Bigelow stretches out for almost twenty minutes rather than elides—but this collapse serves to emphasize the limited place and power of women in mainstream cinema, whether in front of the camera or behind it.

Bigelow's most recent film, *The Hurt Locker* (2008), continues to show her strategy of critiquing the masculine ideology of action genres by working within them, in this case the war film, again providing the genre's pleasures even as it subverts or questions them. The narrative focuses on Bravo Company, a three-man American EOD (Explosive Ordinance Disposal) Unit on patrol in Baghdad. Given its subject, *The Hurt Locker* joins a cycle of recent films about the war against terrorism in Iraq, including *The Battle for Haditha* (2008) and Brian de Palma's *Redacted* (2007), which, with its extended use of YouTube and surveillance videos and digital home movies to tell its story, explores similar but ultimately different territory from Bigelow's film, focusing instead on how experience is mediated by the visual media.

Recalling the beginning of *Strange Days,* there is little offered by way of context, as we join the detail in the process of attempting to diffuse a large bomb planted in a Baghdad street. The leader, responsible for diffusing the bomb, is Sergeant Matt Thompson, played by Guy Pearce, a recognizable star from such action films as the policier *L.A. Confidential* (1997), the horror-western *Ravenous* (1999), and the remake of H. G. Wells's science fiction classic, *The Time Machine* (2002). By comparison, the two other men, Sergeant J. T. Sanborn (Anthony Mackie) and Specialist Owen Eldridge (Brian Geraghty), who maintain a safe perimeter and watch for snipers while Thompson works with the bomb, lack the same degree of star recognition. Hence viewer identification is immediately directed to the character played by Pearce, a spectatorial response further encouraged by showing his face in close-up during this tense scene, and by including in the scene many shots from Thompson's point of view. Here and throughout, *The Hurt Locker* uses a quick editing style, combining mostly hand-held shots from multiple perspectives with quick pans, zooms, and canted angles to express all the soldiers' understandable jumpiness and anxiety about the sudden appearance of potential danger and the constant vigil they must keep in the oppressive heat, but Pearce's star status helps "anchor" our point of view. Thus, even with the film's characteristically edgy style, it is a shock when Thompson fails to defuse the bomb and is blown to bits. Immediately, then, the film offers us a lesson about the pitfalls of spectator identification in the context of violence, as well as placing us in a situation similar to that of the soldiers, who cannot afford to form bonds with Iraqi civilians since anyone is a potential insurgent or the victim of them for colluding with the enemy (as we see when an Iraqi youth, Beckham, who sells DVDs to American soldiers, is killed and a bomb planted in his body).

After Thompson's death, he is replaced by the comparatively reckless Staff Sergeant William James (Jeremy Renner). Boasting that he has diffused more than 800 bombs, Sgt. James takes more chances than his predecessor; he has a seemingly reckless attitude in his approach to bomb situations, to the dismay of Sanborn and Eldridge, who are counting down the days of their rotation and just trying to survive. Tyler's comment in *Point Break* that "there's too much testosterone here for me" would seem to apply perfectly to Sgt. James. A freewheeling cowboy (his name evokes both Billy the Kid and Jesse James), he doesn't hesitate to disconnect his communication equipment in order to ignore warnings from his squad mates to withdraw. *The Hurt Locker* begins with a quotation from Chris Hedges's *War Is a Force That Gives Us Meaning,* a book about the effects of war on the human psyche: "The rush of battle is a potent and lethal addiction, for war is a drug," and it shows us how Sgt. James has become hooked, hot-dogging it each time for yet another adrenalin rush.

At the end of the squad's rotation, Sgt. James goes home but finds it difficult to live a normal life with his family. An addict now, in the film's final shots we see him deplaning back in Iraq, returning for another "fix," just one soldier in formation being deployed. Like Ethan Edwards in John Ford's *The Searchers* (1956), Sgt. James's experiences during war have put him outside the family and home, making him "ride away, ride away."[26] Remembering that President George W. Bush had invoked the rhetoric of the western to build support for the war after 9/11, one might read James's cowboy attitude as a metaphor of American involvement in Iraq and, by extension, elsewhere in the Middle East. From this perspective, the United States barnstorms into sovereign nations, relying once more on its historical tradition of military force as diplomacy.

Just as Sgt. James repeatedly tests himself against potentially deadly bombs, so the United States gambles on its military might to defuse situations in places it regards as powder kegs. In one scene, Sgt. James talks to a panicked man who has been forcibly wired with explosives while he tries to defuse them; the tragic outcome is perhaps a comment on the explosive situation in Iraq, seemingly out of control.

The film does not explicitly address the politics of the Iraqi war, but instead focuses on the experience of counterinsurgency warfare and what it does to those who wage it. And because of war's devastating effects, Bigelow presents the guts without the glory; there are no clear antagonists, little meaningfully "heroic" action in the traditional sense, and no rousing climax. There is riveting suspense, but we are offered no catharsis; we are aware that at any moment Sgt. James might be blown to bits like Thompson, his predecessor. Early on Sgt. James finds himself ensnared within an expanding web of connecting IEDs (improvised explosive devices) buried in the sand, just as he and everyone there becomes enmeshed in the war. The machinery of war is a theater of cruelty that enables men to enact their inherent violent tendencies; it oozes death but lures men in, like the leaking nuclear core that requires Russian sailors deliberately to expose themselves to fatal doses of radiation in a vain attempt to save their ship in Bigelow's preceding film, *K-19: The Widowmaker* (2002). In different ways, men are poisoned by war and militarism.

In a sense, Bigelow's embracing of the action genre's pleasures while simultaneously critiquing them demonstrates a mastery of the master's own language.[27] Although excess is more often associated with melodrama and the musical, it is certainly an important quality of the action film as well. The excess in Bigelow's action films serves as self-reflexive commentary on the genre and the masculine culture it celebrates, much as the excess in Douglas Sirk's melodramas commented on the ideology of the genre in which he was working and the cultural contexts of Eisenhower America. Although Sirk was working within the constraints of the studio system while Bigelow has made her films in the postclassical context of the New Hollywood, the analogy is apt, for both directors exist within the contexts of popular cinema, which is so thoroughly structured at every level by generic principles.

In the introduction to their pioneering anthology, *Screening the Male*, Steven Cohan and Ina Rae Hark note that film theory has for the most part confidently equated the masculinity of the male subject with activity, voyeurism, sadism, fetishism, and story, and the femininity of the female subject with passivity, exhibitionism, masochism, narcissism, and spectacle. In this scheme of homologous differences the power, stability, and wholeness of masculine subjectivity at the expense of femininity seem all too axiomatic and thus, universal and uncontestable.[28]

While many recent action movies have tended to reinscribe traditional patriarchal values,[29] Kathryn Bigelow has made a remarkable series of films that have resisted the genre's conservative thrust. Like the new genre films of the 1970s that John Cawelti described as "set[ting] the elements of a conventional popular genre in an altered context, thereby making us perceive these traditional forms and images in a new way,"[30] Bigelow's action films are generic interventions that invite and encourage speculation about masculine identity and the nature of popular cinema. She uses the action film to address fundamental issues of genre, gender, and spectatorship and to negotiate a place for women both in front of and behind the camera within traditionally masculine discourses. Her films offer one of the most significant negotiations of masculinity yet produced in American cinema and thus a most fitting conclusion to this book.

Notes

Introduction

1. Robin Wood, *Hitchcock's Films Revisited* (New York: Columbia University Press, 1989), 221.
2. Robin Wood, "Ideology, Genre, Auteur," in *Film Genre Reader 3*, ed. Barry Keith Grant (Austin: University of Texas Press, 2003), 70.
3. Wood, *Hitchcock's Films Revisited*, 221.
4. Susan Sontag, *On Photography* (New York: Delta, 1973), 15.
5. Rick Altman, *Film/Genre* (London: British Film Institute, 1999), 189–90.
6. Mark Twain, *Life on the Mississippi* (New York: New American Library, 1961), 265–66. He adds that Scott's retrograde vision, or what he called "the Sir Walter Scott disease," hampered social progress "and out of charity ought to be buried" (266). Appropriately, Twain names the steamship that runs aground in *Adventures of Huckleberry Finn*—the one book from which "all modern American literature comes," according to Ernest Hemingway—the *Sir Walter Scott*. See *Adventures of*

Huckleberry Finn, ed. Sculley Bradley, Richmond Croom Beatty, and E. Hudson Long (New York: Norton, 1961), 62. Ernest Hemingway, *Green Hills of Africa* (New York: Charles Scribner's Sons, 1935), 22.

7. Judith Hess Wright, "Genre Films and the Status Quo," in *Film Genre Reader 3,* ed. Grant, 50.

8. John Fiske, *Reading the Popular* (Boston: Unwin Hyman, 1898), 2.

9. David Bordwell, Janet Staiger, and Kristen Thompson, *The Classical Hollywood Cinema: Film Style and Mode of Production to 1960* (New York: Columbia University Press, 1985), 3, 7.

10. I discuss the generic conventions of these films and others in my *Film Genre: From Iconography to Ideology* (London: Wallflower Press, 2007).

11. Wood, "Ideology, Genre, Auteur," 70, 73.

12. Annalee Newitz, "Serial Killers, True Crime, and Economic Performance Anxiety," in *Mythologies of Violence in Postmodern Media,* ed. Christopher Sharrett (Detroit: Wayne State University Press, 1999), 69, 76.

13. Ibid., 69.

14. These are the terms Robin Wood has so influentially used to discuss the ideology of the horror film. See his essay, "An Introduction to the American Horror Film," in *Planks of Reason: Essays on the Horror Film,* ed. Barry Keith Grant and Christopher Sharrett, rev. ed. (Lanham, MD: Scarecrow Press, 2004), 107–41.

15. Steve Neale, "Masculinity as Spectacle," in *Screening the Male: Exploring Masculinities in Hollywood Cinema,* ed. Steven Cohan and Ina Rae Hark (London and New York: Routledge, 1993), 9–20. Neale's essay was first published in *Screen* 24, no. 6 (1983): 2–16.

16. Peter Lehman, *Running Scared: Masculinity and the Representation of the Male Body,* new ed. (Detroit: Wayne State University Press, 2007), esp. chap. 1.

17. Judith Butler, *Gender Trouble* (New York and London: Routledge, 1990); Gaylyn Studlar, *This Mad Masquerade: Stardom and Masculinity in the Jazz Age* (New York: Columbia University Press, 1966).

18. Frank Krutnik, *In a Lonely Street: Film Noir, Genre, Masculinity* (London and New York: Routledge, 1991), xiii, 91.

19. Neale, "Masculinity as Spectacle," 11.

20. "The sexual confusion at the heart of *Raging Bull* does, I think, put masculinity in crisis, raising the question of what it takes to be a man, and what the alternatives to macho male sexuality might be." Pam Cook, "Masculinity in Crisis?" *Screen* 23, nos. 3–4 (1982): 39.

21. R. W. Connell, *Masculinities* (Berkeley: University of California Press, 1995), 76–77.

22. Ibid., 77.

23. Joan Mellen, *Big Bad Wolves: Masculinity in the American Film* (New York: Pantheon, 1977), 3.

24. Wood, "Ideology, Genre, Auteur," 64, 63.

Chapter 1

1. James Agee, "David Wark Griffith," in *Agee on Film,* vol. 1 (Boston: Beacon Press, 1964), 316–17.

2. Ibid., 314.

3. Andrew Sarris, *The John Ford Movie Mystery* (London: Secker and Warburg; British Film Institute, 1976), 85. For a detailed discussion of Ford as a visual poet, see my "John Ford and Fenimore Cooper: Two Rode Together," in *John Ford Made Westerns: Filming the Legend in the Sound Era,* ed. Gaylyn Studlar and Matthew Bernstein (Bloomington: Indiana University Press, 2001), 193–219.

4. Agee, "Griffith," 317.

5. Neale, "Masculinity as Spectacle."

6. Scott Simmon, "'The Female of the Species': D. W. Griffith, Father of the Woman's Film," *Film Quarterly* 46, no. 2 (1992–93): 9.

7. Lewis Jacobs, *The Rise of the American Film: A Critical History* (New York: Teachers College Press, 1968), 96–97.

8. Lillian Gish, *The Movies, Mr. Griffith, and Me* (Englewood Cliffs, NJ: Prentice-Hall, 1969), 102.

9. Richard Dyer, "A White Star," *Sight and Sound* 3, no. 8 (1993): 24; James Naremore, "*True Heart Susie* and the Art of Lillian Gish," *Quarterly Review of Film Studies* 6, no. 1 (1981): 95.

10. Simmon, "The Female of the Species," 19.

11. Naremore, "*True Heart Susie,*" 83.

12. Robert M. Henderson, *D. W. Griffith: His Life and Work* (New York and London: Garland, 1985), 126.

13. Julia Lesage, "*Broken Blossoms:* Artful Racism, Artful Rape," *Jump Cut* 26 (1981): 51.

14. Karl Brown, *Adventures with D. W. Griffith* (New York: Da Capo, 1976), 241.

15. Dyer, "A White Star," 23.

16. Laura Mulvey, "Visual Pleasure and Narrative Cinema," *Screen* 16, no. 3 (1975): 6–18.

Reprinted in Mulvey, *Visual and Other Pleasures* (London: Macmillan, 1989).

17. John Berger, *Ways of Seeing* (London: British Broadcasting Corporation; Penguin, 1972), 51.

18. Krutnik, *In a Lonely Street*, 190.

19. Robin Wood, *Hollywood from Vietnam to Reagan* (New York: Columbia University Press, 1986), 254.

20. Roland Barthes, *Mythologies*, ed. and trans. Annette Lavers (New York: Hill and Wang), 19, 23.

21. Lesage, "Broken Blossoms," 52.

22. An image of Burrows in the ring appears on the cover of David Gerstner's book *Manly Arts: Masculinity and Nation in Early American Cinema* (Durham, NC: Duke University Press, 2006), although, oddly, the film is not discussed in the book.

23. Dudley Andrew, "*Broken Blossoms:* The Art and the Eros of a Perverse Text," *Quarterly Review of Film Studies* 6, no. 1 (1981): 85.

24. Leger Grindon, "Body and Soul: The Structure of Meaning in the Boxing Film Genre," *Cinema Journal* 35, no. 4 (1996): 54.

25. Simmon, "The Female of the Species," 10.

26. It is probably worth noting that the gun is being wielded by a woman accomplice, although this only demonstrates how thoroughly women are subject to the patriarchal order. On the importance of guns as iconographic representations of phallic power, see chapter 10 on the action films of Kathryn Bigelow.

27. Russell Merritt, "Rescued from a Perilous Nest: D. W. Griffith's Escape from Theater into Film," *Cinema Journal* 21, no. 1 (1981): 18, 3.

28. Lesage, "Broken Blossoms," 52.

29. Mulvey, "Visual Pleasure and Narrative Cinema," 14.

30. Mary Ann, Doane, "Film and the Masquerade—Theorizing the Female Spectator," *Screen* 23, nos. 3–4 (1982): 81–82.

31. Charles Affron, *Star Acting: Gish, Garbo, Davis* (New York: Dutton, 1977), 16.

32. David Cook, *A History of Narrative Film*, 3rd ed. (New York: Norton, 1981), 101.

33. Neale, "Masculinity as Spectacle," 19.

Chapter 2

1. While Rocco's response is, of course, eminently good business in that it encapsulates precisely the governing philosophy of corporations, his answer also

speaks to the gangster genre's relation to the horror film in that the gangster is monstrous to the extent to which his material acquisitiveness is driven by the desires of the id.

2. See Frederick Jackson Turner, "The Significance of the Frontier in American History," in *Frontier and Section: Selected Essays,* intro. Ray Allen Billington (Englewood Cliffs, NJ: Prentice-Hall, 1961), 37–62.

3. F. Scott Fitzgerald, *The Great Gatsby* (New York: Charles Scribner's Sons, 1925), 97.

4. Robin Wood, *Howard Hawks* (Detroit: Wayne State University Press, 2006), 65.

5. Jan Cohn, from *The Palace or the Poorhouse: The American House as Cultural Symbol* (East Lansing: Michigan State University Press, 1979), quoted in Fred E. H. Schroeder, "Houses," in *The Guide to United States Popular Culture,* ed. Ray B. Brown and Pat Brown (Bowling Green, OH: Bowling Green State University Popular Press, 2001), 413; Spiro Kostof, *America by Design* (New York: Oxford University Press, 1987).

6. Gerald Mast, *The Comic Mind: Comedy and the Movies* (Indianapolis: Bobbs-Merrill, 1973), 290–91.

7. Simon Louvish, *It's a Gift* (London: British Film Institute, 1994).

8. Henri Bergson, "Laughter," in *Comedy,* ed. Wylie Sypher (Garden City, NY: Anchor Doubleday, 1956), 73.

9. Royall Tyler, *The Contrast,* in *The Literature of America: Colonial Period,* ed. Larzer Ziff (New York: McGraw-Hill, 1970), 484.

10. Constance Rourke, *American Humor: A Study of the National Character* (Garden City, NY: Anchor Doubleday, 1931), 25, 35. For more on Yankee theater, see Francis Hodge, *Yankee Theater: The Image of America on the Stage, 1825–1850* (Austin: University of Texas Press, 1964).

11. Walt Whitman, "Song of Myself," in *Leaves of Grass,* ed. Sculley Bradley and Harold W. Blodgett (New York: Norton, 1973), 89.

12. Kenneth S. Lynn, ed., *The Comic Tradition in America: An Anthology of American Humor* (New York: Norton, 1958), 149.

13. Ibid., 153–54.

14. Raymond Durgnat, *The Crazy Mirror: Hollywood Comedy and the American Image* (New York: Delta, 1970), 142.

15. Lawrence Alloway, "Lawrence Alloway on the Iconography of the Movies," *Movie* 7 (February–March 1963): 4.

16. Maurice Charney, *Comedy High and Low: An Introduction to the Experience of Comedy* (New York: Oxford University Press, 1978), 82.

17. Mast, *The Comic Mind*, 12, 24.

18. Charney, *Comedy High and Low*, 54.

19. Andrew Sarris, *The American Cinema: Directors and Directions, 1929–1968* (New York: Dutton, 1968), 239.

20. Roland Barthes, "The Grain of the Voice," in *Image-Music-Text*, ed. and trans. Stephen Heath (New York: Hill and Wang, 1977), 179–89.

21. Durgnat, *The Crazy Mirror*, 145.

22. Fitzgerald, *The Great Gatsby*, 177.

23. Sarris, *The American Cinema*, 239.

24. W. C. Fields, with Ronald J. Fields, *W. C. Fields by Himself: His Intended Autobiography* (Englewood Cliffs, NJ: Prentice-Hall, 1973), 81.

25. Donald Deschner, *The Films of W. C. Fields* (Secaucus, NJ: Citadel Press, 1966), 77.

26. Ibid.

27. Sarris, *The American Cinema*, 238; Andrew Bergman, *We're in the Money* (New York: Harper and Row, 1972), 40.

28. Pierre Berton, *Hollywood's Canada: The Americanization of Our National Image* (Toronto: McClelland and Stewart, 1975), 25.

29. Ibid., 25–26.

30. William Cahn, *The Laugh Makers: A Pictorial History of American Comedians* (New York: C. P. Putnam's Sons, 1957), 77.

31. Durgnat, *The Crazy Mirror*, 146.

32. Bergman, *We're in the Money*, 40.

33. Berton, *Hollywood's Canada*, 26.

34. John Cawelti, "*Chinatown* and Generic Transformation in Recent American Films," in *Film Genre Reader 3*, ed. Grant, 243–61.

35. Bergman, *We're in the Money*, 40.

36. Hector St. John de Crèvecoeur, *Letters from an American Farmer* (New York: Dutton, 1975), 36, 40, 39, 48.

Chapter 3

1. Peter Biskind, *Seeing Is Believing: How Hollywood Taught Us to Stop Worrying and Love the Fifties* (New York: Pantheon, 1983), 282; Michael Coyne, *The Crowded Prairie: American Identity in the Hollywood Western* (London and New York: I. B. Tauris, 1997), 56–57.

2. Robert Sklar, "*Red River:* Empire to the West," *Cineaste* 9, no. 4 (1978): 15.

3. Coyne, *The Crowded Prairie,* 54.

4. Chuck Maland, "'Powered by a Ford'?: Dudley Nichols, Authorship, and Cultural Ethos in *Stagecoach,*" in *John Ford's Stagecoach,* ed. Barry Keith Grant (New York and Cambridge: Cambridge University Press, 2003), 48–81.

5. Sklar, "Empire to the West," 15.

6. William R. Meyer, *The Making of the Great Westerns* (New Rochelle, NY: Arlington House, 1979), 171.

7. Wood, *Howard Hawks,* 5.

8. Ian Cameron, *Movie* 1 (June 1962): 9. Reprinted in Ian Cameron, ed., *Movie Reader* (New York: Praeger, 1972), 2.

9. Peter Wollen, *Signs and Meaning in the Cinema,* 3rd ed. (Bloomington: Indiana University Press, 1972), 80.

10. Wood, *Howard Hawks,* esp. 68.

11. Molly Haskell, "The Cinema of Howard Hawks," *Intellectual Digest* 2, no. 8 (1972): 57.

12. Joseph McBride, *Hawks on Hawks* (Berkeley: University of California Press, 1982), 112.

13. Turner, "The Significance of the Frontier in American History," in *Frontier and Section,* 38.

14. Lewis Mumford, *The Golden Day: A Study in American Literature and Culture* (New York: Dover, 1968), 19.

15. Richard Thompson, "Hawks at Seventy," in *Focus on Howard Hawks,* ed. Joseph McBride (Englewood Cliffs, NJ: Prentice-Hall, 1972), 143.

16. Manny Farber, *Movies* (New York: Hillstone, 1971), 30.

17. Marius Bewley, *The Eccentric Design: Form in the Classic American Novel* (New York: Columbia University Press, 1963), 73.

18. Jacques Rivette, "Rivette on Hawks," *Movie* 5 (December 1962): 19.

19. Wollen, *Signs and Meaning,* 81.

20. Hawks admitted that deliberately shooting the scene with Wayne and the passing cloud was consciously inspired by Ford's imagery. "A Discussion with the Audience of the 1970 Chicago Film Festival," in *Focus on Howard Hawks,* ed. McBride, 14–15.

21. Meyer, *Making of the Great Westerns,* 170.

22. D. H. Lawrence, *Studies in Classic American Literature* (New York: Penguin, 1977), 12.

23. James Fenimore Cooper, *The Last of the Mohicans* (Boston: Houghton Mifflin, 1958), 43.

24. Biskind, *Seeing Is Believing*, 282, 281. In this context the casting of the two leads is crucial to the film's meaning. John Wayne is of course the premier icon of rugged American individualism, his image established particularly with *Stagecoach* in 1939 and then solidified in the war films and westerns he made during World War II and into the early '50s. In *The Fighting Seabees* (1944), made during the war, Wayne dies at the end in a deliberate, sacrificial self-immolation on a tractor because he is intractable, too rugged an individual to join the disciplined group effort required of a successful military unit—a theme explored in paradigmatic form in Hawks's *Air Force*, made just one year before *The Fighting Seabees*. By contrast, newcomer Monty Clift, already known for his work in the theater, was an introspective method actor with a more vulnerable and androgynous appeal, prefiguring by a couple of years the popularity of such actors as Marlon Brando and James Dean, and the generational angst they represented.

25. Sklar, "Empire to the West," 16.

26. André Bazin, "The Evolution of the Western," in *What Is Cinema?* vol. 2, ed. and trans. Hugh Gray (Berkeley: University of California Press, 1971), 151, 154.

27. Wollen, *Signs and Meaning*, 88.

28. Peter John Dyer, "Sling the Lamps Low," in *Focus on Howard Hawks*, ed. McBride, 92.

29. Gerald Mast, *Howard Hawks, Storyteller* (New York and Oxford: Oxford University Press, 1982), esp. 314, 321, 325.

30. Janet Bergstrom, "Alternation, Segmentation, Hypnosis: Interview with Raymond Bellour," *camera obscura* 3–4 (1979): 92.

31. Peter Bogdanovich, "Interview with Howard Hawks," *Movie* 5 (December 1962): 15.

Chapter 4

1. Thomas Doherty, *Teenagers and Teenpics: The Juvenilization of the American Movies in the 1950s* (Boston: Unwin Hyman, 1988). See also Pamela Robertson Wojcik and Arthur Knight, eds., *Soundtrack Available: Essays on Film and Popular Music* (Durham, NC: Duke University Press, 2001) and Ian Inglis, ed., *Popular Music and Film* (London and New York: Wallflower Press, 2003).

2. "Of course, the real equation between popular music and anti-social violence would emerge in the rock culture of the 1960s." Jane Feuer, *The Hollywood Musical* (Bloomington: Indiana University Press, 1982), 108. Such a comment begs for elaboration.

3. For example, Richard Staehling, "From *Rock Around the Clock* to *The Trip:* The Truth about Teen Movies," in *Kings of the Bs,* ed. Todd McCarthy and Charles Flynn (New York: Dutton, 1975), 220–51; David Ehrenstein and Bill Reed, *Rock on Film* (New York: Delilah Books, 1982); and Dave Marsh, "Schlock Around the Rock," *Film Comment* 14, no. 4 (1978): 7–13.

4. Rick Altman, "A Semantic/Syntactic Approach to Film Genre," in *Film Genre Reader 3,* ed. Grant, 28.

5. These ideas are explored in Feuer, *The Hollywood Musical,* and in Richard Dyer, "Entertainment and Utopia," and Rick Altman, "The American Film Musical: Paradigmatic Structure and Mediatory Function," in *Genre: The Musical,* ed. Rick Altman (London and Boston: Routledge and Kegan Paul, 1981), 175–89 and 197–207, respectively.

6. As Robin Wood notes in discussing the Astaire-Rogers musicals, for example, the "never never change" sentiment of "The Way You Look Tonight" becomes the musical's equivalent of living happily ever after. "Never Never Change, Always Gonna Dance," *Film Comment* 15, no. 5 (1979): 29–31.

7. Quoted in William Pechter, "Movie Musicals," *Commentary* 53, no. 5 (1972): 78.

8. Feuer, *Hollywood Musical,* 3–7.

9. The subsequent revelation regarding Richard Penniman's (Little Richard) struggle with homosexuality in retrospect provides even further evidence of the extent to which phallic sexuality was performative in early rock 'n' roll.

10. Andrew Dowdy, *The Films of the Fifties: The American State of Mind* (New York: William Morrow, 1973), chap. 7.

11. Michael Wood, *America in the Movies* (New York: Delta, 1976), 153.

12. Dowdy, *Films of the Fifties,* 123.

13. Lee Edward Stern, *The Movie Musical* (New York: Pyramid, 1974), 19.

14. For more on the ideological strategies at work in *The King of Jazz,* see my essay "Jazz, Ideology, and the Animated Cartoon," in *Film's Musical Moments,* ed. Ian Conrich and Estella Tincknell (Edinburgh: Edinburgh University Press, 2006), 17–27.

15. See Staehling, "From *Rock Around the Clock* to *The Trip.*"

16. Steve Chapple and Reebee Garofalo, *Rock 'n' Roll Is Here to Pay: The History and Politics of the Music Industry* (Elmhurst, IL: Music Business Publications, 1977), 246.

17. Gael Sweeney, "The Face on the Lunch Box: Television's Construction of the Teen Idol," *Velvet Light Trap* 33 (Spring 1994): 52–53.

18. Simon Frith and Angela McRobbie, "Rock and Sexuality," in *On Record: Rock, Pop,*

and the Written Word, ed. Simon Frith and Andrew Goodwin (New York: Pantheon, 1990), 378.

19. Sweeney, "Face on the Lunch Box," 51. See also Greg Shaw, "The Teen Idols," in *The Rolling Stone Illustrated History of Rock and Roll,* ed. Jim Miller (New York: Random House, 1980), 97.

20. Frith and McRobbie, "Rock and Sexuality," 375.

21. Sweeney, "Face on the Lunch Box," 51.

22. Frith and McRobbie, "Rock and Sexuality," 375.

23. Theodor Adorno, "On Popular Music," in *On Record,* ed. Frith and Goodwin, 305.

24. "Scott Spenser's Guilty Pleasures," *Film Comment* 17, no. 5 (1981): 22.

25. Altman, "A Semantic/Syntactic Approach to Film Genre," 16.

Chapter 5

1. Jean-Pierre Coursodon, with Pierre Sauvage, *American Directors,* vol. 2 (New York: McGraw-Hill, 1983), 200.

2. Peter Lehman and Susan Hunt, "'The Inner Man': Mind, Body, and Transformations of Masculinity in *The Nutty Professor,*" in *Enfant Terrible! Jerry Lewis in American Film,* ed. Murray Pomerance (New York: New York University Press, 2002), 195.

3. Leonard Maltin, ed., *Leonard Maltin's 2005 Movie Guide* (New York: Plume, 2004), 348.

4. Mast, *The Comic Mind,* 298.

5. Shawn Levy, *King of Comedy: The Life and Art of Jerry Lewis* (New York: St. Martin's Press, 1996), 215.

6. Ibid., 207.

7. Ibid.

8. Dana Polan, "Being and Nuttiness: Jerry Lewis and the French," *Journal of Popular Film and Television* 12, no. 1 (1984): 42–43.

9. Jerry Lewis, *The Total Film-Maker* (New York: Warners Paperback Library, 1973), 82.

10. Ibid., 36.

11. Polan, "Being and Nuttiness," 45.

12. Levy, *King of Comedy,* 227.

13. Durgnat, *The Crazy Mirror,* 234.

14. Barthes, "The Grain of the Voice," in *Image-Music-Text,* 179–89.

15. Doherty, *Teenagers and Teenpics,* 44–46, 51.

16. See, for example, Albert K. Cohen, *Delinquent Boys: The Culture of the Gang* (Glencoe, IL: Free Press, 1955).

17. David Riesman, *The Lonely Crowd* (New Haven, CT: Yale University Press, 1950).

18. William H. Whyte Jr., *The Organization Man* (New York: Simon and Schuster), 1956.

19. Durgnat, *The Crazy Mirror,* 235.

20. Scott Bukatman, "Paralysis in Motion: Jerry Lewis's Life as a Man," in *Comedy/Cinema/Theory,* ed. Andrew S. Horton (Berkeley: University of California Press, 1991), 196.

21. Doherty, *Teenagers and Teenpics,* 44.

22. Jon Lewis, *The Road to Romance and Ruin: Teen Films and Youth Culture* (New York: Routledge, 1992), 3.

23. Staehling, "From *Rock Around the Clock* to *The Trip,*" 230–31.

24. Bukatman, "Paralysis in Motion," 191.

25. Staehling, "From *Rock Around the Clock* to *The Trip,*" 226.

26. Ibid., 236.

27. Levy, *King of Comedy,* 226.

28. Mast, *The Comic Mind,* 79.

29. Claudia Gorbman, *Unheard Melodies: Narrative Film Music* (Bloomington: Indiana University Press, 1997), 86.

30. Levy, *King of Comedy,* 226.

31. Ibid., 227.

32. Bukatman, "Paralysis in Motion," 188, 201.

33. Mast, *The Comic Mind,* 298.

34. Wood, *Hollywood from Vietnam to Reagan,* 46.

35. Sarris, *The American Cinema,* 244.

Chapter 6

1. Stephen Mamber, "The New Documentaries of Frederick Wiseman," *Cinema* 6, no. 1 (1970): 39.

2. See, for example, John Graham, "How Far Can You Go: A Conversation with Fred Wiseman," *Contempora* 1, no. 4 (1970): 33; and Ira Halberstadt, "An Interview with Fred Wiseman," *Filmmakers Newsletter* 7, no. 4 (1974): 25.

3. Over the years it has been announced periodically that Wiseman has been involved

in fiction film projects. In 1970 an interviewer reported that Wiseman was then at work on a script, to be produced in Hollywood, that the filmmaker described as "an adaptation of a novel about a young man who goes AWOL from the army." Donald McWilliams, "Frederick Wiseman," *Film Quarterly* 24, no. 1 (1970): 26. In the same year Wiseman told another interviewer that he was writing a script with a grant from the American Film Institute wherein he wanted to use a documentary approach but also employ "a mosaic technique so the film will not have the conventional story line with beginning, middle and end, but will reveal the relationships of the characters to each other"—which of course is the way Wiseman structures his documentaries. Janet Handelman, "An Interview with Frederick Wiseman," *Film Library Quarterly* 3, no. 3 (1970): 9. Four years later, on the day after the WNET screening of *Primate* (1974), the *New York Times* reported that Wiseman was preparing to make a fiction film tentatively titled *Yes Yes, No No.* The article quotes Wiseman as saying that he has been working on the script intermittently for two years, and that the story is "a contemporary murder-and-trial drama set in Boston." A. H. Weiler, "Wiseman to Make 'Yes Yes, No No,' First Fiction Film," *New York Times,* December 6, 1974, 78. Wiseman did work as co-writer on Norman Jewison's *The Thomas Crown Affair* (1968), and he also wrote an early draft of the successful 1980 feature, *The Stunt Man,* directed by Richard Rush, but was uncredited. Thomas W. Benson and Carolyn Anderson, *Reality Fictions: The Films of Frederick Wiseman* (Carbondale: Southern Illinois University Press, 1989), 32.

4. Benson and Anderson, *Reality Fictions,* 11; and Christina Robb, "Focus on Life," *Boston Globe Magazine,* January 23, 1983, 27.

5. For a detailed analysis of Wiseman's documentaries through *Near Death* (1989), including their relationship to genre conventions, see my *Voyages of Discovery: The Cinema of Frederick Wiseman* (Urbana: University of Illinois Press, 1992).

6. See, for example, Beatrice Berg, "I Was Fed Up with Hollywood Fantasies," *New York Times,* February 1, 1970, sec. 2, 25–26.

7. Donald Bogle, *Toms, Coons, Mulattoes, Mammies, & Bucks: An Interpretive History of Blacks in American Films* (New York: Bantam, 1974), 202.

8. See Warren Miller, "Progress in Documentary," in *The Documentary Tradition: From Nanook to Woodstock,* ed. Lewis Jacobs, 2nd ed. (New York: Norton, 1979), 247–50.

9. Warren Miller, *The Cool World* (New York: Crest, 1965), 26.

10. Anthony Burgess, *A Clockwork Orange* (London: Heinemann, 1962), 184.

11. Quoted in "The Talk of the Town," *New Yorker,* September 14, 1963, 34.

12. Ibid.; Gordon Hitchens, "*The Cool World,*" *Film Comment* 2, no. 2 (1964): 52.

13. Lauren Rabinovitz, *Points of Resistance: Women, Power, and Politics in the New York Avant-Garde Cinema, 1943–71* (Urbana: University of Illinois Press, 1990).

14. Louis Marcorelles, *Living Cinema: New Directions in Contemporary Filmmaking,* trans. Isabel Quigly (London: George Allen and Unwin, 1973).

15. Rabinovitz, *Points of Resistance,* 100.

16. Andrew Sarris, "*The Cool World,*" *Village Voice,* April 23, 1964, reprinted in Sarris, *Confessions of a Cultist: Notes on the Cinema, 1955–1969* (New York: Simon and Schuster, 1970), 135–36; Hitchens, "*The Cool World,*" 53; and Dwight MacDonald, "*The Cool World,*" in *Dwight MacDonald on Movies* (Englewood Cliffs, NJ: Prentice-Hall, 1969), 323–27.

17. Richard Wright, *Native Son* (New York: Harper and Row, 1966), 33.

18. Jonas Mekas, "Notes on the New American Cinema," *Film Culture* 24 (Spring 1962): 6–16.

19. W. E. B. Du Bois, *The Souls of Black Folk,* in *Three Negro Classics* (New York: Avon, 1965), 214–15. See also Thomas Cripps, *Black Film as Genre* (Bloomington: Indiana University Press, 1979), 5.

20. Addison Gayle, ed., *The Black Aesthetic* (Garden City, NY: Doubleday, 1971), xxi.

21. See Henry Louis Gates Jr., *The Signifying Monkey: A Theory of Afro-American Literary Criticism* (New York: Oxford University Press, 1988).

22. Sarris, "*The Cool World,*" 136.

23. Bill Nichols, *Ideology and the Image* (Bloomington: Indiana University Press, 1981), chap. 7.

24. Berg, "I Was Fed Up with Hollywood Fantasies," 25.

25. Harriet Polt, "*The Cool World,*" *Film Quarterly* 17, no. 2 (1963): 34.

26. Bogle, *Toms, Coons, Mulattoes, Mammies, & Bucks,* 284.

27. David Eames, "Watching Wiseman Watch," *New York Times Magazine,* October 2, 1977, 99.

28. Quoted in Benson and Anderson, *Reality Fictions,* 39.

29. Bogle, *Toms, Coons, Mulattoes, Mammies, & Bucks,* 258.

30. Quoted in "Talk of the Town," 35.

Chapter 7

1. See, for example, Evelyn Fox Keller, *Reflections on Gender and Science* (New Haven, CT: Yale University Press, 1985); Donna Haraway, *Simians, Cyborgs, and Women* (New

York: Routledge, 1991); Judith Wajcman, *Feminism Confronts Technology* (University Park: Pennsylvania State University Press, 1991); and Lynn Hankinson Nelson and Jack Nelson, eds., *Feminism, Science, and the Philosophy of Science* (Boston: Kluwer Academic, 1996).

2. Keller, *Reflections on Gender and Science*, 34.

3. Damon Knight, *In Search of Wonder: Essays on Modern Science Fiction,* rev. ed. (Chicago: Advent, 1967), 13.

4. Robert Scholes explains the special dynamic of such fiction this way: "In the worlds of SF, we are made to see the stoniness of a stone by watching it move and change in an accelerated time-scale, or by encountering an anti-stone with properties so unstony that we are forced to reinvestigate the true quality of stoniness." *Structural Fabulation: An Essay on Fiction of the Future* (Notre Dame, IN: University of Notre Dame Press, 1975), 46.

5. See Darko Suvin, *Metamorphoses of Science Fiction: On the Poetics and History of a Literary Genre* (New Haven, CT: Yale University Press, 1979), chap. 1.

6. For an overview of feminist criticism of *Frankenstein,* see Catherine Gallagher and Elizabeth Young, "Feminism and *Frankenstein:* A Short History of American Feminist Criticism," *Journal of Contemporary Thought* 1, no. 1 (1991): 97–109.

7. For a discussion of Hawthorne's science fiction, see H. Bruce Franklin, *Future Perfect: American Science Fiction of the Nineteenth Century* (New York: Oxford University Press, 1966), 3–64.

8. Scholes, *Structural Fabulation*, 15.

9. Hence the number of westerns that have been adapted as science fiction. For more on this, see my "Strange Days: Gender and Ideology in New Genre Films," in *Ladies and Gentlemen, Boys and Girls: Gender in Film at the End of the Twentieth Century,* ed. Murray Pomerance (Albany: State University of New York Press, 2000), 186–88.

10. Stanislaw Lem, *Solaris* (New York: Berkley, 1971), 8–10.

11. Carl Freedman, "Science Fiction and the Triumph of Feminism: Barr's Future Females, the Next Generation," *Science Fiction Studies* 81 (2000): 278.

12. Leslie Fiedler, *Love and Death in the American Novel* (New York: Delta, 1967); Lawrence, *Studies in Classic American Literature*, 40–51.

13. James Tiptree Jr., "The Women Men Don't See," in *The New Women of Wonder: Recent Science Fiction Stories by Women about Women,* ed. Pamela Sargent (New York: Vintage, 1977), 205.

14. Mulvey, "Visual Pleasure and Narrative Cinema."

15. James Cameron's *True Lies* (1994) offers a particularly egregious example of the

same dynamic of recuperation in the overlapping genre of the action film. See my comments on this film in chapter 10.

16. John Cawelti, "*Chinatown* and Generic Transformation in Recent American Films," in *Film Genre Reader 3,* ed. Grant, 251. The only film Cawelti discusses that predates *2001* is Arthur Penn's *Bonnie and Clyde* (1967).

17. James Howard, *Stanley Kubrick Companion* (London: Batsford, 1999), 107.

18. Robert Kolker, *A Cinema of Loneliness: Penn, Stone, Kubrick, Scorsese, Spielberg, Altman,* 3rd ed. (New York: Oxford University Press, 2000), 135.

19. David Bordwell, "Story Causality and Motivation," in Bordwell, Janet Staiger, and Kristin Thompson, *The Classical Hollywood Cinema,* chap. 2.

20. Vivian Sobchack, "The Virginity of Astronauts: Sex and the Science Fiction Film," in *Alien Zone: Cultural Theory and Contemporary Science Fiction Cinema,* ed. Annette Kuhn (New York: Verso, 1990), 107.

21. Bordwell, Staiger, and Thompson, *Classical Hollywood Cinema,* 54.

22. Ibid., chap. 5.

23. Norman Kagan, *The Cinema of Stanley Kubrick* (New York: Grove, 1972), 150.

24. Alexander Walker, *Stanley Kubrick Directs,* expanded ed. (New York: Harcourt Brace Jovanovich, 1972), 259.

25. Mario Falsetto, *Stanley Kubrick: A Narrative and Stylistic Analysis* (Westport, CT: Praeger, 1994), 115–28.

26. Evelyn Fox Keller, *A Feeling for the Organism* (New York: Freeman, 1989). See also Nancy Tuana, "Revaluing Science: Starting from the Practices of Women," in Nelson and Nelson, eds., *Feminism, Science, and the Philosophy of Science,* 22–91.

27. Stan Brakhage, "Metaphors on Vision," *Film Culture* 30 (Fall 1963): n.p.

28. Stanley Kubrick, quoted in Howard, *Stanley Kubrick Companion,* 112.

29. Arthur C. Clarke, "The Sentinel," in *The Making of Kubrick's 2001,* ed. Jerome Agel (New York: New American Library, 1970), 22.

30. Clarke quoted in Howard, *Stanley Kubrick Companion,* 104.

31. Ina Rae Hark, "Animals or Romans: Looking at Masculinity in *Spartacus,*" in *Screening the Male,* ed. Cohan and Hark, 169.

32. Kolker, *A Cinema of Loneliness,* 136–37.

33. H. G. Wells noted this distinctive ability of the new medium of cinema in his first novel, *The Time Machine,* published in 1895, the same year as the first public film screening, where he describes the experience of time traveling as being like watching a speeded-up film.

34. Olaf Stapledon, *Last and First Men: A Story of the Near and Far Future* (New York:

Viking Penguin, 1987), 134. In his preface, Stapledon writes, "To romance of the far future, then, is to attempt to see the human race in its cosmic setting, and to mould our hearts to entertain new values" (11).

Chapter 8

1. Gregory A. Waller, *The Living and the Undead: From Stoker's* Dracula *to Romero's* Dawn of the Dead (Urbana: University of Illinois Press, 1986), 283.
2. Paul Gagne, *The Zombies That Ate Pittsburgh: The Films of George Romero* (New York: Dodd, Mead, 1987), 11; John McCarty, *Splatter Movies: Breaking the Last Taboo of the Screen* (New York: St. Martin's Press, 1984), 58.
3. George A. Romero and Susanna Sparrow, afterword to *Martin* (New York: Day Books, 1980), 209.
4. Wood, *Hollywood from Vietnam to Reagan,* 195.
5. See McCarty, *Splatter Movies,* 1, 5.
6. *Dawn of the Dead,* released without an MPAA rating because of its predecessor's cult reputation, still managed to become, like *Night,* one of the most commercially successful American independent features ever made.
7. I exclude from this series *Diary of the Dead* (2007) and *Survival of the Dead* (2009), the narratives of which intersect with each other and seem to exist in a different diegetic world than the other four films.
8. David Pirie, *The Vampire Cinema* (New York: Crescent Books, 1977), 141; Elliot Stein, "The Night of the Living Dead," *Sight and Sound* 39, no. 2 (1970): 105; Pirie, "New Blood," *Sight and Sound* 40, no. 2 (1971): 73–75; Wood, *Hollywood from Vietnam to Reagan,* 118; Gagne, *Zombies,* 87.
9. Dan Yakir, "Mourning Becomes Romero," *Film Comment* 15, no. 3 (1979): 60–65.
10. John Russo, *The Complete* Night of the Living Dead *Filmbook* (New York: Harmony Books, 1985), 35; Gagne, *Zombies,* 25.
11. Yakir, "Mourning Becomes Romero," 65; Gagne, *Zombies,* 56.
12. Waller, *The Living and the Undead,* 18.
13. Gagne, *Zombies,* 7, 11.
14. Ibid., 108.
15. Wood, *Howard Hawks,* 11.
16. Molly Haskell, "The Cinema of Howard Hawks," 57.
17. See Wood, *Howard Hawks,* esp. chaps. 2 and 3; and Wollen, *Signs and Meaning in*

the Cinema, chap. 2.

18. Naomi Wise, "The Hawksian Woman," *Take One* 3, no. 3 (1972): 17. See also Molly Haskell, *From Reverence to Rape: The Treatment of Women in the Movies* (Baltimore: Penguin, 1974), 208–13.

19. Claire Johnston, "Women's Cinema as Counter Cinema," in *Movies and Methods,* ed. Bill Nichols (Berkeley: University of California Press, 1976), 213; Raymond Durgnat, "Hawks Isn't Good Enough," *Film Comment* 13, no. 4 (1977): 15–16.

20. Durgnat, "Hawks Isn't Good Enough," 9, 11.

21. Waller, *The Living and the Undead,* 310.

22. Linda Williams, "When the Woman Looks," in *The Dread of Difference: Gender and the Horror Film,* ed. Barry Keith Grant (Austin: University of Texas Press, 1996), 15–34.

23. See Williams, "When the Woman Looks"; and Barbara Creed, "Phallic Panic: Male Hysteria and *Dead Ringers,*" *Screen* 31, no. 2 (1990): 125–64. This scene in *Alien* is also discussed in the previous chapter.

24. Robin Wood, "An Introduction to the American Horror Film," in *Planks of Reason,* ed. Grant and Sharrett, 134.

25. Yakir, "Mourning Becomes Romero," 62.

26. R. H. W. Dillard, "*Night of the Living Dead*: 'It's Not Just Like a Wind Passing Through,'" in *Horror Films* (New York: Monarch Press, 1976), 55–82.

27. Robin Wood, "Apocalypse Now: Notes on the Living Dead," in *Hollywood from Vietnam to Reagan,* 114–21.

28. Pam Cook, "Exploitation Films and Feminism," *Screen* 17, no. 2 (1976): 122–27; and Barbara Klinger, "'Cinema/Ideology/Criticism' Revisited: The Progressive Genre," in *Film Genre Reader 3,* ed. Grant, 75–91.

29. Romero and Sparrow, afterword to *Martin,* 210.

Chapter 9

1. Andrew Tudor, *Image and Influence: Studies in the Sociology of Film* (New York: St. Martin's Press, 1975), 208.

2. Rick Altman, "A Semantic/Syntactic Approach to Film Genre," in *Film Genre Reader 3,* ed. Grant, 27–41.

3. Jerry Savells, "Who Are the 'Yuppies'? A Popular View," *International Journal of Comparative Sociology* 27, nos. 3–4 (1986): 234.

4. Jerry Adler et al. "The Year of the Yuppie," *Newsweek,* December 31, 1984, 14–31;

John L. Hammond, "Yuppies," *Public Opinion Quarterly* 50 (Winter 1986): 496.

5. Marissa Piesman and Marilee Hartley, *The Yuppie Handbook: The State of the Art Manual for Young Urban Professionals* (New York: Long Shadow Books, 1984), 12.

6. Adler et al., "Year of the Yuppie," 19.

7. Savells, "Who Are the 'Yuppies'?" 235.

8. Susan Kastner, "So . . . Where Have All the Yuppies Gone?" *Toronto Star,* April 7, 1991, A4.

9. Bruce Kawin, "Children of the Light," in *Film Genre Reader 3,* ed. Grant, 325.

10. John Powers, "Bleak Chic," *American Film* 12, no. 5 (1987): 51.

11. *Obsessed* (2009), a late Obama-period entry in the yuppie cycle, repeats the narrative of *The Temp,* adding the dimension of race by making the young and successful male executive black and the scheming temp a white blond. A number of other horror films have been prompted by the recession that began at the end of the Bush administration in 2008, including Sam Raimi's *Drag Me to Hell* (2009).

12. Wood, *Hollywood from Vietnam to Reagan,* 90; Carol J. Clover, *Men, Women, and Chain Saws: Gender in the Modern Horror Film* (Princeton, NJ: Princeton University Press, 1992), 30.

13. The importance to yuppie horror of Ira Levin's fiction, including *Rosemary's Baby, The Stepford Wives,* and *Sliver,* is significant and certainly a subject for further research.

14. Carol M. Ward, "The Hollywood Yuppie: 1980–88," in *Beyond the Stars: Stock Characters in American Popular Film,* ed. Paul Loukides and Linda K. Fuller (Bowling Green, OH: Popular Press, 1990), 97.

15. Stephen King, *Danse Macabre* (New York: Everest House, 1981), 138.

16. For more on this point, see my "'Sensuous Elaboration': Reason and the Visible in Science Fiction Film," in *Alien Zone II: The Spaces of Science Fiction Cinema,* ed. Annette Kuhn (London and New York: Verso), 16–30.

17. Wood, *Hollywood from Vietnam to Reagan,* 79.

18. Roland Barthes, "Myth Today," in *Mythologies,* 151; Savells, "Who Are the 'Yuppies'?" 235.

19. Pam Cook, "Scorsese's Masquerade," *Sight and Sound* 1, no. 12 (1992): 15; Bruce Kawin, *Mindscreen: Bergman, Godard, and First-Person Film* (Princeton, NJ: Princeton University Press, 1978).

20. It is worth noting that the action in director Adrian Lyne's next film, *Jacob's Ladder* (1990), is revealed explicitly at the end to have occurred entirely in the mind of the protagonist at the moment of his death. The only other similar reading of *Fatal*

Attraction of which I am aware is N. A. Morris's "In Defense of Fatal Attraction," *Movie* 33 (Winter 1989): 53–55.

21. See Kaja Silverman, *The Acoustic Mirror: The Female Voice in Psychoanalysis and Cinema* (Bloomington: Indiana University Press, 1988); and Mary Ann Doane, *The Desire to Desire: The Woman's Film of the 1940s* (Bloomington: Indiana University Press, 1987).

22. Ward, "The Hollywood Yuppie," 106.

23. Adler et al., "Year of the Yuppie," 24.

24. Brett Easton Ellis, *American Psycho* (New York: Vintage, 1991), 375.

25. Ibid., 5, 8, 114. For more on Ellis's novel, see my "American Psycho/sis: The Pure Products of America Go Crazy," in *Mythologies of Violence in Postmodern Media,* ed. Christopher Sharrett (Detroit: Wayne State University Press, 1999), 23–40.

26. Adler et al., "Year of the Yuppie," 19.

27. Elayne Rapping, "*The Hand That Rocks the Cradle,*" *Cineaste* 19, nos. 2–3 (1992): 65.

28. Tzvetan Todorov, *The Fantastic: A Structural Approach to a Literary Genre,* trans. Richard Howard (Ithaca, NY: Cornell University Press, 1975). See also Tom Gunning, "'Like unto a Leopard': Figurative Discourse in *Cat People* and Todorov's The Fantastic," *Wide Angle* 10, no. 3 (1988): 30–39.

29. Fredric Jameson, *Postmodernism, or, the Cultural Logic of Late Capitalism* (Durham, NC: Duke University Press, 1992), 291.

30. Wood, *Hollywood from Vietnam to Reagan,* 78.

31. In the context of romantic comedy, Steve Neale argues that the end of *Something Wild* "manoeuvres its couple . . . into an 'old-fashioned,' 'traditional' and ideologically conventional position." "The Big Romance or Something Wild? Romantic Comedy Today," *Screen* 33, no. 3 (1992): 297.

32. Jameson, *Postmodernism,* 289–90.

33. George F. Will, "Reality Says You Can't Have It All," *Newsweek,* February 3, 1986, 78.

34. Adler et al., "Year of the Yuppie," 14.

35. Hammond, "Yuppies," 496.

36. Kastner, "So . . . Where Have All the Yuppies Gone?," A4.

37. Altman, "Semantic/Syntactic Approach," 39.

38. King, *Danse Macabre,* 138.

39. Altman, "Semantic/Syntactic Approach," 36.

Chapter 10

1. Anna Powell, "Blood on the Borders—*Near Dark* and *Blue Steel*," *Screen* 35, no. 2 (1994): 136.

2. Christina Lane discusses some of these comments in *Feminist Hollywood: From Born in Flames to Point Break* (Detroit: Wayne State University Press, 2000), 103–4.

3. Neale, "Masculinity as Spectacle," 11.

4. Laura Rascaroli, "Steel in the Gaze: On POV and the Discourse of Vision in Kathryn Bigelow's Cinema," *Screen* 38, no. 3 (1997): 232.

5. "Momentum and Design: Kathryn Bigelow Interviewed by Gavin Smith," *Film Comment* 31, no. 5 (1995): 46.

6. Barbara Creed, "From Here to Modernity: Feminism and Postmodernism," *Screen* 28, no. 2 (1987): 65.

7. Yvonne Tasker, *Spectacular Bodies: Gender, Genre, and the Action Cinema* (London and New York: Routledge, 1993); Susan Jeffords, *Hardbodies: Hollywood Masculinity in the Reagan Era* (New Brunswick, NJ: Rutgers University Press, 1994).

8. Peter N. Chumo II, "At the Generic Crossroads with *Thelma and Louise*," *Post Script* 13, no. 2 (1994): 5.

9. Rebecca Bell-Metereau, *Hollywood Androgyny*, 2nd ed. (New York: Columbia University Press, 1993), 248.

10. Brian Henderson, "Towards a Non-Bourgeois Camera Style," *Film Quarterly* 24, no. 2 (1970–71): 2–14.

11. Lane, *Feminist Hollywood*, 110.

12. See, for example, Jim Kitses, *Horizons West* (Bloomington: Indiana University Press; London: British Film Institute, 1970), chap. 1; and Robin Wood, "An Introduction to the American Horror Film," in *Planks of Reason*, ed. Grant and Sharrett, esp. 107–15.

13. Susan Sontag, "The Imagination of Disaster," in *Against Interpretation and Other Essays* (New York: Delta, 1966), 213.

14. Christopher Sharrett, "The Horror Film in Neoconservative Culture," in *The Dread of Difference*, ed. Grant, 259–61. For Robin Wood's distinction between "progressive" and "reactionary" horror films, see Wood, "Introduction to the American Horror Film."

15. Allen Ginsberg, "Wichita Vortex Sutra," *Planet News* (San Francisco: City Lights, 1968).

16. Powell, "Blood on the Borders," 145.

17. Ibid., 147. See also Clover, *Men, Women, and Chain Saws.*

18. Tasker, *Spectacular Bodies,* 147.

19. Kathleen Murphy describes the scene as "berserker campaign iconography promising good times, a tiger in every tank." "Black Arts," *Film Comment* 31, no. 5 (1995): 53.

20. Interestingly, Reeves would later star in an even more apt role as *Johnny Mnemonic* (1995).

21. See Cynthia J. Fuchs, "The Buddy Politic," in *Screening the Male,* ed. Cohan and Hark, 194–210.

22. "Momentum and Design," 48.

23. Robin Wood, "The Spectres Emerge in Daylight," *Cineaction* 43 (1997): 7.

24. Wood, *Hollywood from Vietnam to Reagan,* 46.

25. "Momentum and Design," 49.

26. Amy Taubin, "Hard Wired: Kathryn Bigelow's *The Hurt Locker,*" *Film Comment* 45, no. 3 (2009): 35.

27. As this book was going to press, *The Hurt Locker* won Academy Awards for both Best film and Best Director for Bigelow, beating out, among the other nominated films, ex-husband James Cameron's *Avatar* (2009). Among the several ironies involved in the film's upset win is the fact that Bigelow's work has now come to be embraced by the industry mainstream.

28. Steven Cohan and Ina Rae Hark, "Introduction" in *Screening the Male: Exploring Masculinities in Hollywood Cinema,* 2.

29. See Karen Schneider, "With Violence If Necessary: Rearticulating the Family in the Contemporary Action-Thriller," *Journal of Popular Film and Television* 27, no. 1 (1999): 2–11.

30. John Cawelti, "Chinatown and Generic Transformation in Recent American Films," in *Film Genre Reader 3,* ed. Grant, 251.

Filmography

Among the many films discussed in this book, the following are considered in some detail.

Broken Blossoms, or The Yellow Man and the Girl (D. W. Griffith Productions/Paramount/ United Artists, 1919). Director, Producer: D. W. Griffith. Screenplay: D. W. Griffith, based on the story "The Chink and the Child" by Thomas Burke. Photography: G. W. "Billy" Bitzer. Cast: Richard Barthelmess (Cheng Huan), Donald Crisp (Battling Burrows), Lillian Gish (Lucy).

The Fatal Glass of Beer (Paramount, 1933). Director: Clyde Bruckman. Producer: Mack Sennett. Screenplay: W. C. Fields. Cast: W. C. Fields (Pa Snavely), Rosemary Theby (Ma Snavely), George Chandler (Chester), Rychard Cramer (Mountie).

Go West (MGM, 1940). Director: Edward Buzzell. Producer: Jack Cummings. Screenplay: Irving Brecher. Photography: Leonard Smith. Music: George Bassman, George Stoll. Cast: Groucho Marx (S. Quentin Quayle), Chico Marx (Joe Panello), Harpo Marx (Rusty Panello).

Shadow of a Doubt (Universal, 1943). Director: Alfred Hitchcock. Producer: Jack H.

Skirball. Screenplay: Thornton Wilder, Alma Reville, Sally Benson. Photography: Joseph Valentine. Music: Dimitri Tiomkin, Charles Previn. Cast: Joseph Cotten (Uncle Charlie Oakley), Teresa Wright (Young Charlie Newton), Macdonald Carey (Jack Graham), Patricia Collinge (Emma Newton), Henry Travers (Joseph Newton), Hume Cronyn (Herbie Hawkins), Wallace Ford (Fred Saunders), Edna Mae Wonacott (Ann Newton).

Red River (Monterey Productions/United Artists, 1948). Director, Producer: Howard Hawks. Screenplay: Borden Chase, Charles Schnee, from the novel *The Chisholm Trail* by Chase. Photography: Russell Harlan. Music: Dimitri Tiomkin. Cast: John Wayne (Tom Dunson), Montgomery Clift (Matthew Garth), Walter Brennan ("Groot" Nadine), John Ireland (Cherry Valance), Joanne Dru (Tess Millay), Noah Berry, Jr. (Buster), Harry Carey (Mr. Melville), Harry Carey, Jr. (Dan Lattimer), Chief Yowlachi (Quo).

The Delicate Delinquent (Paramount, 1957). Director, Screenplay: Don McGuire. Producer: Jerry Lewis. Photography: Haskell B. Boggs. Music: Buddy Bregman. Cast: Jerry Lewis (Sidney L. Pythias), Darren McGavin (Mike Damon), Martha Hyer (Martha Henshaw).

Lonely Boy (National Film Board of Canada, 1962). Director: Wolf Koenig, Roman Kroitor. Producer: Roman Kroitor, Tom Daly. Photography: Wolf Koenig. With Paul Anka.

The Cool World (1964). Director: Shirley Clarke. Producer: Frederick Wiseman. Screenplay: Shirley Clarke, Carl Lee, based on the novel by Warren Miller. Photography: Baird Bryant. Music: Mal Waldron. Cast: Hampton Clanton (Duke), Carl Lee (Priest), Yolanda Rodriquez (Luanne), Clarence Williams III (Blood), Gary Bolling (Littleman), Bostic Felton (Rod).

2001: A Space Odyssey (MGM, 1968). Director, Producer: Stanley Kubrick. Screenplay: Stanley Kubrick and Arthur C. Clarke. Photography: Geoffrey Unsworth. Cast: Keir Dullea (Dave Bowman), Gary Lockwood (Frank Poole), William Sylvester (Dr. Heywood Floyd).

Night of the Living Dead (The Latent Image, Inc./Hardman Associates, Inc., 1968). Director, Photography: George A. Romero. Producer: Russell Streiner, Karl Hardman. Screenplay: George A. Romero, John A. Russo. Cast: Duane Jones (Ben), Judith O'Dea (Barbara), Karl Hardman (Harry Cooper), Russell Streiner (Johnny), Marilyn Eastman (Helen Cooper), Keith Wayne (Tom), Judith Ridley (Judy), Kyra Schon (Karen Cooper).

Dawn of the Dead (Laurel Entertainment, 1978). Director, Screenplay: George A. Romero. Producer: Richard P. Rubinstein. Photography: Michael Gornick. Music: The

Goblins, with Dario Argento. Cast: David Emge (Stephen), Ken Foree (Peter), Scott Reiniger (Roger), Gaylen Ross (Fran), David Crawford (Dr. Foster).

Knightriders (Laurel Entertainment, 1981). Director, Screenplay: George A. Romero. Producer: Richard P. Rubinstein. Photography: Michael Gornick. Music: Donald Rubinstein. Cast: Ed Harris (Billy David), Gary Lahti (Alan), Tom Savini (Morgan), Amy Ingersol (Linet), Patricia Tallman (Julie), Christine Forrest (Angie), Warner Shook (Pippin), Brother Blue (Merlin), Cythia Adler (Rockie), John Amplas (Whiteface), Scott Reiniger (Marhalt), Ken Foree (Little John).

The Loveless (Pioneer/Atlantic, 1982). Director, Screenplay: Kathryn Bigelow, Monty Montgomery. Producer: Grafton Nunes, A. Kitman Ho. Photography: Doyle Smith. Music: Robert Gordon. Cast: Willem Dafoe (Vance), Robert Gordon (Davis), Marin Kanter (Telena).

Day of the Dead (Laurel Entertainment, 1985). Director, Screenplay: George A. Romero. Producer: Richard P. Rubinstein. Photography: Michael Gornick. Music: John Harrison. Cast: Lori Cardille (Sarah), Terry Alexander (John), Joseph Pilato (Capt. Rhodes), Richard Liberty (Dr. Logan), Howard Sherman (Bub), John Amplas (Fisher).

Fatal Attraction (Paramount, 1987). Director: Adrian Lyne. Producer: Stanley R. Jaffe, Sherry Lansing. Screenplay: James Dearden. Photography: Howard Atherton. Music: Maurice Jarre. Cast: Michael Douglas (Dan Gallagher), Glenn Close (Alex Forrest), Anne Archer (Beth Gallagher).

Near Dark (Anchor Bay Entertainment, 1987). Director: Kathryn Bigelow. Producer: Steven-Charles Jaffe. Screenplay: Eric Red, Kathryn Bigelow. Photography: Adam Greenberg. Music: Tangerine Dream. Cast: Adrian Pasdar (Caleb Colton), Jenny Wright (Mae), Lance Henriksen (Jesse Hooker), Bill Paxton (Severen), Jenette Goldstein (Diamondback).

Night of the Living Dead (21st Century Film Corp., 1990). Director: Tom Savini. Producer: John A. Russo, Russ Streiner. Exec Producer: Menahem Golan and George A. Romero. Screenplay: George A. Romero. Photography: Frank Prinzi. Music: Paul McCollough. Cast: Tony Todd (Ben), Patricia Tallman (Barbara), Tom Towles (Harry Cooper), McKee Anderson (Helen Cooper), William Butler (Tom), Katie Finneran (Judy Rose), Bill Mosley (Johnnie), Heather Mazur (Sarah Cooper).

Blue Steel (Vestron/Lightning Pictures/Precision Films, 1990). Director: Kathryn Bigelow. Producer: Edward R. Pressman, Oliver Stone. Screenplay: Kathryn Bigelow, Eric Red. Photography: Amir Mokri. Music: Brad Fiedel. Cast: Jamie Lee Curtis (Megan Turner), Ron Silver (Eugene Hunt), Clancy Brown (Nick Mann).

Point Break (20th Century Fox, 1991). Director: Kathryn Bigelow. Producer: Peter Abrams, Robert L. Levy. Screenplay: W. Peter Iliff. Photography: Donald Peterman. Music: Mark Isham. Cast: Patrick Swayze (Bohdi), Keanu Reeves (Johnny Utah), Gary Busey (Pappas), Lori Petty (Tyler).

Strange Days (UIP/Lightstorm, 1995). Director: Kathryn Bigelow. Producer: Steven-Charles Jaffe, James Cameron. Screenplay: Jay Cocks, Kathryn Bigelow, James Cameron. Photography: Mathew F. Leonetti. Music: Graham Revell. Cast: Ralph Fiennes (Lenny Nero), Angela Bassett (Lornette "Mace" Mason), Juliette Lewis (Faith Justin), Tom Sizemore (Max Peltier), Michael Wincott (Philo Gant).

The Hurt Locker (Summit Entertainment, 2008). Director: Kathryn Bigelow. Producer: Kathryn Bigelow, Mark Boal, Nicolas Chartier, Greg Shapiro. Photography: Barry Ackroyd. Music: Marco Beltrami, Buck Sanders. Cast: Jeremy Renner (SSgt. William James), Anthony Mackie (Sgt. J. T. Sanborn), Brian Geraghty (Spc. Owen Eldridge), Guy Pearce (Sgt. Matt Thompson), Ralph Fiennes (Contract Team Leader).

Bibliography

Adler, Jerry, et al. "The Year of the Yuppie." *Newsweek,* December 31, 1984, 14–31.

Affron, Charles. *Star Acting: Gish, Garbo, Davis.* New York: Dutton, 1977.

Agee, James. "David Wark Griffith." *The Nation,* September 4, 1948. Reprinted in *Agee on Film,* vol. 1, 313–18. Boston: Beacon Press, 1964.

Agel, Jerome, ed., *The Making of Kubrick's 2001.* New York: New American Library, 1970.

Alloway, Lawrence. "Lawrence Alloway on the Iconography of the Movies." *Movie* 7 (February–March 1963): 4–6. Reprinted in Ian Cameron, ed., *Movie Reader* New York: Praeger, 1972, 16–18.

Altman, Rick, ed. *Genre: The Musical.* London and Boston: Routledge and Kegan Paul, 1981.

Andrew, Dudley. "*Broken Blossoms:* The Art and the Eros of a Perverse Text." *Quarterly Review of Film Studies* 6, no. 1 (1981): 81–90.

Barthes, Roland. *Image-Music-Text.* Edited and translated by Stephen Heath. New York: Hill and Wang, 1977.

———. *Mythologies.* Edited and translated by Annette Lavers. New York: Hill and Wang, 1972.

Bazin, André. "The Evolution of the Western." In *What Is Cinema?* vol. 2, edited and translated by Hugh Gray, 149–57. Berkeley: University of California Press, 1971.

Bell-Metereau, Rebecca. *Hollywood Androgyny.* 2nd ed. New York: Columbia University Press, 1993.

Benson, Thomas W., and Carolyn Anderson. *Reality Fictions: The Films of Frederick Wiseman.* Carbondale: Southern Illinois University Press, 1989.

Berg, Beatrice. "I Was Fed Up with Hollywood Fantasies." *New York Times,* February 1, 1970, sec. 2, 25–26.

Berger, John. *Ways of Seeing.* London: British Broadcasting Corporation; Penguin, 1972.

Bergman, Andrew. *We're in the Money.* New York: Harper and Row, 1972.

Bergson, Henri. "Laughter." In *Comedy,* edited by Wylie Sypher, 61–190. Garden City, NY: Anchor Doubleday, 1956.

Bergstrom, Janet. "Alternation, Segmentation, Hypnosis: Interview with Raymond Bellour." *camera obscura* 3–4 (1979): 71–103.

Berton, Pierre. *Hollywood's Canada: The Americanization of Our National Image.* Toronto: McClelland and Stewart, 1975.

Bewley, Marius. *The Eccentric Design: Form in the Classic American Novel.* New York: Columbia University Press, 1963.

Biskind, Peter. *Seeing Is Believing: How Hollywood Taught Us to Stop Worrying and Love the Fifties.* New York: Pantheon, 1983.

Bogdanovich, Peter. "Interview with Howard Hawks." *Movie* 5 (December 1962): 8–18.

Bogle, Donald. *Toms, Coons, Mulattoes, Mammies, & Bucks: An Interpretive History of Blacks in American Films.* New York: Bantam, 1974.

Bordwell, David, Janet Staiger, and Kristin Thompson. *The Classical Hollywood Cinema: Film Style and Mode of Production to 1960.* New York: Columbia University Press, 1985.

Brakhage, Stan. "Metaphors on Vision." *Film Culture* 30 (Fall 1963): unpaginated.

Brown, Karl. *Adventures with D. W. Griffith.* New York: Da Capo, 1976.

Brown, Ray B., and Pat Brown, eds. *The Guide to United States Popular Culture.* Bowling Green, OH: Bowling Green State University Popular Press, 2001.

Burgess, Anthony. *A Clockwork Orange.* London: Heinemann, 1962.

Burke, Thomas. *Limehouse Nights.* New York: Robert M. McBride, 1922.

Cahn, William. *The Laugh Makers: A Pictorial History of American Comedians.* New York: C. P. Putnam's Sons, 1957.

Cameron, Ian, ed. *Movie Reader.* New York: Praeger, 1972.

Chapple, Steve, and Reebee Garofalo. *Rock 'n' Roll Is Here to Pay: The History and Politics of the Music Industry.* Elmhurst, IL: Music Business Publications, 1977.

Charney, Maurice. *Comedy High and Low: An Introduction to the Experience of Comedy.* New York: Oxford University Press, 1978.

Chumo, Peter N., III. "At the Generic Crossroads with *Thelma and Louise.*" *Post Script* 13, no. 2 (1994): 3–13.

Clover, Carol J. *Men, Women, and Chain Saws: Gender in the Modern Horror Film.* Princeton, NJ: Princeton University Press, 1992.

Cohan, Steven, and Ina Rae Hark, eds. *Screening the Male: Exploring Masculinities in Hollywood Cinema.* London and New York: Routledge, 1993.

Cohen, Albert K. *Delinquent Boys: The Culture of the Gang.* Glencoe, IL: Free Press, 1955.

Cohn, Jan. *The Palace or the Poorhouse: The American House as Cultural Symbol.* East Lansing: Michigan State University Press, 1979.

Connell, R. W. *Masculinities.* Berkeley: University of California Press, 1995.

Cook, David. *A History of Narrative Film.* 3rd ed. New York: Norton, 1981.

Cook, Pam. "Exploitation Films and Feminism." *Screen* 17, no. 2 (1976): 122–27.

———. "Masculinity in Crisis?" *Screen* 23, nos. 3–4 (1982): 39–46.

———. "Scorsese's Masquerade." *Sight and Sound* 1, no. 12 (1992): 14–15.

Cooper, James Fenimore. *The Last of the Mohicans.* Boston: Houghton Mifflin, 1958.

Coursodon, Jean-Pierre, with Pierre Sauvage. *American Directors.* 2 vols. New York: McGraw-Hill, 1983.

Coyne, Michael. *The Crowded Prairie: American Identity in the Hollywood Western.* London and New York: I. B. Tauris, 1997.

Creed, Barbara. "From Here to Modernity: Feminism and Postmodernism." *Screen* 28, no. 2 (1987): 47–67.

———. "Phallic Panic: Male Hysteria and *Dead Ringers.*" *Screen* 31, no. 2 (1990): 125–64.

Crèvocoeur, J. Hector St. John de. *Letters from an American Farmer.* New York: Dutton, 1975.

Cripps, Thomas. *Black Film as Genre.* Bloomington: Indiana University Press, 1979.

Deschner, Donald. *The Films of W. C. Fields.* Secaucus, NJ: Citadel Press, 1966.

Dillard, R. H. W., ed. *Horror Films.* New York: Monarch Press, 1976.

Doane, Mary Ann. *The Desire to Desire: The Woman's Film of the 1940s.* Bloomington: Indiana University Press, 1987.

———. "Film and the Masquerade—Theorizing the Female Spectator." *Screen* 23, nos. 3–4 (1982): 74–87.

Doherty, Thomas. *Teenagers and Teenpics: The Juvenilization of American Movies in the 1950s.* Boston: Unwin Hyman, 1988.

Dowdy, Andrew. *The Films of the Fifties.* New York: Morrow, 1975.

Du Bois, W. E. B. *The Souls of Black Folk.* In *Three Negro Classics,* 207–389. New York: Avon, 1965.

Durgnat, Raymond. *The Crazy Mirror: Hollywood Comedy and the American Image.* New York: Delta, 1972.

———. "Hawks Isn't Good Enough." *Film Comment* 13, no. 4 (1977): 15–16.

Dyer, Richard. "Entertainment and Utopia." *Movie* 24 (Spring 1977): 2–13.

———. "A White Star." *Sight and Sound* 3, no. 8 (1993): 22–24.

Eames, David. "Watching Wiseman Watch." *New York Times Magazine,* October 2, 1977, 96–102, 104, 108.

Ehrenstein, David, and Bill Reed. *Rock on Film.* New York: Delilah Books, 1982.

Ellis, Brett Easton. *American Psycho.* New York: Vintage, 1991.

Falsetto, Mario. *Stanley Kubrick: A Narrative and Stylistic Analysis.* Westport, CT: Praeger, 1994.

Farber, Manny. *Movies.* New York: Hillstone, 1971.

Feuer, Jane. *The Hollywood Musical.* Bloomington: Indiana University Press, 1982.

Fiedler, Leslie. *Love and Death in the American Novel.* New York: Delta, 1967.

Fields, W. C., with Ronald J. Fields. *W. C. Fields by Himself: His Intended Autobiography.* Englewood Cliffs, NJ: Prentice-Hall, 1973.

Fitzgerald, F. Scott. *The Great Gatsby.* New York: Charles Scribner's Sons, 1925.

Forster, E. M. *Aspects of the Novel.* New York: Harcourt, Brace and World, 1927.

Franklin, H. Bruce. *Future Perfect: American Science Fiction of the Nineteenth Century.* New York: Oxford University Press, 1966.

Freedman, Carl. "Science Fiction and the Triumph of Feminism: Barr's *Future Females, The Next Generation.*" *Science Fiction Studies* 81 (2000): 278–89.

Frith, Simon, and Andrew Goodwin, eds. *On Record: Rock, Pop, and the Written Word.* New York: Pantheon, 1990.

Gagne, Paul. *The Zombies That Ate Pittsburgh: The Films of George Romero.* New York: Dodd, Mead, 1987.

Gallagher, Catherine, and Elizabeth Young. "Feminism and *Frankenstein:* A Short History of American Feminist Criticism." *Journal of Contemporary Thought* 1, no. 1 (1991): 97–109.

Gates, Henry Louis, Jr. *The Signifying Monkey: A Theory of Afro-American Literary Criticism.* New York: Oxford University Press, 1988.

Gayle, Addison, ed. *The Black Aesthetic.* Garden City, NY: Doubleday, 1971.

Gerstner, David. *Manly Arts: Masculinity and Nation in Early American Cinema.* Durham, NC: Duke University Press, 2006.

Ginsberg, Allen. *Planet News.* San Francisco: City Lights, 1968.

Gish, Lillian. *The Movies, Mr. Griffith, and Me.* Englewood Cliffs, NJ: Prentice-Hall, 1969.

Gorbman, Claudia. *Unheard Melodies: Narrative Film Music.* London: British Film Institute; Bloomington: Indiana University Press, 1987.

Graham, John. "How Far Can You Go: A Conversation with Fred Wiseman." *Contempora* 1, no. 4 (1970): 30–33.

Grant, Barry Keith. *Voyages of Discovery: The Cinema of Frederick Wiseman.* Urbana: University of Illinois Press, 1992.

Grant, Barry Keith, ed. *The Dread of Difference: Gender and the Horror Film.* Austin: University of Texas Press, 1996.

———. *Film Genre Reader 3.* Austin: University of Texas Press, 2003.

———. *John Ford's* Stagecoach. New York and Cambridge: Cambridge University Press, 2003.

Grant, Barry Keith, and Christopher Sharrett, eds. *Planks of Reason: Essays on the Horror Film.* Rev. ed. Lanham, MD: Scarecrow Press, 2004.

Grindon, Leger. "Body and Soul: The Structure of Meaning in the Boxing Film Genre." *Cinema Journal* 35, no. 4 (1996): 54–69.

Gunning, Tom. "'Like unto a Leopard': Figurative Discourse in *Cat People* and Todorov's *The Fantastic.*" *Wide Angle* 10, no. 3 (1988): 30–39.

Halberstadt, Ira. "An Interview with Frederick Wiseman." *Filmmakers Newsletter* 7, no. 4 (1974): 19–25.

Hammond, John L. "Yuppies." *Public Opinion Quarterly* 50 (Winter 1986): 487–501.

Handleman, Janet. "An Interview with Frederick Wiseman." *Film Library Quarterly* 3, no. 3 (1970): 5–9.

Haraway, Donna. *Simians, Cyborgs, and Women.* New York: Routledge, 1991.

Haskell, Molly. "The Cinema of Howard Hawks." *Intellectual Digest* 2, no. 8 (1972): 56–58.

———. *From Reverence to Rape: The Treatment of Women in the Movies.* Baltimore: Penguin, 1974.

Henderson, Brian. "Towards a Non-Bourgeois Camera Style." *Film Quarterly* 24, no. 2 (1970–71): 2–14.

Henderson, Robert M. *D. W. Griffith: His Life and Work.* New York and London: Garland, 1985.

Hitchens, Gordon. "*The Cool World.*" *Film Comment* 2, no. 2 (1964): 52–53.

Hodge, Francis. *Yankee Theater: The Image of America on the Stage, 1825–1850.* Austin: University of Texas Press, 1964.

Horton, Andrew S., ed. *Comedy/Cinema/Theory*. Berkeley: University of California Press, 1991.

Howard, James. *Stanley Kubrick Companion*. London: Batsford, 1999.

Jacobs, Lewis. *The Rise of the American Film: A Critical History*. New York: Teachers College Press, 1968.

Jameson, Fredric. *Postmodernism, or, the Cultural Logic of Late Capitalism*. Durham, NC: Duke University Press, 1992.

Jeffords, Susan. *Hardbodies: Hollywood Masculinity in the Reagan Era*. New Brunswick, NJ: Rutgers University Press, 1994.

Johnston, Claire. "Women's Cinema as Counter Cinema." In *Movies and Methods,* edited by Bill Nichols, 208–17. Berkeley: University of California Press, 1976.

Kagan, Norman. *The Cinema of Stanley Kubrick*. New York: Grove Press, 1972.

Kastner, Susan. "So . . . Where Have All the Yuppies Gone?" *Toronto Star,* April 7, 1991, A1, A4.

Kawin, Bruce. *Mindscreen: Bergman, Godard, and First-Person Film*. Princeton, NJ: Princeton University Press, 1978.

Keller, Evelyn Fox. *A Feeling for the Organism*. New York: W. H. Freeman, 1983.

———. *Reflections on Gender and Science*. New Haven, CT: Yale University Press, 1985.

King, Stephen. *Danse Macabre*. New York: Everest House, 1981.

Kitses, Jim. *Horizons West*. Bloomington: Indiana University Press; London: British Film Institute, 1969.

Knight, Damon. *In Search of Wonder: Essays on Modern Science Fiction*. Rev. ed. Chicago: Advent, 1967.

Kolker, Robert. *A Cinema of Loneliness: Penn, Stone, Kubrick, Scorsese, Spielberg, Altman*. 3rd ed. New York: Oxford University Press, 2000.

Kostof, Spiro. *America by Design*. New York: Oxford University Press, 1987.

Krutnik, Frank. *In a Lonely Street: Film Noir, Genre, Masculinity*. London and New York: Routledge, 1991.

Kuhn, Annette, ed. *Alien Zone: Cultural Theory and Contemporary Science Fiction*. New York: Verso, 1990.

———. *Alien Zone II: The Spaces of Science Fiction*. London and New York: Verso, 1999.

Lane, Christina. *Feminist Hollywood: From* Born in Flames *to* Point Break. Detroit: Wayne State University Press, 2000.

Lawrence, D. H. *Studies in Classic American Literature*. New York: Penguin, 1977.

Leach, Jim, and Jeannette Sloniowski, eds. *Candid Eyes: Essays on Canadian Documentaries*. Toronto: University of Toronto Press, 2003.

Le Guin, Ursula. *The Left Hand of Darkness*. New York: Ace, 1969.

Lehman, Peter. *Running Scared: Masculinity and the Representation of the Male Body.* New ed. Detroit: Wayne State University Press, 2007.

Lem, Stanislaw. *Solaris.* New York: Berkley Books, 1971.

Lesage, Julia. "*Broken Blossoms:* Artful Racism, Artful Rape." *Jump Cut* 26 (1981): 51–55.

Levy, Shawn. *King of Comedy: The Life and Art of Jerry Lewis.* New York: St. Martin's Griffin, 1997.

Lewis, Jerry. *The Total Film-Maker.* New York: Warners Paperback Library, 1973.

Lewis, Jon. *The Road to Romance and Ruin: Teen Films and Youth Culture.* New York: Routledge, 1992.

Loukides, Paul, and Linda K. Fuller, eds. *Beyond the Stars: Stock Characters in American Popular Film.* Bowling Green, OH: Popular Press, 1990.

Louvish, Simon. *It's a Gift.* London: British Film Institute, 1994.

Lynn, Kenneth S., ed. *The Comic Tradition in America: An Anthology of American Humor.* New York: Norton, 1958.

MacDonald, Dwight. "*The Cool World.*" In *Dwight MacDonald on Movies,* 323–27. Englewood Cliffs, NJ: Prentice-Hall, 1969.

Maltin, Leonard. *Leonard Maltin's 2005 Movie Guide.* New York: Plume, 2004.

Mamber, Stephen. "The New Documentaries of Frederick Wiseman." *Cinema* 6, no. 1 (1970): 33–40.

Marcorelles, Louis. *Living Cinema: New Directions in Contemporary Filmmaking.* Translated by Isabel Quigly. London: George Allen and Unwin, 1973.

Marsh, Dave. "Schlock Around the Rock." *Film Comment* 14, no. 4 (1978): 7–13.

Mast, Gerald. *The Comic Mind: Comedy and the Movies.* Indianapolis: Bobbs-Merrill, 1973.

———. *Howard Hawks, Storyteller.* New York and Oxford: Oxford University Press, 1982.

McBride, Joseph, ed. *Focus on Howard Hawks.* Englewood Cliffs, NJ: Prentice-Hall, 1972.

———. *Hawks on Hawks.* Berkeley: University of California Press, 1982.

McCarthy, Todd, and Charles Flynn, eds. *Kings of the Bs.* New York: Dutton, 1975.

McCarty, John. *Splatter Movies: Breaking the Last Taboo of the Screen.* New York: St. Martin's Press, 1984.

McWilliams, Donald. "Frederick Wiseman." *Film Quarterly* 24, no. 1 (1970): 17–26.

Mekas, Jonas. "Notes on the New American Cinema." *Film Culture* 24 (Spring 1962): 6–16.

Mellen, Joan. *Big Bad Wolves: Masculinity in the American Film.* New York: Pantheon, 1977.

Merritt, Russell. "Rescued from a Perilous Nest: D. W. Griffith's Escape from Theater into Film." *Cinema Journal* 21, no. 1 (1981): 2–30.

Meyer, William R. *The Making of the Great Westerns.* New Rochelle, NY: Arlington House, 1979.

Miller, Jim, ed. *The Rolling Stone Illustrated History of Rock and Roll.* New York: Random House, 1980.

Miller, Warren. *The Cool World.* New York: Crest, 1965.

———. "Progress in Documentary." In *The Documentary Tradition: From Nanook to Woodstock,* edited by Lewis Jacobs, 2nd ed., 247–50. New York: Norton, 1979.

Morris, N. A. "In Defense of *Fatal Attraction.*" *Movie* 33 (Winter 1989): 53–55.

Mulvey, Laura. "Visual Pleasure and Narrative Cinema." *Screen* 16, no. 3 (1975): 6–18. Reprinted in Mulvey, *Visual and Other Pleasures,* 14–26. London: Macmillan, 1989.

Mumford, Lewis. *The Golden Day: A Study in American Literature and Culture.* New York: Dover, 1968.

Murphy, Kathleen. "Black Arts." *Film Comment* 31, no. 5 (1995): 51–53.

Naremore, James. "*True Heart Susie* and the Art of Lillian Gish." *Quarterly Review of Film Studies* 6, no. 1 (1981): 91–104.

Neale, Steve. "The Big Romance or Something Wild? Romantic Comedy Today." *Screen* 33, no. 3 (1992): 284–99.

Nelson, Lynn Hankinson, and Jack Nelson, eds. *Feminism, Science, and the Philosophy of Science.* Boston: Kluwer Academic, 1996.

Nichols, Bill. *Ideology and the Image.* Bloomington: Indiana University Press, 1981.

Pechter, William. "Movie Musicals." *Commentary* 53, no. 5 (1972): 77–81.

Piercy, Marge. *Woman on the Edge of Time.* New York: Fawcett Crest, 1977.

Piesman, Marissa, and Marilee Hartley. *The Yuppie Handbook: The State of the Art Manual for Young Urban Professionals.* New York: Long Shadow Books, 1984.

Pirie, David. "New Blood." *Sight and Sound* 40, no. 2 (1971): 73–75.

———. *The Vampire Cinema.* New York: Crescent Books, 1977.

Polan, Dana. "Being and Nuttiness: Jerry Lewis and the French." *Journal of Popular Film and Television* 12, no. 1 (1984): 42–46.

Polt, Harriet. "*The Cool World.*" *Film Quarterly* 17, no. 2 (1963): 33–35.

Pomerance, Murray, ed. *Enfant Terrible! Jerry Lewis in American Film.* New York: New York University Press, 2002.

———. *Ladies and Gentlemen, Boys and Girls: Gender in Film at the End of the Twentieth Century.* Albany: State University of New York Press, 2001.

Powell, Anna. "Blood on the Borders—*Near Dark* and *Blue Steel.*" *Screen* 35, no. 2 (1994): 135–56.

Powers, John. "Bleak Chic." *American Film* 12, no. 5 (1987): 47–51.

Rabinovitz, Lauren. *Points of Resistance: Women, Power, and Politics in the New York Avant-Garde Cinema, 1943–71.* Urbana: University of Illinois Press, 1990.

Rapping, Elayne. "*The Hand That Rocks the Cradle.*" *Cineaste* 19, nos. 2–3 (1992): 65–66.

Rascaroli, Laura. "Steel in the Gaze: On POV and the Discourse of Vision in Kathryn Bigelow's Cinema." *Screen* 38, no. 3 (1997): 232–46.

Riesman, David. *The Lonely Crowd.* New Haven, CT: Yale University Press, 1950.

Rivette, Jacques. "Rivette on Hawks." *Movie* 5 (December 1962): 19–20.

Robb, Christina. "Focus on Life." *Boston Globe Magazine,* January 23, 1983, 26–34.

Romero, George A., and Susanna Sparrow. *Martin.* New York: Day Books, 1980.

Rourke, Constance. *American Humor: A Study of the National Character.* Garden City, NY: Anchor Doubleday, 1931.

Russ, Joanna. *The Female Man.* New York: Bantam, 1975.

Russo, John. *The Complete* Night of the Living Dead *Filmbook.* New York: Harmony Books, 1985.

Sargent, Pamela, ed. *More Women of Wonder: Science Fiction Novelettes by Women about Women.* New York: Vintage, 1976.

———. *The New Women of Wonder: Recent Science Fiction Stories by Women about Women.* New York: Vintage, 1978.

———. *Women of Wonder: Science Fiction Stories by Women about Women.* New York: Vintage, 1975.

Sarris, Andrew. *The American Cinema: Directors and Directions, 1929–1968.* New York: Dutton, 1968.

———. *Confessions of a Cultist: Notes on the Cinema, 1955–1969.* New York: Simon and Schuster, 1970.

———. *The John Ford Movie Mystery.* London: Secker and Warburg; British Film Institute, 1976.

Savells, Jerry. "Who Are the 'Yuppies'? A Popular View." *International Journal of Comparative Sociology* 27, nos. 3–4 (1986): 234–41.

Schatz, Thomas. *Hollywood Genres: Formulas, Filmmaking, and the Studio System.* New York: Random House, 1981.

Schneider, Karen. "With Violence If Necessary: Rearticulating the Family in the Contemporary Action-Thriller." *Journal of Popular Film and Television* 27, no. 1 (1999): 2–11.

Scholes, Robert. *Structural Fabulation: An Essay on Fiction of the Future.* Notre Dame, IN: University of Notre Dame Press, 1975.

Sharrett, Christopher, ed. *Mythologies of Violence in Postmodern Media.* Detroit: Wayne State University Press, 1999.

Silverman, Kaja. *The Acoustic Mirror: The Female Voice in Psychoanalysis and Cinema.* Bloomington: Indiana University Press, 1988.

Simmon, Scott. "'The Female of the Species': D. W. Griffith, Father of the Woman's Film." *Film Quarterly* 46, no. 2 (1992–93): 8–20.

Sklar, Robert. "*Red River:* Empire to the West." *Cineaste* 9, no. 4 (1978): 14–19.

Smith, Gavin. "Momentum and Design: Kathryn Bigelow Interviewed by Gavin Smith." *Film Comment* 31, no. 5 (1995): 46–50.

Sontag, Susan. *Against Interpretation and Other Essays.* New York: Delta, 1966.

Spencer, Scott. "Scott Spenser's Guilty Pleasures." *Film Comment* 17, no. 5 (1981): 21–23.

Stapledon, Olaf. *Last and First Men: A Story of the Near and Far Future.* New York: Viking Penguin, 1971.

Stein, Elliott. "*The Night of the Living Dead.*" *Sight and Sound* 39, no. 2 (1970): 105.

Stern, Lee Edward. *The Movie Musical.* New York: Pyramid, 1974.

Studlar, Gaylyn. *This Mad Masquerade: Stardom and Masculinity in the Jazz Age.* New York: Columbia University Press, 1996.

Studlar, Gaylyn, and Matthew Bernstein, eds. *John Ford Made Westerns: Filming the Legend in the Sound Era.* Bloomington: Indiana University Press, 2001.

Suvin, Darko. *Metamorphosis of Science Fiction: On the Poetics and History of a Literary Genre.* New Haven, CT: Yale University Press, 1979.

Sweeney, Gael. "The Face on the Lunch Box: Television's Construction of the Teen Idol." *Velvet Light Trap* 33 (Spring 1994): 49–59.

"The Talk of the Town: New Producer." *New Yorker,* September 14, 1963, 34.

Tasker, Yvonne. *Spectacular Bodies: Gender, Genre, and the Action Cinema.* London and New York: Routledge, 1993.

Taubin, Amy. "Hard Wired: Kathryn Bigelow's *The Hurt Locker.*" *Film Comment* 45, no. 3 (2009): 31–32, 34–35.

Todorov, Tzvetan. *The Fantastic: A Structural Approach to a Literary Genre.* Translated by Richard Howard. Ithaca, NY: Cornell University Press, 1975.

Tudor, Andrew. *Image and Influence: Studies in the Sociology of Film.* New York: St. Martin's Press, 1975.

Turner, Frederick Jackson. "The Significance of the Frontier in American History." In *Frontier and Section: Selected Essays,* 37–62. Introduction by Ray Allen Billington. Englewood Cliffs, NJ: Prentice-Hall, 1961.

Tyler, Royall. *The Contrast.* In *The Literature of America: Colonial Period,* edited by Larzer Ziff, 483–526. New York: McGraw-Hill, 1970.

Wajcman, Judith. *Feminism Confronts Technology.* University Park: Pennsylvania State University Press, 1991.

Walker, Alexander. *Stanley Kubrick Directs.* Expanded ed. New York: Harcourt Brace Jovanovich, 1972.

Waller, Gregory A. *The Living and the Undead: From Stoker's* Dracula *to Romero's* Dawn of the Dead. Urbana: University of Illinois Press, 1986.

Weiler, A. H. "Wiseman to Make 'Yes Yes, No No' First Fiction Film." *New York Times,* December 6, 1974, 78.

Wells, H. G. *The Time Machine.* In *Seven Famous Novels by H. G. Wells.* New York: Knopf, 1934.

Whitman, Walt. *Leaves of Grass.* Edited by Sculley Bradley and Harold W. Blodgett. New York: Norton, 1973.

Whyte, William H., Jr. *The Organization Man.* New York: Simon and Schuster, 1956.

Will, George F. "Reality Says You Can't Have It All." *Newsweek,* February 3, 1986, 78.

Wise, Naomi. "The Hawksian Woman." *Take One* 3, no. 3 (1972): 17.

Wollen, Peter. *Signs and Meaning in the Cinema.* 3rd ed. Bloomington: Indiana University Press, 1972.

Wood, Michael. *America in the Movies.* New York: Delta, 1976.

Wood, Robin. *Hollywood from Vietnam to Reagan.* New York: Columbia University Press, 1986.

———. *Howard Hawks.* London: British Film Institute, 1981. Reprint, Detroit: Wayne State University Press, 2006.

———. "Never Never Change, Always Gonna Dance." *Film Comment* 15, no. 5 (1979): 29–31.

———. "The Spectres Emerge in Daylight." *Cineaction* 43 (1997): 4–13.

Wright, Richard. *Native Son.* New York: Harper and Row, 1966.

Yakir, Dan. "Mourning Becomes Romero." *Film Comment* 15, no. 3 (1979): 60–65.

Index

Italicized page numbers indicate photographs.